DREAM
FACTORIES

DREAM
FACTORIES

Why Universities Won't Solve
the Youth Jobs Crisis

KEN S. COATES AND BILL MORRISON

TAP
BOOKS

DUNDURN
TORONTO

Editor: Diane Young
Design: Laura Boyle
Printer: Webcom
Cover Design: Sarah Beaudin
Cover Image © WestLight/iStockphoto.com

Library and Archives Canada Cataloguing in Publication

Coates, Kenneth, 1956-, author
    Dream factories : why universities won't solve the youth jobs crisis /
Ken S. Coates and Bill Morrison.

Includes bibliographical references.Issued in print and electronic formats.

ISBN 978-1-4597-3377-0 (paperback).--ISBN 978-1-4597-3378-7 (pdf).--ISBN 978-1-4597-3379-4 (epub)

1. College graduates--Employment. 2. Youth--Employment. 3. Education, Higher--Social aspects.
4. Universities and colleges.I. Morrison, William R. (William Robert), 1942-, author II. Title.

HD6277.C62 2016   331.11'445   C2016-900383-3
                                  C2016-900384-1

1 2 3 4 5   20 19 18 17 16

We acknowledge the support of the **Canada Council for the Arts** and the **Ontario Arts Council** for our publishing program. We also acknowledge the financial support of the **Government of Canada** through the **Canada Book Fund** and **Livres Canada Books**, and the **Government of Ontario** through the **Ontario Book Publishing Tax Credit** and the **Ontario Media Development Corporation**.

Care has been taken to trace the ownership of copyright material used in this book. The author and the publisher welcome any information enabling them to rectify any references or credits in subsequent editions.

— *J. Kirk Howard, President*

The publisher is not responsible for websites or their content unless they are owned by the publisher.

Printed and bound in Canada.

VISIT US AT
www.dundurn.com/TAPbooks

TAP Books Ltd.
3 Church Street, Suite 500
Toronto, Ontario, Canada
M5E 1M2

CONTENTS

Note that the words "university" and "college" are used interchangeably in this book to refer to degree-granting institutions of higher learning.

PREFACE

During the first 2015 Democratic presidential debate, Senators Hillary Clinton and Bernie Sanders struggled to outdo each other with grandiose visions for free public university and greatly enhanced loans and bursaries for students from poor families. On October 21, 2015, Joe Biden, vice-president of the United States, outlined his devotion to college education, while announcing his decision not to run for the presidency. North of the border, Justin Trudeau, during his successful campaign to become prime minister of Canada, extolled the virtues of expanding access to universities. If there is consensus about anything in North America, it is that a college or university education is a "good thing" for contemporary youth.

Indeed, heading off to college is one of North America's signature rites of passage. Everyone knows the routine: evaluating colleges, cramming to get the high-school grades necessary to get into the best universities, waiting for the admission (or rejection) letters, tearful farewells for those leaving, and move-in day at the college residence. And then the studying begins.

What happens after that is also well known: four or five years of college (with the bright ones staying on for graduate school or a professional degree), the stress of job applications, the choice of employer, and settling into a career. Traditionally, the career-work continuum is followed by marriage, house purchase, and children.

This new American Dream is founded on a firm belief in the efficacy of a *Learning = Earning* formula where the number of years of post-secondary study provide an assurance of an ever-higher income. It appears to be a worthy successor to the dreams of earlier generations who built their futures and fortunes on agriculture, industrial labour, entrepreneurship, or the combination of unionized and government work that propelled prosperity in the post–World War II era.

But what if this belief is not true? What if the formula is wrong? What if the actual experience of North American students deviates dramatically from the image that has sustained the optimism and dreams of young people for the past three generations? For those who have saved for years to pay for a college education, who have pinned their hopes on the career potential of a university degree, the formula is intensely personal. What if *Learning* does not equal *Earning*?

Rumblings are getting louder that all is not well in college-land. Sociologists Richard Arum and Josipa Roksa have provided an invaluable service to the research-based understanding of contemporary post-secondary education in their provocative studies of the actual experiences of American college students. Their first book on this theme, *Academically Adrift: Limited Learning on College Campuses*, examined how much students actually took away, intellectually, from the college experience. Their depressing study argued that most students showed surprisingly little gain, even after they had completed their degrees.

In *Aspiring Adults Adrift: Tentative Transitions of College Graduates,* Arum and Roksa looked at the employment experiences of a group of university students who graduated in 2009, a time of serious economic difficulty in America. The book observed that college graduates did much better than those without a college education, but also documented the severe challenges facing young adults. The researchers found that for those unemployed at the time of the spring 2011 survey, 40 percent had been unemployed for six months or more. Almost a quarter of the respondents who were unemployed in 2011 had also been unemployed when surveyed in the spring of 2010. Others were underemployed, with 4 percent working fewer than twenty hours per week. The remaining 89 percent of graduates had found either full-time employment or close to it, but many were in low-paid jobs. Fifteen percent of college graduates were in full-time positions that paid less than $20,000 per year, and 15 percent were in positions that paid between $20,000 and $30,000 per year.

Considered as a whole, 53 percent of the college graduates who had not re-enrolled full-time in school were unemployed, employed part-time, or employed in full-time jobs that paid less than $30,000 annually.

College and university has never been one thing or a single kind of institution. In his excellent and affectionate commentary on the American college, called simply *College*, Andrew Delbanco, a Columbia University professor, observed:

> For a relatively few students, college remains the sort of place that Andrew Kronman, former dean of Yale Law School, recalls from his days at Williams, where his favorite class took place at the home of a philosophy professor whose two golden retrievers slept on either side of the fireplace "like bookends beside the hearth" while the sunset lit the Berkshire Hills "in scarlet and gold." For many more students, college means the anxious pursuit of marketable skills in overcrowded, under-resourced institutions, where little attention is paid to that elusive entity sometimes call the "whole person." For still others, it means travelling by night to a fluorescent office building or to a "virtual classroom" that exists only in cyberspace. It is a pipe dream to imagine that every student can have the sort of experience that our richest colleges, at their best, provide. But it is a nightmare society that affords the chance to learn and grow only to the wealthy, brilliant, or lucky few. Many remarkable teachers in America's community colleges, unsung private colleges, and underfunded public colleges live this truth every day, working to keep the ideal of democratic education alive.[1]

But the actual outcomes should give us pause. Consider the following information. These figures are for the state of Missouri, admittedly not the economically strongest part of the United States. For every hundred students who enter high school, seventy-eight will graduate, of whom forty-seven will enter college. Of these, only sixteen will earn a Bachelor's degree, with another six earning an associate degree. Unless you read the statistics, you would never guess that only about a third of those entering college would reach the Holy Grail of a degree in a timely fashion.

But, as the TV pitchmen say, there's more. Among college graduates in the United States, with the number varying according to the vagaries of the national and global economy, around 10 percent cannot immediately find work at all. And it gets worse from there. Go back to our sixteen college graduates. Of these, fully a third will end up underemployed, meaning that they will have a job that does not require a four-year degree to hold down the position.

Of one hundred high school graduates, only sixteen will finish a first degree and only eleven will be employed in a job appropriate to their college education. Think about it. From a hundred high school graduates, we are down to eleven young men and women who completed their degrees in a timely fashion, moved into the workforce, and found a job commensurate with their education and experience.

Look for depressing statistics like these ones in the recruitment and promotional literature for a college or university close to you. Look really hard. You will rarely find them. Show us the political platform that proudly proclaims that the world's largest, most comprehensive, and best post-secondary education system produces a positive outcome for as many as a third of those who attend it. Sounds a little underwhelming, doesn't it? The Canadian results are better, in part because of a strong high school system and a lower participation rate. But the general direction is much the same.

Of course, this being contemporary North America, opportunity and outcomes are not equally shared. The percentage of students at elite universities who experience desired outcomes—quick passage through college and a shift into paid employment in a decent job—is much higher, probably in the order of 60 percent or more of the total. (Following the Missouri example, if a hundred high school graduates go to an elite institution, at least ninety will complete their first year, close to eighty will finish their degrees, and at least sixty will find promising work.)

The opposite is true at the weaker, open-entry institutions and many of the for-profit places. Here, dropout rates in the first year can reach 50 percent or more. In the worst examples, as few as 15 to 20 percent will actually complete a degree in institutions of this type. And these graduates are likely to have greater difficulty translating a degree from a little-known and low-ranked school into a stable career with a decent income. If 60 percent of elite students achieve the twenty-first-century version of the American Dream, it is probably less than half that at the much more numerous, lower-ranked institutions.

Colleges and universities have numbers of their own. For years, they have boasted that their graduates earn much more over the course of their careers than non-college graduates. There are serious problems with this assertion (which we will discuss later), some of them obvious, others less so. First, individual ability, family circumstances, and motivation account for a significant portion of the income differential between high school graduates and college graduates. Second, people with degrees are on the whole—but of course not always—smarter, harder-working, and more talented than those without them. Is it the degree that produces income, or is it the abilities of the individuals that matter most? It seems that income for college graduates is strongly correlated to parental income. Not only that, but it's possible that rich people's kids are actually smarter, as a study recently argued.[2] Ask the disadvantaged in North America. Will they be surprised that rich kids stay rich and even get richer?

Data put out by universities conveniently leave out those who start a college degree, but don't finish it. (Remember that this accounts for about 10 to 40 percent of the total, depending on the institution.) In any other field of public policy evaluation, this is called cooking the books. Always remember that averages are just averages. They encompass the high earnings of doctors, Wall Street minions, a handful of millionaire professional football players, and a minority of lawyers. These numbers offset the hundreds of thousands of university graduates working for rental-car companies and retail stores. Average tells you what happens to a broad, diverse cohort and provides a vague guide for the individual student.

Ah, Canadians say with standard sanctimoniousness, the situation is better north of the border. And so it is, but only by a little, and mostly because the preoccupation with university is not as strong in Canada as in the United States, and not as high a percentage of the population goes to college, although the gap seems to be closing. Canadians at elite private schools and the best public schools share a passion for the top-ranked American colleges and universities and are well served at home by the country's best schools. Canada also has an excellent set of polytechnics, or high-quality technical schools, which have strong connections to the major employers. But Canadians have little to boast about, and the same job dynamics hold in this country too.

College and university propaganda often fails to acknowledge the impact of additional training and education on the outcomes they so glowingly advertise. Some graduates stay in the academy and go on to either graduate school or professional studies programs, particularly in Education or Master of Business Administration. Others go back to a community college or a polytechnic to get a more career-oriented credential. When a student who failed to find a good job based on his BSc gets an electrical technician's diploma at a community college, he shows up in the employment and income statistics as a "success" for the university credential. As always, statistics have to be read with great care.

Maybe institutions and governments consider these career outcomes to be acceptable. Perhaps the purpose of the university system in North America is to give people a chance to test their potential to see what they are capable of achieving. It is an awfully expensive way—for students, families, governments, and institutions—to indulge a young person's over-estimation of his or her abilities, interests, and motivation. Our point is this: young adults and their parents rarely have this information in front of them when they consider college or university as an option. If they had it, perhaps they would make different choices.

Here's another statistic that you won't hear from American colleges and universities: of those who enter them, 53 percent don't complete their degrees. Some countries do worse: the figure for Italy is 55 percent, while others, notably Japan at 10 percent, do better. The average for the OECD is 31 percent. What a sad result from the expenditure of all that hope and effort and money.[3]

The USA and Italy are real outliers, with Canada doing considerably better, but the university dropout rate in Canada is still close to three times the rate for Japan. (The data are not directly comparable, so precise comments are impossible.) Studies of the Canadian and American situations point to two main issues, one of which can be readily fixed and another that is more intractable. First, students admitted with low high school grades (under 75 percent) do poorly, with the dropout rate increasing as the entering grades fall. The solution to this problem is to raise entrance standards or create separate entry and/or remedial programs for students who have failed to perform at an acceptable level. Second, poorer students tend to drop out more often, in part because of financial difficulties and shortcomings in earlier education. The solution in this case is to improve the quality of high school education and provide more financial assistance for students from less-advantaged families.

The situation is, of course, very complicated. Some students drop out and then re-enter later, in a different program or at a different institution. Mobility is the hallmark of youth educational explorations.

These numbers bother us profoundly, and they should bother you as well. They should make us think seriously about the role and value of the modern university. College degrees are completely worthwhile if the goal of earning them is education, learning, and citizenship—and if students actually capitalize on the intellectual and social opportunities that are available to them. (Of course many don't and didn't, even in the legendary ivory-tower days of previous generations.) On the other hand, if university attendance is seen primarily as a ticket to middle-class prosperity and security, then its value has seriously weakened over the last decade or two. The problem is that the universities haven't told this to their customers. That's what this book is about. Like Paul Revere, we ride to shout an alert: colleges are increasingly turning into factories selling a dream that is disconnected from reality. Be warned!

INTRODUCTION

All people dream—of love, of fame, of wealth, of a happy life—and none more so than the young, who have yet to learn that not all things are possible in this world. This book deals with a dream that is almost universal among them: that they will grow into successful, self-sufficient, prosperous adults, independent of their parents, able to stand on their own. Throughout history people have found various ways to achieve this dream, most of which involved entering the workforce early, taking over the family farm, or learning the techniques of hunting or the family trade. Other avenues involved immigrating to new lands, rising in the church or the military, or engaging in some other adventure. Today, however, in the world's urbanized society, the dream is increasingly focused on education in universities and colleges.

There are over 150 million students attending colleges, technical schools, and universities worldwide. They are part of a social revolution and an impressively risky social experiment: the democratization of university education in a manner comparable to the spread of mass elementary and secondary education throughout much of the world during the twentieth century. Going to college has been transformed during the past two generations from a privilege available only to the Western or Westernized elite into something that is almost viewed as a right. This movement and investment, this commitment of the young talent of so many nations to the classroom, represents one of the most profound transformations of the modern era.

In 1950, there were many fewer colleges in the world. The institutions currently in operation range from the oldest (Bologna in Italy and Oxford in England) to the hastily built research and technical institutions founded in the USA after World War II or created from polytechs in the United Kingdom in the late twentieth century. By 2000, there were more than twelve thousand colleges, with hundreds more under development, particularly in China, India, and the Middle East, and with for-profit institutions competing in ever-larger numbers with increasingly overcrowded publicly funded colleges.

Everywhere around the world, young adults—eighteen and nineteen years or older—stand on the precipice of adulthood, faced with decisions that will affect the rest of their lives. In the industrialized world, they must choose between joining the workforce, travel, attending a college or university, or entering a trade college or an apprenticeship program. Those who dropped out of high school have already made a different choice, one that has severely limited their options. For the rest, the pressure to make the right decision is intense.

This preoccupation with academic study leading to a career is nothing new, much as advocates for post-secondary education like to think higher education is primarily for expanding the mind, improving public discourse, and celebrating the world of ideas. The growth of colleges in all countries has been tied to the economy since the end of World War II. Companies and the public sector, the argument goes, need highly qualified personnel—mostly college graduates. Governments want a strong, modern economy, which most authorities see as tied to the training of young people and the creation of intellectual prosperity in the laboratories and field stations of research-intensive institutions. Eighteen- and nineteen-year-olds desire careers freed from physical labour—jobs that are often called "meaningful" by student advocates and the politicians of the left. Globally, it can be argued that this generation is the softest generation of all, desperate to escape from agrarian or low-end industrial futures and eager for white-collar opportunities or, for the tiny creative elite, for entrepreneurial activities. Students in China, India, and Vietnam tackle their studies with a ferocity and competitiveness that most Western students find alarming; but then, for American and European students, the rice paddy or the sweatshop is not the alternative to a college education. From South Africa to Thailand, Finland to Bulgaria, the most-motivated and hardest-working young people are determined to find brain work and to avoid physical labour. The test of the college system, then, is the degree to which opportunities for graduates match with graduates' abilities and expectations.

In rich countries, these young adults—often poorly prepared for the choices they now must make—face a bewildering set of options. If they possess extraordinary abilities or if their parents have money, they can select from several world-class universities, believed to be fast-tracks to prosperity and career success. If they come from poor families or are of average intelligence or ability, their options will be more limited: Oxford, Harvard, and the Sorbonne are not likely possibilities for them. But even here, a long list of universities, colleges, for-profit institutions, and the like compete for their attention and tuition dollars.

Their counterparts in the developing world have fewer choices. Here, the decision is a harsher one, often amounting to education or a life of factory work or subsistence agriculture. But here, too, the dream is very much alive. Children of the wealthy or well-connected, prodigies, or those educated in elite private schools have significant options, many outside their home countries. For the children of ambitious middle-class or working-class parents, the best opportunities lie overseas, where post-secondary education may lead to immigration to a more prosperous nation. For the rest, village agriculture or industrial labour beckons.

Earlier generations, too, had their dreams, but they did not often involve universities. Centuries ago, these institutions had a very narrow focus—they served mostly as training places for jobs that required a high degree of literacy: the clergy and, to a lesser degree, the law. Young adults (until late in the nineteenth century they were almost always male) would have scoffed at the idea that universities were the best road to a successful career of any kind. Of the great "robber barons" of the early American industrial age—Astor, Vanderbilt, Carnegie, Rockefeller, Morgan—only the last had a university education, and that was because his father was wealthy. Even law and medicine were not professionalized until the late 1800s. It was quite possible to become a lawyer by apprenticing yourself in your teens to a practising lawyer—John A. Macdonald, the first prime minister of Canada, did that, and Abraham Lincoln read law books after a day's work—or to become a doctor by spending a short time at some more or less respectable medical academy.

Many young people tried to escape the dead-end drudgery of rural life by taking factory work in cities, but this often did not improve their lives, only substituting one kind of proletarian existence for another. Emigration provided better opportunities for those who dreamt of religious freedom, social liberation, private land, or economic opportunity in North America, Brazil, Australia, New Zealand, and elsewhere. America, launched in part as a "city on the hill" for religious dissenters, became a global magnet for people seeking prosperity and better prospects. For young men in countries with empires, the dream often involved military or administrative service in the colonies or working in an institution such as the East India Company.

Rapid post–World War II industrialization created a new set of dreams, offered to eager families in the form of secure factory jobs, suburban tract homes, and the domestic tranquility of the consumer age. These were times of simpler dreams, supported by widespread prosperity and growing economic opportunity. It was possible to fulfill one's dream while working for a company such as General Motors, Ford, or Chrysler, which, mostly thanks to trade unionization, provided middle-class opportunities for working people. Universities were for those heading for the learned professions, for those with sufficient family money to spend four years in a pleasant finishing school, and for those—always a minority—who were genuinely fired with a thirst for academic knowledge. Today's world is much more muddled, with far greater returns for those who chose the right track, and serious career dangers for those who choose unwisely. For young people and their parents around the world, the dream of personal opportunity and well-being is focused, obsessively, we argue, on university and college education.

It was during this postwar era that the universities began to grow into Dream Factories, first with the influx of war veterans, and then with the tsunami of baby boomers that descended on them after 1960. They began to position themselves as the logical, and increasingly the only, or at least the preferred, route to prosperity. More and more it became clear to young people that universities, not the shop floor and certainly not striking out on their own for new lands or distant opportunities, held the key to their dreams.

An example of this process is the professionalization of school teachers, particularly at the elementary level. Before World War II few teachers in the lower grades went to university. At most they went to a "Normal School," as teachers' colleges were sometimes called, for a year's course. Often those who taught in the one-room country schools had only a high school education. This is why it was common to see classrooms in these schools presided over by teachers, often women, who were twenty years old or even younger. Then, partly as a means of raising salaries, elementary education became "professionalized," to the point where five years or more of post-secondary education is now required to teach the basics to six-year-olds. Today, if your dream is to be a teacher, there is only one path to achieve it (although some American schools, particularly in poorer districts, are so desperate to find teachers that they are fudging this requirement).

At the same time, the earlier paths to success gradually began to fade. Immigrating to America remains something of a global fantasy, but not for all those who once dreamt of it. Elsewhere, the cities in the developing world hold out hope for the desperate and the ambitious. The "arrival cities" in the sprawling slums around the major cities in the developing world are one of the most important phenomena of our generation, but the prospects for immediate improvement are minimal and uncertain, as any visit to Lagos, Mumbai, or Cairo will attest. Industrial labour, strengthened by a long run of union empowerment, has crumbled, largely due to the unique blend of global competition and technological transformation. There are fewer entry points and fewer opportunities each year.

Where, then, do the dreamers look? Where do people seek opportunity and the promise of well-being and wealth? What do you say to teenagers about their future? That the world is full of endless opportunities? That they can be anything they want to be? That the twists and turns of the global economy have created more uncertainty than we have seen in decades? That they will have a brighter and richer future than their parents? That the lives of today's adults are no roadmap for the future? It is hard to know how to arm young people for prosperity, opportunities, and a high quality of life in the midst of the constant economic and technological turmoil that engulfs the modern world. For many people, the answer is simple: universities.

To their proponents, universities are the Dream Factories of the twenty-first century, ideally suited to the desires of the current and future generations. This is the time of the "knowledge economy," where innovation and human creativity seem to have replaced natural resources and industrial strength as the foundation for personal and national prosperity. This is the age where smart people rule, where companies like Google, Facebook, Rakuten, Skype, and Alibaba rise from obscurity into global prominence. This is the generation where national boundaries have declined in significance, where the mobility of labour is rushing to catch up with the mobility of news, celebrity, influence, and, most of all, capital. In the global swirl that wipes out old wealth and creates new with dazzling speed, young adults and their parents search for the golden ticket, the assured path forward, that will ensure their family's place in the new economy.

The university degree is widely believed to be that golden ticket. Within two generations or so, universities have been transformed from largely Western, elite, and male-dominated institutions into truly global, multicultural, gender-neutral, and increasingly open-access platforms for personal growth and exploration. It seems that China is building universities as fast as the United States once opened McDonald's franchises. India's aggressively mediocre university system expands apace, relying more on unchecked private-sector growth than quality-focused public-sector expansion. Nigeria, with one of the most undependable university systems in the world, has seen its undergraduate population grow from seventeen thousand in 1970 to 1.7 million in 2012—a one-hundred-fold increase—before starting to slide in the face of demoralizing career results for graduates.[1] Even the United States, which is watching century-old private, rural, religious, and liberal-arts colleges close for lack of students, is supporting a rapid expansion of its highly variable and questionable for-profit university system.

Every generation needs and wants a focus for its dreams. And universities are perfect for this. Given enough money, there is, in theory, a university seat for every student who wants one, without, of course, any reference to intellectual ability or scholarly interest. There are grand schools, with impeccable pedigrees, that cater to the truly talented. Others are places for the offspring of the *nouveau riche* or the socially ambitious. Still others, with failure rates that defy belief, accept all comers and watch them be thrown onto the intellectual and career junk heap, degreeless and branded as failures. Even worse are those places all over the world, public and private, that move all tuition-paying students through their studies, granting degrees to individuals of minimal achievement who have severe deficiencies in their basic skills. Worse still is the distressingly extensive culture of lying, academic fraud, cheating, and fabrication of transcripts that increasingly mars the credibility of the global university system.

Like all of the grand dreams that have driven global affairs, modern universities display a mix of achievement and failure. There's plenty of the former, but plenty of the latter too. Much as a goldfield produces a handful of rich deposits and thousands of empty shafts and the high-tech incubator generates two successful companies for every hundred that enter, universities produce a small percentage of winners. Some universities produce graduates of world-changing potential. Many others—including some of the famous as well as the obscure campuses—generate degree holders who work as taxi drivers, waiters, and retail clerks, hardly the stuff of parental dreams and childhood ambition. The odds are better than in a lottery, but nowhere near the slam-dunk of common belief.

For young adults, their families, and countries around the world, the Dream Factories have become a central solution to the uncertainties of the twenty-first century. While there are many examples of university graduates going on to great careers and productive lives, there is also ample evidence that the global system has grown too fast. There are only so many people with the talent to succeed at university. There are only so many jobs and opportunities that benefit from a university degree. And yet these institutions continue to be built by governments, private-sector speculators, and well-meaning philanthropists, all of whom embrace the belief in the unlimited absorptive capacity of the modern economy for university graduates. And they are embraced by young people and parents, eager to escape from physical or outside work, people who believe that universities hold the key to success.

Universities continue to be touted as the flagship opportunity-producing machines of the twenty-first century, but in reality they fall far short of delivering what they promise. There is nothing inherently wrong with them. For smart, motivated, and attentive students, a university degree can bring a wonderful education, a life-changing social experience, and the foundation for a highly successful career. The problem lies with two things: the uneven quality of the university experience and the global disconnect between the mass production of university graduates and the needs of the modern economy.

So here is the reality that is rarely discussed. Across the United States and Western Europe, there are huge numbers of unemployed and underemployed university graduates. In Asia, thousands of graduate degree holders, even those in the so-called career-ready fields of engineering, computer science, and mathematics, find a tight if not closed job market. Nigerian university graduates actually earn average salaries below those of high school graduates, so flawed is that country's university system. And the Arab Spring was, researchers have discovered, an uprising driven significantly by the unrealized dreams of thousands of university graduates who could not find work in the stalled Middle Eastern economies.

The global university system needs a reset, as do the expectations of young people, their families, and governments. Governments need to stop expanding the system. Universities need to change their focus from the production of more graduates to a greater concentration on the quality of the system. Employers need to speak clearly to universities, young people, parents, and governments about their medium- and long-term employment needs. Young people and their parents must look far more carefully at the abilities of young adults and the realities of the twenty-first century economy. The system can be fixed, although the self-interest and autonomy of most institutions militate against responsiveness. The harsh truth is that universities will reform only when governments change their policies, and, even more rapidly, when young people pursue other means of preparing themselves for the future.

But here is the greater challenge. The young need a new dream, because the old one that has served for the past fifty or sixty years no longer works. The global population of young people is higher than ever. The technological and competitive transitions in the world economy have rarely been greater. Millennials, looking forward, are bewildered by the new realities. Their parents, scared about the prospects for their children and even for themselves, turn back to what worked in the past, namely university degrees. If every generation needs a dream, the tragedy of the twenty-first century is that young adults have had to borrow the vision of opportunity that sustained their parents. The Dream Factories are proving to be more ephemeral and less real than anyone thought. Dealing with this reality may well be the transformative challenge of our time.

1

THE DREAM FACTORIES

The world's universities and colleges are in turmoil. In a little over a generation, they have been transformed from training grounds for professionals, the curious, the gifted, and the wealthy into expensive extensions of high schools, designed to educate a broad range of people and prepare them for stable middle-class opportunities. The transformation has its roots in the post–World War II era, starting in the USA with opportunities for returned servicemen, then growing there and elsewhere during the 1950s and 1960s with the "space race" and the search for sustained economic growth.

The dream of universities as the guaranteed road to prosperity—an idea that grew first and fastest in North America—delivered on what it promised, at least at the beginning. An expanding professional and scientific economy produced many opportunities for young adults, who found that a college degree provided a reliable and useful ticket to the middle class. The convergence between post-secondary studies and employment opportunities, while not ideal, was nonetheless impressive and, for those intellectually and financially able to consider college, rewarding. But the result has been an institutional sea-change. Universities, once "ivory towers," have increasingly become Dream Factories, educational institutions dependent for their revenues and thus their existence on selling their product—their dream—to an ever-wider audience.

THE GROWTH OF MASS EDUCATION

The roots of the current situation go back about a hundred years. In 1900, college education was restricted to a tiny minority of the population, and even a high school education was not common: in the United States in about 1900, fewer than 5 percent of the population graduated from high schools, which often had entrance examinations and charged fees. After World War I, governments in the industrial world, especially in the United States, accepted the premise that economic prosperity required an educated and well-trained workforce. All over the industrialized world, governments invested in a massive expansion of elementary and secondary school education. Countries moved quickly toward universal schooling, ensuring that young boys and girls had the rudiments of writing, arithmetic, and basic civics. This happened at different times in different countries: in the UK, for example, it did not occur until after World War II. Many children moved from classroom to the industrial workforce, even in their early teens, but societies declared mass education to be an essential prerequisite for a modern economy. From a standing start in the mid-nineteenth century, public elementary education expanded rapidly to become virtually commonplace, at least in the world's wealthier countries.

In the 1960s and after, as the complexity of the modern world increased, societies doubled down on the educational commitment. Publicly funded, universally accessible high school education came into vogue worldwide, as it had already done in the United States. Governments that had invested massively in elementary school classrooms and teachers now raced to build high schools to accommodate the millions of teenagers seeking a high school education. The systems varied, with Germany leading the way in incorporating industrial and skills training in the advanced school system, and countries like the USA, the UK, and Japan focusing more on general education. But the expansion of the high school system was remarkable, with millions of children who, in previous generations, would have entered the workforce in their early teens, continuing their studies at an advanced level. By the 1970s, high school participation had become as commonplace as going to elementary school had been two generations earlier. By the 1990s, in countries like the USA, Canada, the UK, Japan, South Korea, and across Scandinavia, university became the new preoccupation, with governments opening up millions of spaces for young people anxious to join the expanding professional class. Mass education had more than arrived; it had leapt up the age ladder into the early twenties.

The resulting global university system is an incredible mishmash, with public and private institutions of widely differing quality, and now, particularly in the United States, for-profit schools as well. The University of Phoenix is the flag-bearer for this quintessential contemporary private-sector institutional model. It is listed on NASDAQ, has produced many millions of dollars of profit for its shareholders, provides student-centric education, without spending money on such things as academic graduate programs or faculty research. Courses are offered where and when students want to take them, not according to faculty biorhythms and preferences. It is also now the largest university in the United States, with close to four hundred thousand students. The University of Phoenix's parent organization—the Apollo group—is one of a substantial number of for-profit educational deliverers, including the American InterContinental University, Capella University, and Walden University, several of which have expanded operations internationally.

Not all for-profit institutions have operated ethically, particularly in the USA. The University of Phoenix has run into substantial difficulties, closing many physical campuses, facing legal challenges, and seeing its stock price plummet. Several private universities figured out how to capitalize on the generous Pell Grants, a program expanded by President Obama to ensure that any student who could spell "university" got to go. Unscrupulous recruiters convinced students to sign up for expensive for-profit education, without telling them that they had to pay back any money borrowed under the system. The for-profit movement has expanded internationally, with new institutions springing up from Malaysia (Multimedia University) to Grenada (St. George's University) and Spain (Universidad Europea de Madrid), as well as elsewhere. With governments rushing to meet demand in most countries, it is not clear how much further the for-profit movement will spread at present.

New technologies have accelerated the growth even more. Massive online and distant-education universities, with student populations counted in the hundreds of thousands, offer hundreds of degrees to off-campus learners. If participation and enrolment are proper markers of success, students love them. The largest institutions, located in India, Pakistan, Iran, and Turkey, have over a million students. Many of these universities have tens, if not hundreds, of thousands of enrollees, all studying online and most working toward a university degree. Not a great deal is known about the quality and career impact of these institutions. Suffice it to say that digital technology is allowing governments to deliver advanced learning to literally millions of students who would not otherwise be able to attend a standard university. If a student from Pakistan presented a degree from Anadolu University in Turkey, how many employers would know that this institution, with over one million students, served only twenty-two thousand students on-site and educated the rest at a distance? Would it matter? Academics debate and study the quality of the online learning experience and have yet to reach an absolute consensus about the utility of this type of education. For governments unable to cover the costs of regular universities, and for students unable to participate in standard education processes, distance learning is a godsend.

While college conversions, distance education, and private universities all played a role in the growth of the post-secondary system, one of the greatest contributors to university expansion came from institutions already in place. From the 1960s onward, existing universities the world over built new facilities to house the influx of students who swarmed onto campuses and to provide research space for the faculty hired to teach them. (Politicians like new campus buildings almost as much as they celebrate expansion in student numbers.) Money was forthcoming for the laboratories, libraries, classrooms, residences, and other facilities deemed essential for the modern research-intensive university. The results were often spectacular. Moscow State University, operating since the eighteenth century, has grown to an amazing complex of over a thousand buildings covering some one million square metres, more than 40 percent larger than the Pentagon, the world's largest office building. In many instances—the King Abdullah University of Science and Technology in Saudi Arabia being one of the latest examples—governments and donors have produced eye-popping architectural masterpieces to grace university campuses. In the vast majority of the cases, however, the buildings had the aesthetic of a nineteenth-century prison or an early twentieth-century factory. Only rarely has design overcome financial considerations, resulting in a network of institutions that lack the intellectual impact of the stunning artistry of the facilities at the University of Leuven, the cold rigour of Cambridge, the majesty of Duke, or the dignity of college campuses like Swarthmore, Middlebury, and Dartmouth.

DECLINING STANDARDS

These places differ profoundly in history, design, and ambiance, but they are all Dream Factories, institutions devoted to a simple concept: guaranteeing a successful life to those who pay to attend them. Their promotional materials, full of photographs of happy students studying with classmates and enjoying the bucolic campus life, promise great careers and a golden ticket to the middle class. They are the quintessential institution of the twenty-first-century knowledge economy, tackling the challenges of the high-tech, globalized economy and the realities of an international workforce in rapid transition.

It took close to a century for high school graduation to become almost universal in first-world countries. Regular schooling did not suit all students equally, particularly those who were inclined toward the skilled trades. Governments generally did not fund high schools equally, resulting in substantial educational gaps among poor, rural, and minority populations. Equally, the rapid expansion of the post–World War II industrial economy, which drew heavily on low-skilled and semi-skilled labour in the factories and construction trades, meant that it was still possible, in the 1950s and 1960s, for young people, particularly men, to make a good living without a high school education. Many left high school without graduating, often following their fathers' paths to plants, mines, or construction sites. The gathering strength of unions, combined with an abundance of low-skill/high-wage work, ensured that these jobs paid well and carried generous benefits. As a result, high school graduation rates did not rise as rapidly as early high school attendance.

The situation became more complicated by the early twenty-first century, as a pattern of "social passes," particularly in the United States and Canada, produced a steadily increasing number of high school graduates who got through school without learning much of anything. Consider these depressing facts. Among American high school graduates, only

40 percent have age-appropriate reading skills and only 25 percent have appropriate mathematical skills.[1] The situation in Canada is not much better. The high school completion rate has increased in recent years for a number of reasons, one of them being massive government encouragement to stay in school; another presumably being a lowering of standards for graduation. The percentage of young adults (age twenty-five to thirty-four) who have "attained at least upper secondary education" is, according to the OECD, fairly even across Western industrialized countries, with Canada, at 92 percent, having one of the highest completion rates. In comparison, the percentage of Americans who graduate stands at 89. In both Turkey and Mexico it is 46 percent.[2]

Japan and Germany have higher and more standardized academic accomplishments, as do South Korea, Finland, Singapore, and Taiwan. In China, a country that has made massive investments in high school education over the past thirty years, educational fraud and manipulation of transcripts is so widespread as to make it difficult to assess educational achievement. Many Chinese proudly carry high school diplomas that provide no assurance that they have the abilities and learning that have, since World War II, been associated with a high school degree. But, of course, the same is true in the United States.

College and university education is now replicating the high school experience. A new focus on higher education has occurred as job opportunities for high school dropouts have declined and opportunities for high school graduates have shrunk in the face of the collapsing power of trade unions and the disappearance of traditional low-skill/high-wage work. Naturally and inexorably, governments, parents, and young people have begun to focus on post-secondary education.

The inflation in education has been steady. Before 1920, most students stopped their studies after elementary school. Before the 1960s, they stopped after high school. In the last third of the twentieth century, in a fit of educational optimism that gripped much of the world, attention shifted to community colleges, colleges, and universities, with the latter representing the gold standard for those who felt that they had the skills, determination, and ability to prosper. A quick look at the same industrial nations illustrates the degree to which college and university preparation swept the wealthiest countries.

As with the high school systems after World War II, the colleges and universities took in many more students than they graduated. The percentage of those not finishing increased over time, primarily because the standards of the advanced educational institutions proved to be less flexible than the high schools'. This is an important point. Governments rejoice that 90 percent of the population has at least a high school education, but we may ask this question: How much of an achievement is it to earn a qualification that nine-tenths of the population also earns? High school graduation is almost universal in a country such as Canada and even more so in Scandinavia, South Korea, Singapore, and Japan. Largely because of public, government, and parental pressure, high schools have lowered educational standards to ensure more students graduate—literate and numerate or, in the case of all too many, not. For the time being (with variations between institutions), colleges and universities have maintained higher academic standards and resisted the pressure—also from the public, governments, parents, and students—to pass those who fail to meet clear and objective standards of academic achievement.

HIGHER EDUCATION GENERATES MIXED REVIEWS

Not surprisingly, universities generate mixed reviews. Some people, like President Obama, believe that universities are central to personal success and national prosperity. Enthusiasm is particularly strong among organizations of university presidents and teachers. Andrew Hacker, a well-known American "public intellectual" and emeritus professor of political science at Queen's College, New York, baldly states that "everyone has the capacity to succeed at college and benefit from what it has to offer." "*All* young people," he says, and he puts the word in italics, have "knowledge-thirsty minds that can be awakened and encouraged to examine the world they inhabit."[3] Others are more skeptical and are beginning to question the contribution that those currently being urged to get a degree will make to economic, social, and cultural success. Angela Merkel, solid where Obama wanders into the fantasy world of Garrison Keller's Lake Wobegone (where everyone is above average), demonstrates the uncertainty and caution of a thoughtful leader:

We have committed a lot of resources to increasing interest in mathematical, engineering and scientific training courses, and will continue to do so. We have too few students, rather than too many, in these subjects. If we wish to maintain prosperity and living standards in our countries, it thus behooves us to encourage the enjoyment of science education. Taking a degree in the natural and engineering sciences is considered to be rather precarious. In terms of career prospects, experience has repeatedly shown that whilst the take-up of people trained in these professions is very good during economically buoyant periods, during a recession these people will experience considerable difficulties in finding a job. This is why it is also the job of business and education institutions to ensure there is a permanent shoring up, so to speak, of career prospects for graduates from the mathematics and natural science disciplines. Scientific knowledge has a very short sell-by-date, which is why we cannot afford to have gaps in the provision of qualified scientists.[4]

A smaller number are increasingly skeptical about university education. Few are as blunt as Simon Dolan, United Kingdom multi-millionaire high school dropout and author of *How to Make Millions Without a Degree: And How to Get By Even If You Have One*:[5] "I feel University only prepares students for a very specific set of circumstances. I'm not sure if it robs them of life skills, but it certainly delays the point at which they attain those life skills. By life skills, I mean work skills, be that in an office or in a factory or whatever—the key is that work skills can only be learned through real work. These are skills that you don't learn from a book; you learn them by getting out there and doing them." Peter Thiel, co-founder of PayPal, has gone a step further, offering to pay young people $100,000 to not attend university for two years and instead to pursue their business ideas. As Thiel, who believes that universities are oversold and headed for a crash, told *TechCrunch* in 2011, "A true bubble is when something is overvalued and intensely believed. Education may be the only thing people still believe in in the United States. To question education is really dangerous. It is the absolute taboo. It's like telling the world there's no Santa Claus."

The more young people who go, or who ponder going, to college, the louder the debate grows. On one side, people claim that those with university degrees make more money in their lifetimes than those without them (true as an average, but not for individuals, and each would-be student is an individual). The case is forcefully put, with charts, by Mark Gongloff in *The Huffington Post*.[6] The contrary case is made by two scholars in a paper published by the Brookings Institution,[7] an argument that we will explore in a later chapter.

The debate about the value of a university education is carried on worldwide. In Vietnam, Pham Chi Lan, the former president of the Vietnam Chamber of Commerce and Industry, is a dynamo, with an energy and verve that belies her seventy-plus years. Her keynote address to the hundred or so academics and government officials gathered in a posh Hanoi hotel to discuss the Asian innovation environment contradicted all the stereotypes of an officially Communist state. Vietnam, she said, was taking on the world. The country had what it took to succeed: the prodigious work ethic of the people married with foreign investment, government support, and Vietnamese ingenuity.

She flashed charts and tables about competitive pricing, low labour costs, and urban developments, the like of which few countries outside China have attempted, as well as a regulatory environment that was becoming more capitalist by the month. She spoke about the application of new scientific and technological discoveries to Vietnamese agriculture and fisheries and described the country's efforts to attract high-technology businesses. She wowed the audience, as much by her confidence and determination as by the clearly promotional tour of Vietnam's new economy. People were impressed.

During the question period, a visiting scholar asked about something she had not covered in the speech: the role of university research and university graduates in Vietnam's innovation efforts. It was a standard question, likely to draw a standard answer. The audience knew that national innovation systems draw on the powerful combination of the academy, government, and business to prepare a country for global competitiveness and prosperity. They also knew that the Vietnamese government was investing heavily in research and post-secondary education. A science city under development within a dozen miles of the conference hotel had attracted a $1 billion in investment and would, if finished as planned, host over a million people in a new economic powerhouse. The once-isolationist government had even permitted foreign institutions, led by Royal Melbourne Institute of Technology University, to set up operations in both Ho Chi Minh City and Hanoi. The audience relaxed, ready for the latest morale-boosting tribute to the modern university. They were in for a shock.

To the surprise of the audience, Pham stepped aside from the podium—almost as tall as she was—and launched into a savage critique of Vietnam's universities. She described them as next to useless. Their researchers did little work that had any value to the business community or to the country. The business community clamored for graduates with practical skills, while the universities produced young people with traditional classical educations. As a result, businesses rarely looked to universities to help solve commercial problems. The government was unhappy with the return on their investment. Her diatribe dripped with frustration and criticism of an ossified and unproductive university system. The audience, unused to the spectacle of an Asian leader dissecting a national institution in public, was uncharacteristically quiet. The academics among them all believed as a matter of faith that universities were central to dreams of national prosperity. Was there really something wrong with the country's universities? Or was it simply that this businesswoman failed to appreciate the many benefits of university training and research to an emerging economy?

Some 3,500 miles west of Hanoi, on the edge of a desert, another nation had a different approach. In the ultra-modern, energy boom-town of Doha, Qatar, two young hijab-clad women offered a portrait of the role of universities and university graduates in their country's future. Education City, located less than ten miles from Doha's city centre, demonstrated how fossil-fuel revenues can drive national change. Because the country's little-known University of Qatar lacked the global prestige and scientific expertise of foreign universities, the country opted to buy skill and status rather than build it slowly from within. The Qatar Foundation for Education, Science and Community Development, extremely well funded and with strong political connections, sponsored the initiative, seeking to vault Qatar's university system from virtually nowhere into international prominence.

The multi-billion dollar campus made itself available for a number of programs offered by first-rate international institutions. Virginia Commonwealth University offered a fine arts program. Cornell University delivered a medical program and Texas A&M gave students a chance to study chemical, electronic, mechanical, and petroleum engineering. Business and computer science degrees were available through Carnegie Mellon University, with Northwestern University offering journalism and communication studies, and Georgetown University's School of Foreign Service delivering its prestigious foreign service degree. HEC Paris, one of the top-ranked business schools anywhere, provided executive education programs and another of the world's great universities, University College of London, delivered graduate degrees in museum and heritage studies. A national university program—the Qatar Faculty of Islamic Studies—operated on the site. Nearby, in one of the most unusual international initiatives anywhere, the College of the North Atlantic from Newfoundland offered a full range of college and trades programs in a $2 billion campus.

The billions pumped into this university by the Qatari government have bought some pretty impressive facilities. The campus is designed to minimize the effects of the 35+°C (95+°F) temperatures—during the cool season—and to show off the educational opportunities available for Qatar's elite students. A well-designed student service centre offers everything from a bowling alley to high-end gyms and swimming pools (separate ones for women and men). No harsh words here for the unique Education City experiment, which government officials and business leaders praise endlessly and finance at a remarkable level, with high standards but the constraints that are common in a Middle Eastern nation.

The two students assigned to take a small group of visitors around Education City lauded the facilities. The participating universities, they said proudly, were among the best in the world. They explained how each international participant tried to replicate the culture and ambiance of its home institution by ensuring that top-quality faculty taught the classes, and that the educational standards were the same as at home. Both students had started in Cornell's pre-medicine program, but found the courses not to their liking. They opted instead for Texas A&M's engineering degree.

Bright, engaging, and well informed, the students fit in comfortably with the unusual mixture of Qatari nationals, home campus visitors, and foreign students studying at Education City.

Their take on Education City could not have been more different from the Vietnamese business leader's condemnation of her country's university system. The satellite campuses brought prestige and opportunity to Qatar. Neither one of them, they said, would have been permitted by their parents to study outside the country. Yet the national university lacked the stature and credibility their parents sought for them. The satellites offer them the benefits of a foreign education without having to leave home. As was the norm for Qataris, neither student wanted for much—both were chauffeured to and from the campus each day—and neither one would have been out of place in a top-flight university located elsewhere in the world. Obviously smart, they knew that they were preparing for one of the most lucrative employment markets in the world. They chuckled when asked if they worried about finding work after graduation. Both had high-paying jobs lined up, even though they were still in their third year.

Vietnam and Qatar represent polar opposites of the current university reality: on one hand, damning criticism of a system that is poorly connected to the national business community and underperforming from an economic perspective, and on the other, praise for institutions that promise to produce the leaders and commercial discoveries of tomorrow.

WORLD HUNGER FOR THE DREAM

Like a storm gathering its strength from the ocean's energy, the tempest bearing down on the universities takes its energy from young people's yearnings for a good and prosperous life. It is as regular and predictable as the tides. Every year, all over the world, seventeen- and eighteen-year-olds perform a ritual. Its details differ from country to country, but there is a common goal: to ensure success in life by getting into a top university. In Japan, students work themselves into exhaustion studying for nation-wide high school–leaving examinations. When the results are posted (and in Japan they are posted publicly), careers and lives are made or blighted, because the tests determine which students get into the best schools and which ones are destined for the factory floor. The winners in Britain's endless educational class wars emerge from their A-level tests, heading for the top schools, while the losers go on to less prestigious institutions or directly into the low-paid workforce. American parents hire advisors, letter-writers, and test coaches to help their offspring work through the maze of college and university admission procedures. In China, where until recently only 2 percent of high school graduates got into a domestic university, wealthy parents set aside up to $200,000 to give their child a shot at completing a four-year degree overseas. South African students, particularly black youngsters struggling to overcome the legacy of apartheid, are desperate to get into an institute of higher learning.

In most African nations, where only a minority gets to go to high school and only a fraction of these have the chance to go to university, the pursuit of a post-secondary education is usually a distant dream, dependent on personal connections. Harvard accepts about 7 percent of those who apply, but that is almost an open-entry institution compared to the situation in India. Indian students compete through rigorous examinations for a place in the Indian Institutes of Technology, campuses with such intense competition for entry that they make the admissions standards at Harvard and Oxford look easy in comparison. In 2012, half a million people wrote the national IIT entrance exam, and the success rate was 2 percent.[8] At Nanjing University of China, one of the top schools in an education-hungry nation, fewer than 1 percent of applicants are accepted, making it even tougher to get into than the IITs.

Ever wonder why people attach a premium to top institutions? The race to get in is a key reason. At many of the world's universities, high school graduation and the ability to pay tuition is sufficient for entry. Take it for granted that students are not banging down the doors to get into the University of Kinshasa, currently ranked 5,959th in the world (but top of the mountain in the Congo). Not surprisingly, parents who want their children to get into the top institutions invest heavily in entrance-examination preparation and pre-testing exercises. In contrast, South Korea and Taiwan, like the United States, have places for almost every high school graduate; there is intense competition for a handful of elite schools, but it's easy to get into one of the public and private universities in the country. Germany, in contrast, identifies academic potential early on, moving high-quality students into academic streams in their early teens and herding the less bookish into technical and trades programs.

This being the age of universities, however, there are always workarounds. Cannot get into the University of Chicago law school? Go to the University of Windsor, not so far away in Canada and less than a quarter the cost. Turned down for medical school at USC or UCLA? Why not try the University of Guadalajara, which uses the same curriculum and many of the same instructors? Cannot get into a prime law school in the United Kingdom or Canada? The private Bond University—one of the few places named after a convicted felon—offers internationally transportable law degrees. One of the simple truths of this age is that all universities are not created equal and that students in pursuit of a specific credential can often find it—for a price—somewhere in the world.

But universities have some tricks up their sleeves, particularly when governments insist on accessibility as a prime value. Some countries—the Netherlands and Portugal being good examples—believe that accessibility to university is as much of a right as high school attendance. Institutions cope with this intellectually irrational proposition by making a simple point: admission is not a guarantee of graduation. So institutions and programs in high demand among entering students— engineering, design, digital media, and other market-ready programs are currently popular—admit hundreds and hundreds of students, then use the first-year experience to cull the number to a manageable level. Second-year cohorts, entrance to which is closely guarded by program directors, might be limited to 10 percent or fewer of the first-year students. Students who fail to meet the threshold—and clearly they are numbered in the many hundreds—are redirected to lower-demand (and often lower-quality) programs. If the university does not need the extra bodies to cover institutional costs, having sucked government grants and often tuition fees from the first-year students, they can simply let the students leave the university.

The success of colleges and universities in North America has produced many global imitators over the past three decades. While countries with strong resource economies lagged behind—largely because of the continuation of high-wage/low-skill work—nation after nation invested in the rapid expansion of its college and university system. The growth in the wealthier nations was dramatic, building off an institutional base that, in some quarters, was hundreds of years old.

But consider what has occurred at the same time in the developing world. The colonial powers created universities in their overseas possessions, usually training the children of elite families to take their place in the colonial business and governance systems and sending the best of them back to institutions in the mother country. These former colonies, struggling to adjust to industrial competition and globalization, have seized on advanced education as a means of achieving individual and collective prosperity. With many of these countries coping with widespread poverty, serious infrastructure challenges, and limited government resources, distance-education systems and online educational delivery have provided a means of extending advanced education to villages and towns outside of the capital cities. The result has been a massive global increase in the total number of universities and university students.

This expansion has been fraught with irony and contradiction. The colonial powers financed the early stages of the system and trained many faculty and staff members who subsequently found work in developing world institutions. Industrial-world philanthropy, often through global governance organizations such as the United Nations, UNESCO, the World Bank, and private donors, provided further assistance to the international effort. When the system worked—and there were many individual and institutional success stories among a global university system marked by serious inconsistencies in standards and effectiveness—these colleges and universities converted bright young students into globally competitive graduates. To put it bluntly, the leading universities in the leading industrial nations trained their competitors, transferring a significant portion of the educational advantage enjoyed by the West to the emerging economies. India is an excellent example of this process in action. This act of educational philanthropy improved the global economy, strengthening the training in these countries through lifelong commercial and professional contacts with their graduates. Overall, the primary impact was to improve their economic prospects dramatically.

At the individual level, the growing universities of India, China, and other countries are classic Dream Factories, converting potential into achievement and opportunity into personal success, though not necessarily at home. Africa, in recent years, has seen upwards of thirty-five thousand of its best-trained graduates leave the continent each year for further study in first-world institutions or jobs in wealthier countries. Turkey has, over the past decade, financed a ferocious expansion of its university system, focusing largely on engineering and technology, predicated on the belief that these graduates will find work in the European Union, send money home, and eventually return to bolster the country's economy. Worldwide, more than 4.5 million students are enrolled in university-level education outside their home country, a number that is predicted to rise to 8 million by 2025.[9] The country with the highest percentage of international students studying in its universities is, perhaps surprisingly, Australia—surprising until one thinks of its geographical location.

One of the imperatives behind studying overseas is the idea, particularly strong in China, that young graduates would either enjoy a decided employment advantage when they returned home, or would be able to gain a working visa that could lead to permanent residency in the country of their education. Nations such as Canada, the United States, Germany, Australia, New Zealand, and the United Kingdom have for several decades capitalized on the talent and education of foreign-born students to buttress their economies, particularly in high-technology sectors.

The commitment to college and university expansion has rested on more than the opportunities for personal advancement. Many countries, observing closely the success of scientific and technological innovation in North America, Japan, East Asia, and northern Europe, and desiring rapid economic expansion, concluded that major commitments to an education and research-rich society would produce favourable economic outcomes for the society as a whole. Countries that had lagged far behind in competitiveness and productivity caught up rapidly. Singapore, Taiwan, and South Korea, to use East Asian examples, were transformed as the rapid improvement of the education system underpinned an increasingly technologically proficient society. Other countries, from Finland to Israel, also capitalized on the advanced education of their citizens to create globally competitive economies, in both of these cases underpinned by high-technology industries.

By the early twenty-first century, almost every country in the world believed that national prosperity rested on an expansion of the post-secondary system. The commitment to national innovation through advanced education and basic research became a global mantra, adopted from Greenland to Botswana, with policy manifestations in most nations. (This phenomenon raises the question of how national innovation policies can be "innovative" when they are the same everywhere, copying standard global practice.) The explosion in the number of universities, the number of students, the number of graduates, the number of postgraduate students, the number of faculty members, the amount of research activity and expenditures, and the volume of academic publication has been truly impressive.

Indeed, recent estimates suggest that the knowledge base in the world doubles every five years, a growth rate that boggles the mind. If the total volume of knowledge (judged by published research) stood at 100 in 1980—near the real starting point of the global expansion of universities and colleges—then it would have increased to 12,800 in 2015—128 times in a generation. Some of this research is in fields of no economic importance, that will never reach more than a handful of readers—there have been many thousands of scholarly publications about William Shakespeare in the past few decades[10]—but the significance in computer science, engineering, medicine, and other practical fields is considerable.[11] So, the results are impressive: more students, more research, more publications and, as a quick look around the modern economy demonstrates, rapid technological and commercial innovation.

But there is no linear or simple relationship between post-secondary education and economic advancement. Consider the characteristics of the following country:

Population: 11.2 million
Trading population within a three-hour flight: 500+ million
High school graduation rate: 94 percent
Number of universities and colleges: 47
Total student enrolment: 112,000
Number of medical graduates: 10,500 (half are international students)

By any global standard, this country is perfectly aligned for global competitiveness and leadership in the new economy. But the nation languishes, with a per-capita income that is only 10 percent of that of the United States,[12] major deficiencies in infrastructure, high unemployment, and large-scale overseas employment of the country's well-trained professionals. The country is Cuba, an ideologically frozen country caught in a half-century-long conflict with the United States that is only now warming. Mass advanced education has not saved Cuba from the dual burdens of ideology and politics. Much the same is true of Russia, a nation with a distinguished history of mathematical and scientific education and high participation rates—but with a cramped economy. Mass education is no guarantee of national economic success, especially when trumped by politics.

The outcomes of mass education are similar in many emerging economies as well. China has doubled its university and college system to about 2,400 institutions in the past ten years. In 2014, China graduated 7.26 million students from its universities, seven times the number of 1999.[13] Around 9 percent of Chinese have at least some college education, twice the percentage in 2000. In 2012–2013 there were a quarter of a million Chinese students studying at American universities.[14] At present, its university graduates are facing high rates of underemployment and unemployment, since there is a misalignment of the national economy and the education provided to Chinese youth. Put simply, the country does not have enough middle-management positions or even technology-based jobs for the young people streaming out of the universities. Remember those students going overseas to get an international degree? They are referred, upon returning to China, as *haigui* or sea turtles, and find that their degrees are not an assured ticket to career opportunities.

Chinese university graduates are not alone. South Korea has one of the highest university participation rates in the world (80 percent of high school graduates continue on to university). The country has some 3 million (as of 2014) inactive university graduates, because, policy-makers believe, of the oversupply of job-hungry young people. Steadily rising unemployment rates among university graduates have started to level off in Japan. But the country continues to wrestle with a massive oversupply of PhDs, many of them in the high-technology, computing, and engineering jobs that are supposed to be at the centre of the technologically-rich "new economy." Singapore, with a robust economy, still saw graduate unemployment jump significantly, if only to 3.6

percent. Unlike other countries, however, the government responded by capping total university enrolment in Singapore at 25 percent of the high school graduating class.[15]

Nigeria, on the other hand, with about six hundred thousand university and college students in 2010 (down substantially from three years earlier),[16] has created a system wracked by corruption, mismanagement, and low quality. About a third of school-age children are not in school. The system is so dysfunctional that alert employers and universities in other parts of the world discount Nigerian grades and credentials substantially. The situation is similar in Egypt and other North African states that bit into the golden apple of post-secondary education. They have discovered that a functioning higher education system cannot be wished into existence in the absence of a strong national infrastructure, no matter how badly their citizens want to attend university, and that in any case the regional economy cannot accommodate most of the system's graduates.

So, for every Israel and Finland, both advanced countries that prospered through education-driven growth, or Taiwan, Singapore, and South Korea, which built twenty-first-century economies off advanced education and training, there are others like Greece, Vietnam, India, Egypt, Zambia, Spain, South Africa, Nigeria, and Mexico that have not yet seen the growth expected from unleashing a flood of university graduates into the economy. In Portugal, the graduates from a large and academically solid university system cannot find work in the moribund national economy. Instead, they look to France, Germany, and Brazil for employment, as their working-class parents and grandparents did in earlier times. This has not stopped the expansion, however, because parents and young people alike still consider a college or university degree as the most promising— even if not assured—path to a comfortable life. The dream is international.

THE LEARNING = EARNING EQUATION

Why the enthusiasm for higher education? There are three basic reasons: first, sustained evidence that a university degree produces highly beneficial results, if not for everyone, then at least on average; second, major shifts in the industrial workforce; third, changing attitudes toward work in the contemporary world. We will discuss the first reason in detail later, but for now we note the following: there is substantial statistical evidence that students with degrees (especially if they have more than one degree) fare much better on average in the modern workforce than people who lack such degrees. Some reasons for this are obvious: doctors make more money than retail clerks and they require more than one degree in most countries; teachers generally have higher incomes than taxi drivers; and engineers enjoy better salaries than hairdressers. Those who went through universities and colleges in the 1950s and 1960s—when there were not many graduates and when the expanding economy desperately required hundreds of thousands of managers and easily trained white-collar workers—have generally been blessed with stable employment, decent incomes, and middle-class lives, at least in the leading industrial nations.

It is important to note, however, the qualification "on average." The equation *Learning* = *Earning* is not universally true. Graduates in the fine arts do not make more money than unionized heavy-duty mechanics or workers in the oilfields, and many other similar comparisons could be made. Ask the 25 percent of retail workers or the 15 percent of taxi drivers in the United States who held college degrees in 2010.[17] The American Bureau of Labor Statistics gives a surprising estimate of the number of other "low-skill" jobs held by college graduates: 1 in 6 bartenders, 1 in 4 amusement park attendants, and 1 in 5 telemarketers all have at least one degree.

Some of this has carried forward into the 2010s. Graduates in fields in high demand continue to enjoy wage premiums and diverse opportunities for work, while the prospects for those pursuing general degrees and study in fields disconnected from the workforce (Film Studies, anyone?) have diminished in recent years. Nor are degrees from all colleges worth the same in the workforce. Contrast the contemporary career prospects of a Yale graduate in economics or finance or a Harvard graduate in law on the one hand, with those of someone with a Bachelor of Science in Biology from North Arizona University. Or those of an engineer from the National University of Singapore, a globally elite institution, with those of a Bachelor of History from University of Wisconsin-Parkside, a fine open-access college that makes a real effort to assist students from less-prosperous backgrounds. This part of the university equation has not filtered down to the consciousness of the general public, where the belief that a college or university degree—any degree—offers a major career boost remains illogically strong.

Some of the enthusiasm for college and university rests with the erosion of other opportunities. Imagine being a high school graduate in Flint, Michigan, or Oshawa, Ontario, in 1955. Automotive manufacturers had a huge hunger for hard-working young men—although not many women—at that time. A young man in Grade 10 or 11 faced a choice: accept a high-wage factory job with good union-inspired benefits or invest four years in a degree. Many opted for the former and, until the 1990s, could be confident that they had made the right economic decision. Leap forward fifty years. Similar high school students in these now post-industrial cities can see the employment devastation and industrial wasteland around them. Few employers are offering high-wage, secure employment to high school graduates. The local industrial option has faded dramatically in appeal in contrast to the promise that a degree appears to offer. With the division of employment into low-wage service work and diminished industrial work on the one hand, and well-paid employment for professionals and the technologically skilled on the other, the appeal of a university education is now evident.

Attitudes to work have also shifted, with strong manifestations of this change in the developing world. While romantics love to idealize the lives of coal miners, factory workers, and farmers, the reality is these are hard, often dirty, and frequently dangerous jobs. For generations, people have sought easier lives, adopting new technologies that removed the more difficult elements of pre-industrial and industrial labour. The glorification of office work and the declining enthusiasm for outdoor and physical labour have convinced parents the world over to invest heavily in their children's education.

The dreams of university do not play out equally. In the West, college or university education has become a rite of passage, something parents plan and save for throughout their children's youth. In other nations, however, getting into a degree-granting institution is no real accomplishment; entrance standards have fallen to derisory levels at many public and some private institutions. In richer countries, getting into the "right" institution—Oxford rather than the University of Arts London, Stanford over Clark Atlanta University of Georgia, University of Toronto over Algoma University—is the real struggle. Many families spend tens of thousands of dollars in trying to game the admissions system in order to secure a coveted spot in an elite institution. But still young people go to universities, even those of low and dubious abilities, in ever-increasing numbers.

Nowhere is the mystique of the Dream Factory more firmly entrenched than in the developing world, even though the local institutions, even the elite ones, are markedly inferior to the best universities elsewhere. Families spend enormous sums on prestigious local preparatory schools, often English-language and typically internationally-branded, in the hope that this will help their sons and daughters win admission to Oxford or Stanford or MIT. They then hand over large amounts of money to agents, some of whom are of dubious quality, who help children prepare for international admissions processes. They are met by hundreds of college and university recruiters, desperate for the high-fee-paying international students they increasingly rely on to pay their institutions' bills.

The international-student recruitment process has turned into a high-stakes dating game. The students—and their parents—have their eyes on the elite institutions and the preferred countries (the USA, UK, Australia, Canada, Germany and New Zealand, but China and Japan are increasingly attractive as well). There are family dreams and a great deal of money at stake—an international student will, over four years, pay more than US$200,000 in tuition at a top-ten American school, £40,000 to £140,000 in the UK, AUS$120,000 in Australia and as much as CDN$140,000 in Canada, depending on the program. But there is no lack of students. China sends over 275,000 students per year to the United States, representing over 30 percent of the international student total. India is in second place, at about 12 percent.

While rich families can afford the price of attending a Dream Factory— each year Harvard, Oxford, and the Sorbonne welcome dozens of the children from the world's wealthiest families—middle-class and working-class families often mortgage the future of the extended family to make attendance possible. Recruiting agents, frequently paid by both the families and the recruiting institutions, try to align interests, abilities, and admission standards. The dependence on a single country can lead to questionable behaviour at the institutional level. One American school created a real stir when it was revealed that the university was adjusting entrance grades and taking extraordinary steps to ensure that the students stayed on campus, primarily to ensure a steady flow of international-student cash. One can only imagine the educational and financial calculus of international families as they balance savings, a child's academic record, the admission standards of thousands of overseas institutions, the educational and career interests of the student, and the family's strategy for migration and/ or employment.

But as parents and young people began vigorously pursuing a limited number of places at the very best universities, other institutions saw an opportunity, expanding to meet a seemingly inexhaustible demand. Aggressive as well as prestigious institutions, particularly from the United States, Australia, and the United Kingdom, opened campuses overseas. New York University brought its high-quality, high-cost liberal-arts education to Dubai and Singapore. Monash opened campuses in Malaysia and South Africa. James Cook University, a rising but little-known institution in Queensland that focuses on tropical areas, has campuses in Cairns, Townsville, and Brisbane, and overseas facilities in Singapore. George Mason University in Virginia has a campus in Songdo, South Korea. Some of these have foundered, including the University of Waterloo's effort in Dubai and some costly experiments by British universities in China.

PROFITING FROM THE DREAM

But even with a few faltering steps, the trajectory remained the same: students from around the world were clamoring for higher education. Universities salivated at the possibilities, domestically because this justified rapid expansion, and internationally because the high tuition paid in most nations underpinned the increasingly precarious financial situation on campuses.

Governments loved the expansion as well. The arrival of thousands of international students, many of them well-heeled, did more than expand the university enrolments. The students spent money on everything from housing and food to cars and entertainment—and more than a little on alcohol—boosting the local and national economies in the process. Hosting international students became an industry in its own right. Australia declared international students to be worth AUS$16.3 billion in 2013–14.[18] Other countries, aided by bean-counting university organizations, spoke enthusiastically about the $7.7 billion Canadian sector,[19] the

$22 billion brought into the United States,[20] and the £2.3 billion contributed to the United Kingdom's economy every year.[21]

The situation seemed like a match made in heaven. Young people wanted to go to university. Their parents were willing to foot the bill to send them overseas. The receptor universities were happy to welcome them, with the elite institutions selecting some of the brightest (and wealthiest) students on the planet and the lower-ranked universities hoovering up thousands of full-fee-paying students, albeit often of lower academic standing. Governments bought in big time, welcoming the annual infusion of cash into the local economies. Few complained—and surprisingly little thought was given to the simple question of whether or not this massive expansion in university attendance was connected to the needs of the national and global economies.

Others saw commercial opportunities in the global preoccupation with the Dream Factories. A massive industry of agents grew up around the world, with specialists, some qualified and honest, others not, promising parents and students access to the best universities. No one really knows the balance between those with integrity and those who are simply eager for cash. Add to this the privately run housing units, immigration lawyers (it is not automatic that the students admitted to even a top university will get the appropriate visas in a timely fashion), travel agents, and the like who cluster around the international-student industry. Not surprisingly, fraudsters gathered. Recently Mark Zinny, an ex-Harvard teacher and "educational consultant," was sentenced in Boston to five years in prison for scamming a Chinese family for $2 million in fees and bribes to get their sons into top prep schools and colleges. The *Boston Globe* commented that "the case calls attention to the dark side of a growing international admissions consulting industry, as more foreign families seek to send their students to elite US schools at any cost."[22]

The private sector has also stepped in to compete with public institutions for fee-paying students. The for-profit companies engage at many levels in the educational process. Private secondary schools offer students from non-Western countries high-quality, internationally recognized diplomas that give them a leg up on students graduating from domestic high schools. There is a large global network of English-language training centres, most operating on a for-profit basis and many targeted at helping would-be international students pass their Test of English as a Foreign Language (TOEFL) or other language competency examination. (There is a much smaller industry associated with helping students improve their skills in German, Spanish, French, and Chinese.) China alone claims more than three hundred million people are studying English; Japan has millions taking English lessons. Private and public institutions in Western countries also offer pre-university English-language programs, primarily focused on university entrance, another lucrative sideline for the global education industry.

The involvement of for-profit institutions goes much further than these preparatory stages, however. Private for-profit colleges, often brokering programs from established and accredited institutions, recruit, teach, and graduate their own students, or aid them in transferring mid-program into the more prestigious non-profit institutions. For-profit institutions have proliferated around the world, ranging from the University of Phoenix, Laureate Education, Corinthian Colleges, and University Canada West to hundreds of private institutions in countries such as China, Pakistan, Nigeria, and others. Indeed, the Indian private universities market is growing so rapidly and with so little oversight that it is effectively out of control, as well as of doubtful quality.

But there is money—often big money—to be made in education. And not all of the university aspirants can get into Princeton, UCLA, Cambridge, or the University of British Columbia. When students can't get into a high-ranking institution but still want a degree, they will find many others, both national and international, that are happy to oblige them for a price. With a university degree almost fully commoditized, and with high status attached to the top schools, many students who dream of getting into elite institutions end up going downmarket from the top one hundred, to the top one thousand, and eventually to a low-ranking institution that will accept any international applicant with enough money to pay its fees.

To capitalize on the global opportunities, universities have expanded their international recruiting offices, sent recruiters to high schools in countries where there is a high demand, and participated in massive university and college fairs that attract thousands of eager—even desperate—students and their parents. Recruiting for the Dream Factories has become an industry its own right, with associations, specialized training, conferences, professional associations, marketing divisions, trade magazines, and the other accoutrements of a multi-billion-dollar a year industry. At the most aggressive universities, students define their interests by answering a brief questionnaire. Thanks to digital technology, each student then receives a personalized newsletter from the recruiting office that highlights campus activities, services, and personnel connected to the applicant's preferences. Consider the situation from the university's perspective. An international student attending a top American university might pay more than $50,000 a year in tuition and another $20,000 in other expenses, for each of the four to six years it takes successful students to complete a degree. A smart university would happily pay $10,000 or more for an accepted and con-firmed applicant, and is therefore quite willing to spend aggressively on recruiters, agents, participation in recruiting fairs, outreach to parents, promotional material, and personalized websites.

Is college worth it? A couple of years ago the *New York Times* posed this question, quoting William J. Bennett, secretary of education under President Reagan, and Jeffrey Selingo, an editor at *The Chronicle of Higher Education*, both of whom believe the American college system is self-destructing. Bennett, a conservative, believes too many people are going to college, and Selingo says those who do go aren't getting their money's worth for the debt they are accumulating. He cited the 645-foot-long river-rafting feature in the "leisure pool" at Texas Tech to support his claim that students are going into debt for needless frills. The *Times* takes a more benign view: "… most colleges are filled with hard-working students and teachers. At underfunded, overcrowded com-munity colleges, which enroll more than a third of the almost 18 million American undergraduates, there aren't many leisure pools."[23]

New technologies have permitted another route to the Dream Factories, albeit one that has not yet reached its potential. The Internet and digital course delivery have accelerated the pace of university growth, permitting the more prestigious institutions to reach students around the world, new institutional aspirants to carve out a market niche, and socially-aware universities to provide high-quality education to non-wealthy students worldwide. A decade ago, as enthusiasm for Massive Open Online Courses (MOOCs) surged, promoters forecast the demise of brick-and-mortar universities (they were wrong) and a rapid shift to Internet-based courses and universities. On many campuses, residential students do enrol in online courses instead of rousing themselves from bed to take a regular class (at Canada's most innovative university, the University of Waterloo, more than 80 percent of online course registrations are from on-campus students). Online and distance learning has taken off dramatically in the developing world, where most of the largest universities are Internet-based, allowing students who otherwise could not have aspired to university attendance to start their studies.

Rarely has a single dream been embraced so widely, so enthusiastically, and so uncritically, as that of the modern university. There was enough evidence, particularly in the life and work histories of the baby boomers, to "prove" that a university degree would unlock opportunity, careers, and lifelong stability. The closest historical parallel to the race to universities in energy, commitment, and personal investment is perhaps the monumental global migration boom of the late nineteenth and early twentieth centuries, which sent millions from Europe to seize land and opportunities in the USA, Canada, Australia, New Zealand, Brazil, Argentina South Africa, Rhodesia, and a handful of other countries or colonies. Access to free or cheap land was the global ladder to opportunity in the industrial age. A century later, at the end of the twentieth and early twenty-first centuries, universities have become the object of global dreams and aspirations.

Don't underestimate the anxiety that underscores the attempt to gain access to a university. In January 2012, one person died in a stampede set off when students panicked about admission to the College of Johannesburg in South Africa. With more than ten thousand students vying for one of eight hundred spots, the assembled youth rioted. The conflict started when the government, seeking to respond to the inequities created by an unjust and unequal high school system, lowered the passing grades for math from 50 percent to 30 percent, instantly making thousands of new aspirants eligible for admission. Sbahle Mbambo, a young woman, was one of those desperate for a place. "Everyone in this country wants to be educated," she said. "They want to be independent, and to get proper jobs."[24] South Africa's anxieties peaked again in October 2015 when planned tuition hikes sent tens of thousands of angry students, mostly black, to the streets to protest what they saw as the growing inaccessibility of a university education.

The metrics of this application process are quite remarkable. In Japan, students pay an application fee of up to ¥10,000 (or more than US$1,000) for many universities. In India, middle-class parents with talented children work tirelessly to get them accepted into the career-making IITs, among the hardest universities in the world to get into. The tiger mothers immortalized by Amy Chua devote much of their energy to ensuring their little treasures have their choice of the very best schools. Getting a young adult into Oxford or Cambridge typically requires careful attention to the elementary and secondary school that the children attend, for few graduates from mediocre high schools make it into a top British university. In country after country, getting into an elite institution is seen as a sure road to career success and personal wealth.

No one, however, does it quite like the Americans. The USA has the world's most remarkable and diverse university system. Everyone knows about the elite Ivy League universities, the superb public research institutions (Wisconsin-Madison and UC-San Diego are among the best universities anywhere), and even the truly special liberal-arts colleges, like Wellesley, Bates, Lewis and Clark, and Reed. Many fewer people have ever heard of the vast array of mid-ranked institutions, from Bowling Green to the University of Alaska-Fairbanks, that provide top-flight research to their regions and a decent education to their students. Almost no one has heard of the large number of aggressively mediocre institutions that admit all comers, graduate only a small percentage of their students, and give them little of value while they are there. While we forebear to name the universities in this last category, they are often in the news for their high attrition rates, poor student-satisfaction results, and financial crises.

It's also worth noting that the image of cutthroat competition to get into a top institution is more hokum than reality. The top schools—Harvard, UC-Berkeley, Middlebury, and the like—are truly difficult to impress. Harvard accepts fewer than 7 percent of those who apply, and there is a careful self-selection process that winnows down the applicant pool to a small group of truly talented individuals. The mystique of Harvard—of which more later—is such that American parents are, like their Japanese counterparts, prepared to devote large sums of money and years of planning to line their children up for such an opportunity.

But beyond the top hundred universities in the country (or, in truth, the top fifty), the competition to get in is not terribly intense. Even the so-called "selective" institutions offer places to upwards of 75 percent of all applicants. An institution like Colorado College—an impressive place to be sure—makes offers to over 70 percent of applicants, meaning that it's reaching a bit to call it "selective." Similarly, Canada's highly ranked and aggressively entrepreneurial University of Waterloo accepts close to 75 percent of the students who apply. Many of the institutions with quite flexible approaches to admission, particularly when trying to balance the entry class by gender and race, are truly fine institutions, offering an educational environment as good, if not better, than the allegedly elite institutions that garner the headlines. But, truth be told, a strong high school graduate, with an average of over 80 percent will get into almost all of the universities she or he applies for—outside the top hundred—and might even squeeze into the very top institutions, provided the goal is not a particularly high-demand program. Smart applicants realize that they can often apply for a low-demand program, sadly, in the arts at most institutions, and wrangle a transfer later into a high-demand offering, like business.

Despite this, American parents devote a remarkably large amount of time and money preparing their children for admission to the right school. They send them to after-school programs—called *juku* (cram) schools in Japan, but available in countries around the world, particularly through the now-ubiquitous Sylvan Learning Centres—to overcome the perceived and actual liabilities of most high schools. They pay for SAT (the Scholastic Aptitude Test) preparation classes, aiming to get their children into the 1,200+ score category that opens a lot of campus doors. These same students are counselled to volunteer, excel in sports, run for student council, help the needy, write a screenplay, sing on Broadway, or otherwise demonstrate to the admissions officers that they are real firebrands, worthy of entrance to a high-profile university. With many of the best schools requiring a formal letter of application, parents also pay for a coach to help draw up the all-important document, outlining the applicant's stellar citizenship, legacy of overcoming personal crises, humanitarian zeal, and intellectual gifts. These same aggressive, overbearing, and highly protective parents then accompany their children on extensive campus tours, visiting top choices (and a couple of "safety schools," institutions that are sure to admit them in case the top ones send rejection letters) and seeking to impress admissions officers.

The United States is not the only country that has developed an entire industry around preparing children for admission into elite universities, but it is the one that does it most openly, at the highest expense, and with the greatest public awareness of the topic. Parents have come to view the investment in admission coaches as akin to a form of career health care, evidence that they are loving and devoted to their kids. Focusing on the USA, however, overshadows the increasingly global nature of this student-focused enterprise. In the Middle East, wealthy families also spend very large sums to support their children at overseas universities. In China and Hong Kong, where the value of a top-flight technical (that is, engineering, math, science, accounting, or business) education is valued more than anywhere on earth perhaps, parents of all social classes invest heavily in the academic careers of hard-working youngsters. The growing African middle class, likewise, seeks out international opportunities for its children, despite the high costs and long periods away from the home country. So it goes in Brazil, where the intellectual allure of the former imperial power, Portugal, draws hundreds of students across the Atlantic each year—aided now by a multi-billion dollar scholarship program to send undergraduates and graduates overseas. In Brazil, as well, the academically elite public university system attracts a great deal of attention, with parents pushing their students to excel in high school so that they can avoid the much higher fees at the country's private institutions.

Many countries—Canada, Scandinavia, Russia, Spain, Portugal, South Africa, Australia, and New Zealand among others—take great pride in their egalitarian university systems, with the quality of teaching, research, and facilities varying relatively little across a wide range of institutions. In these countries, parents can rest much easier and can feel comfortable about sending their children to the local publicly funded university, although this is starting to change as national and international ranking systems become all the rage in the pursuit of advancement for young adults.

Parents are important simply because they play two crucial roles in determining the shape of the global university system. They influence the choice of institution and they finance (or refuse or are unable to finance) the undergraduate education for many students. Their preoccupation with the world of work leads them to press for admission to a prestigious university and enrolment in a market-related field. Parents from China and those of Chinese ancestry of place exceptional pressure on their children to take a science, business, or technical program. European families are far more comfortable with arts-based education. A Chinese family, facing massive and even multi-generational investment in a single child, cheer the decision to go to CalTech or to study computer science at the University of Hong Kong. It is often considered an extended family failure if a son or daughter ends up at Brandon University or Newcastle in the UK. A Western family is likely to be happy with admission into any field at Yale, Swarthmore, or Auckland; if the young adult is only able to get into the University of Pennsylvania at Bradford or Charles Darwin University (Australia), it is much preferred that they take a practical field, such as math or education. University is a family matter, starting with the enforcement of parental expectations from a very young age, establishment of an education trajectory, selection of a university, and financing.

There is a gripping illustration—tragic in so many ways—of how this works out in America, and this story can be replicated in dozens of countries around the world. *Waiting for Superman* is a documentary film indictment of public education in the United States. In the process of critiquing the existing school system, director Davis Guggenheim follows dozens of children entered into a lottery to get into a prestigious and high-quality charter school. The calculus from here is devastatingly simple. Get accepted and the student is on track to university admission and the prospect of a good life. Get turned down and the student is sentenced to a lifetime of mediocrity and poverty, based on attendance at a substandard public school. The faces of the parents—and by extension, their children—as the lottery names are called, passing over one after the other, speak volumes about the crisis of expectations. With so many North American families assuming that their children have to go to university in order to succeed, the failure to get into a good feeder school at the age of eight or nine years is viewed as a family catastrophe.

As for the agents who help with getting them into a good college, a distressing number of them are apparently willing to fabricate or alter high school transcripts and other documents in order to get past admissions officers and visa officials. Often, the universities pay the agents as well, creating impressive cash flows and potential conflicts of interest all around. The result can be spectacular abuse, such as the 2012 scandal that hit Dickinson State University in North Dakota, where it was discovered that dozens of students had been let in inappropriately and were then shepherded through the degree process in questionable ways. Or worse, the 2011 scandal involving Tri-Valley University of California, accused of collecting fees from foreign students but not requiring them to attend class so that they could work throughout the country on student visas.[25]

While most Western countries have fairly straightforward systems of admission—those with the highest grades get in—the United States has a bewildering array of institutional choices and admission procedures. Here, as in China, admission agents have proven extremely popular. Agents advise about where to volunteer, how to broaden the resumé, and how to shape the all-crucial letter of application to suit institutional expectations. There are shady dealings here as well. Some high school seniors have been directed to faux humanitarian projects, allowing the students to stay in nice accommodations while getting their pictures taken with orphans and AIDS sufferers. Amazingly, and perhaps providing proof of their poor fit at a top institution, the applicants and their parents seem to believe that the universities don't know about these scams. Outsourcing both the selection process—agents are supposed to find the best school that will accept the student—and the work needed to get into that school undercuts one of the core purposes of the admission process. Universities want to know (or they should want to know) that the student is really interested in attending their institution; not that their parents can afford to hire an agent to fill in the forms, edit the letter of application, and charm the admissions officers.

In an age of egregiously spoiled children—one outcome of small family size and two-career families—it's hardly surprising that parents devote a great deal of effort to the admissions process. But there are deeper issues at play here. While the reality is less impressive than the myth, most wealthy parents buy into some variant of the double-dipper myth of university attendance. The first, and widely shared, element is that a university degree creates job opportunities and therefore a steady adult income, and even a rewarding career, although that is becoming secondary. Second, there is the belief that attendance at the "right" university will bring prestigious opportunities, through personal connections (maybe your son will marry the daughter of a billionaire or your daughter's roommate will become a senior executive at Procter & Gamble) and the glamour of the degree. That 40 percent of the graduating class from Yale University found work in the financial industry—despite the moral bankruptcy of the sector in the last decade—is a clarion call to parents: "Get your kids into Yale and they will be rich!"

Other countries offer variations on the same theme. Attendance at a top Japanese school is often a precondition for a great job in the civil service, where power rests in Japan. In India, graduating from an IIT produces a badge of honour that the individual and the extended family carry for life. Every country has its institutional hierarchy, which in the minds of parents relates far more to career opportunities and income forecasts than the universities would like to believe; their commitment is to the ideal of high education, world-class research, and a stimulating intellectual environment. The *Times Higher Education Supplement* produces a widely distributed annual ranking of the top four hundred universities in the world. Grabbing a spot near the top—"the 400" represents about half of one percent of the world's universities—pushes an institution to the forefront of parents' minds. The rankings, won by academic success and determined by peer reviews, have their primary value in recruiting students (and donors) to the institution. In much the same way, the *U.S. News & World Report*'s rankings industry shapes and distorts institutional expenditures and planning, all with a view to making the universities more attractive to students and their parents.

THE RATIONALE FOR INVESTING IN HIGHER EDUCATION

Accept, if you will, that there are parents who truly wish their students to have a challenging intellectual experience, to study at the feet of the masters, and to graduate from universities with a well-developed world view and a broad understanding of the human condition and/or the natural world. Recognize that these parents are in the minority. Parents are prepared to invest very heavily—up to $60,000 a year for a top American private university and $20,000 a year for a high-ranked public institution, when living costs are factored in.

Why do they pay so much? Because they want their children to get a job and earn a high income. (Or, to be frank, if the family is truly wealthy and the teenagers will never have to work for a living, the goal is largely pride and bragging rights.) They have sipped the university Kool-Aid for decades and perhaps benefited from university attendance themselves, when participation rates were much lower and the job market much more favourable. Or sometimes they ante up because they can see no other alternative. We live in an age that prioritizes white-collar office work and that unwittingly deprecates blue collar or physical labour, even if such work produces higher and steadier incomes. Finally, parents are willing to pay up because they know that few children have the entrepreneurial spirit and drive to produce their own jobs and careers. So, in an age of rampant credentialism, when a university degree is a prerequisite for the most basic, entry-level jobs—rental-car clerk, telephone operator, and the like—when they are bombarded by promises about the knowledge economy, when government leaders speak about the high value attached to post-secondary education, and when everyone is encouraged to enrol in university, they do the obvious thing.

Politicians reinforce these parental obsessions when they speak in boosterish terms about the "knowledge economy" and the open-ended opportunities that lie before college and university graduates. As companies such as Microsoft, Cisco, Sun Computer Systems, DoCoMo, Samsung, Alibaba, Nokia, and thousands of others displaced the big industrial firms at the top of the corporate order, it seemed that new technologies and their applications would define the evolving global economy. The global expansion of university education, both domestically and in terms of the annual migration of millions of international students, has been tied to the assumption that the high-tech economy of the twenty-first century would easily absorb all of the graduates from the world's universities. This is proving to be only partly true.

DIVERSITY IN SIZE, DIVERSITY IN QUALITY

Savour for a moment the diversity of these Dream Factories. Universities are to cities, regions, and countries what a degree is to the student: a promise of prosperity and opportunity. There are more than thirty thousand degree-granting universities operating around the world, not counting a growing and unknown number of private-sector, for-profit institutions. These universities range in size from tiny specialist religious universities in the United States, such as the City University in Kansas City, Missouri, which has twelve students, to massive online universities in the developing world. Indira Gandhi National Open University, based in Delhi, India, enrolls 3.5 million students. They vary just as widely in quality, with Harvard University, Oxford University, and the University of Tokyo emerging from the same academic tradition as the New England Institution of Art (rated as the worst college in the United States by *Washington Monthly* and ranked poorly in terms of student satisfaction). These thirty thousand institutions are all universities, in the legal and technical definition of the term, but they are as different from one another as soccer is from roller derby.

The transformation that has occurred in higher education during the last five or six decades has been almost universally viewed as a positive social change. Universities have evolved from what they once were—reclusive places of intellectual contemplation—into modern institutions. Yet some have also become degree mills that are destroying the reputation of university education around the world. Discovering that the transition is, in numerical terms, largely a function of the last sixty years and, in quality and impact, the last twenty years, should be reason to pause. In less than a century, universities have emerged from their impressive foundation in North America and Western Europe, beyond the toehold created in Asia and the European colonies, into global ubiquity.

Once elite, aloof, and unique, universities are now democratic, accessible, and commonplace. Every town and city of substantial size—and many unsubstantial places—expects to have a publicly funded university. Universities emerged, with little fanfare, as one of the central instruments of state educational, economic, and social planning and have become a major force for change around the globe.

Celebrated as a universal "good thing," universities are reshaping pathways to careers and adulthood for hundreds of millions of young people. Their presence transforms communities and changes the way that employers recruit, train, and hire young people. More importantly, they have become repositories for the dreams of millions of young adults, their parents, their communities, and their nations. The world has embraced these institutions in a remarkable, uncritical, and highly enthusiastic way. Now the young, their families, and their countries are slowly discovering that these dreams are compromised, that the promise of personal and collective opportunity has been seriously exaggerated, and that the unchecked and ill-managed growth of the university system has developed without much reference to the job market or the global economy. But they sure are popular.

2

AWAKENING FROM THE DREAM

The Italian university graduate, visiting North America as a volunteer camp counsellor, laughed when asked if he had a job at home lined up for the fall. "I have an undergraduate degree," he said. "No one in Italy gets a job with only an undergraduate degree." Even with a degree in economics, one of the more marketable fields of study, he had been warned not to anticipate full-time work. So he applied for entry to graduate study in International Management at the Rotterdam School of Management, Erasmus University, and was waiting to learn if he had been accepted. "With a Master's degree," he said hopefully, "at least I have a shot at a decent career." Given that more than half of Italian students drop out of university without a degree, you would think that the careers of those who persisted and earned an undergraduate degree would have a better outcome. Not so, it seems.

Not all Italians have such a dismal result after four years of academic study, of course. Some graduates get good jobs and solid careers, but this young man's observations reflected the experience of many of his generation. Consider this surprising commentary, which shows that it's actually more difficult for Italians to get a job with a university degree than without one:

> Italy is the European country with the lowest number
> of "tertiary" graduates—meaning anyone with a univer-
> sity or university-like degree. Yet despite relatively low

supply, one in three tertiary graduates between 20 and 24 (33.3%, up from 27.1% in 2011) remains out of work, according to Eurostat—even higher than their peers with just a high-school level degree, whose unemployment rate is 30.4%.

Italian companies actually seem to favor workers with lower levels of education: 37% of those employed in managerial positions hold only the minimum compulsory level of education, compared with 15% who hold a bachelor's degree or above, according to AlmaLaurea, an Italian institution run by a consortium of universities and the Ministry of Education that gathers statistics on education.[1]

The problem, it seems, is that Italian undergraduates favour the Humanities and the law, areas that are disconnected from the contemporary European economy. But give some thought to the Italian realities. One-third of graduates were without work in 2013, only a small proportion move into management positions, and only slightly more than half of those who start out to get a degree actually complete their studies. If this is not an educational crisis, it's hard to know what would be.

NEW REALITIES: UNEMPLOYMENT AND UNDEREMPLOYMENT

The Italian situation is a good example of two new global realities: university graduate unemployment and the equally important pattern of sustained underemployment. Unemployment is easily understood. Students graduate and head into the job market, only to receive a cold reception. They cannot find work, struggle with living costs, and often move back home. The highly anticipated launch into adulthood has been postponed. Underemployment is equally devastating, but a little different. Many university graduates do find work, but not of the type and with the income that they had been led to expect. This produces underemployment, where university graduates find jobs but in positions that do not require the skills and expertise learned in their academic studies. A political science student driving a bus is employed, certainly, and perhaps even reasonably well paid, but in terms of the utilization of his or her skills is clearly under-employed. So it is with the hundreds of thousands of university graduates employed as retail clerks, taxi drivers, office support staff, hotel or airline representatives, or otherwise doing decent and useful work, but work that they could easily have done immediately after leaving high school.

According to *The Economist*, graduate unemployment and under-employment are significant around the world.[2] In country after country, graduate underemployment has become commonplace. In China, even before the financial slowdown hit in 2015, the chaotically expanding university systems—founded on a firm belief in the *Learning = Earning* mantra—had gotten well out of sync with the national labour force. New graduates struggled to find work. Graduates returning with for-eign degrees found the market potency of the diploma greatly dimin-ished. It turns out that China's manufacturing-based economy did not demand an endless supply of university graduates, even in such previ-ously high-demand fields as engineering.

The situation is not the same everywhere. In countries that limit university enrolment, as in Germany and Scandinavia, where the skilled trades enjoy considerable status and decent incomes, graduate unemployment rates are significantly lower. The American situation, however, is stunning. In 2013, according to Richard Vedder and his colleagues with the Center for College Affordability and Productivity, 48 percent of college graduates were underemployed, and 37 percent of college graduates held positions that did not require a high school degree to perform the job properly. Collectively, that added up to five million American college graduates holding jobs across the coun-try that did not require even a high school diploma, let alone a col-lege degree. As they reported, ominously, "Past and projected future growth in college enrolments and the number of graduates exceeds the actual or projected growth in high-skilled jobs, explaining the develop-ment of the underemployment problem and its probable worsening in future years."[3] The situation eased in the United States as the economy rebounded in 2015, but became worse across Europe and in many parts of Asia, particularly in China. The *National Post* reported that "stu-dents have high expectations that their university degrees will amount to a job fairly soon after graduation ... To the statement 'obtaining a post-secondary degree ensures I will have a job in my field of study after graduation,' the average response was 4.57 out of 10—meaning about half of the students strongly felt their degree would fairly easily score them work."[4]

So, what went wrong? How did the dream of a university education become so substantially disconnected from the reality? It is important to realize that the focus on the experiences of college and university graduates actually understates the problem significantly. Imagine, if you will, that a hospital reported the success rates of open-heart surgeries basing its data entirely on the health outcomes of those who walked out of the medical centres on their own within a few weeks of the operation. This would be absurd, of course, for it would exclude those who died or became sicker in the hospital after their operations and those who were not helped by the procedures. The statistics, obviously, would be a success story, skewed in favour of the hospitals and their medical professionals.

But universities do this all the time. Statistical reports, particularly those issued by universities or academic associations, routinely focus on university graduates—the ones who enrol and then continue through to the end of their programs, graduating as planned. These are the patients who walked out of the hospital on their own, in other words. But what about those who fall by the wayside? In the United States, over half of those who start a college or university program do not complete their degrees within seven years. And the dropout statistics vary according to institution and race: the rate is much lower for Harvard and much higher for two- and four-year community colleges. "Traditionally Black colleges" in the USA have a six-year graduation rate of only 39 percent.[5] David Leonhardt, writing in the *New York Times* on September 9, 2009, reports that "only 33 percent of the freshmen who enter the University of Massachusetts, Boston, graduate within six years. Less than 41 percent graduate from the University of Montana, and 44 percent from the University of New Mexico. The economist Mark Schneider refers to colleges with such dropout rates as 'failure factories' and they are the norm." If universities are going to take credit for the employment outcomes of their graduates, then surely they should also be morally responsible for students who are admitted into programs of study but drop out for academic, financial, or personal reasons.

EDUCATIONAL OUTCOMES

Educational outcomes vary widely across and within countries. Canadian universities do better than those in the United States, on average, although approximately 30 percent of Canadian first-year students do not graduate. At India's highly regarded IITs, dropout rates are low, as they are in most elite universities. High-quality institutions, like Hong Kong Polytech, Cambridge, Stanford, and Swarthmore, have very low (as in less than 10 percent) dropout rates after admission. There is a simple lesson here. If you are juggling statistics to favour universities, you should select smart, highly motivated, and hard-working students at high-end institutions. Then graduation outcomes and employment outcomes will certainly tend to make the system look good.

At the other end of the spectrum lie America's open-entry institutions, where graduation rates are routinely under half and occasionally lower than one-quarter of all entrants. In northern Europe (Germany and Scandinavia), doubly blessed with excellent high school systems and selective admissions to universities, dropout rates are under 10 percent. The United Kingdom, which raised its university fees dramatically in recent years, has a dropout rate under 9 per cent, much lower than France's free and open university system, which loses about half of its students after first year. The message here? If an institution accepts poorly prepared and struggling students, even if it provides substantial assistance and support along the way (and some don't), it will have trouble getting its students through to graduation. The top employers know these realities, and thus recruit heavily in the best colleges and universities, leaving graduates from the lower-tier and low-status institutions to fend for themselves in the workplace.

The global preoccupation with universities as a means to employment has introduced yet another worrisome element into the evaluation of the college and university system: declining standards. Recent studies of the American university system have produced disturbing insights into the limited learning that occurred among many students, and the low skill levels among both entering and graduating students. This is also seen anecdotally in, for instance, the notorious YouTube video in which undergraduates at Texas Technical University are asked the question "Who won the Civil War?"

and a disheartening number don't know.[6] The nature of the modern academy, where the expansion has been fuelled by an increasing commitment to accessibility, is such that the quality of the education provided has come under intense scrutiny. The picture that emerges is not pretty, for it describes (for American students and for many of their counterparts in other countries), serious problems with the students' basic skills, limited curiosity, lack of commitment to studies, and disengagement from learning as a whole.

There is another set of issues related to the faculty members that includes an overemphasis on research and professional engagement; a surge of political correctness and sensitivity to issues of gender, ethnicity, class, and the like; the intellectual turmoil associated with post-modernism; and a publish-or-perish mindset that detracts from faculty commitment to the university experience. The struggle to reassert the primacy of college teaching is shaping up as one of the epic professional battles of the twenty-first century.

But governments, to say nothing of parents and students, want results. And just as the commitment to universal high school education has led to a gradual reduction in the quality and academic standards of the secondary system, so are pressures to retain and graduate students from universities resulting in noticeably lower standards for course work and eventual graduation. The one place where this really attracts attention in the United States relates to college athletics, particularly basketball and football, with a regular cycle of scandals relating to "bird" courses, assistance in writing papers and examinations, special concessions from faculty members, and other measures designed to keep the student athletes in school and eligible for competition (and, less urgently, on track to graduating from college). The worst current example is the appalling scandal at the University of North Carolina at Chapel Hill, where football students for years took fake courses to retain their eligibility to play.[7]

At many institutions, faculty members are under various forms of pressure, subtle and otherwise, to allow students to progress so they stay eligible to play, with many non-elite colleges and universities mirroring the behaviour of public schools in their desire to reach performance targets. That keeping students in programs adds to the institutions' financial bottom line and therefore pays for faculty and staff salaries is an additional incentive to let academic standards sag.

Overall, the picture from the perspective of student success is not a happy one. Certainly it is far removed from the cheerful pictures in the recruiting brochures and the promises to students and their parents about supportive academic environments. Some American institutions—places like Reed College, Colorado College, St. John's College, and the members of the Colleges of Distinction consortium—uphold the spirit of the learning-centred academy (as opposed to that of places focusing on preparation for careers; for instance, a teachers' college or a law school), but they are clearly the exception rather than the norm in the modern university system. What this means, to be blunt, is that many students—the number unknown and likely unknowable—have mediocre college and university experiences, do not see their skills improve significantly, and are not well positioned for the transition to the workplace. Some universities do much better than others. Elite technical institutions, such as MIT, CalTech, and Waterloo, for example, and specialized universities like Juilliard (fine and performing arts), Rensselaer (technology), and the Colorado School of Mines, attract focused, eager, and career-oriented students and, not surprisingly, produce graduates whom companies, government agencies, and organizations find very attractive.

But too few people have noticed the unfolding of a basic economics lesson: the production of millions of university graduates, in numbers beyond the capacity of the labour force to absorb them, has lowered their value overall and individually, especially at the bottom end. Richard B. Freeman, a Harvard-based labour economist, fears that American college graduates may suffer further from international competition. As he noted, "The college graduate situation has a global dimension—6 million bachelor's graduates in China that affect the U.S. market as well—which is very different than in the past."[8] Freeman is right. But add in millions more from Turkey, India, Spain, Portugal, Brazil, and many other countries. In the 1960s, as we showed earlier, North American and northern European countries had the global lead on post-secondary education. Now, North American graduates are swimming in what looks like an ocean full of fish with mortarboards on their heads. Companies looking to build high-tech operations near a pool of skilled labour can choose among a few key sites in North America, but they can also go to Hong Kong, Melbourne, Oulu, Stockholm, or Copenhagen; to several cities in Germany or Istanbul; or to leading high-tech and higher-education urban areas in India. And the choices don't end there.

In technology, North America set the gold standard immediately after World War II and held pride of place into the 1970s. But its leadership has steadily eroded—despite the continued success of Stanford, University of Texas at Austin, University of San Diego, Waterloo, MIT, Harvard, Duke, University of North Carolina–Chapel Hill, and several other major centres. Imagine, if you will, a global firm (say a former American-centric multinational like Sun Computer Systems that now has much of its research capacity in Asia) trying to decide on the best location for a new digital research centre. Their eyes—if they are smart—will scan a few American hotspots, contemplate Bangalore, consider London or a European centre, and then take a good hard look at China. A quick check of Beijing would reveal dozens of excellent universities, topped by Tsinghua University, one of China's best and a world leader in engineering, math, computer science, and other scientific fields. A check of the student population and workforce will reveal thousands of creative, eager, highly skilled workers who are willing to work for wages that are lower than those in the West. North American schools produce many graduates of comparable quality—Tsinghua is on par with Stanford, Princeton, Waterloo, and Toronto in this area—with the important caveat that many of the undergraduate and graduate students in these institutions were born in Asia, too.

THE EMPLOYMENT CRISIS

The employment crisis has hit unevenly. For graduates with specialized degrees—from Accounting and Electrical Engineering to Medicine and Digital Communications—the evolving scientific and technological economy still provides excellent opportunities. High incomes, multiple job offerings, and rapid advancement exist in the world of Google, Apple, Microsoft, and Cisco. But many of the jobs in the evolving "new economy" belong to the service sector. While some young adults—most notably in the deservedly derided finance sector—discovered world-class opportunities for wealth and advancement, the majority left university to find that most jobs offered low incomes, short-term contracts, and insecurity.

Having gone into debt to pay for their degrees, the graduates find themselves in low-paying, undependable jobs with few prospects for advancement. Not many parents and young people expected that four to six years of academic study would lead to work as a cashier, though in 2008 more than 356,000 cashiers had college degrees, up from 132,000 in 1992.[9] Of course, as Matt Gurney points out in the *National Post*, there's a fairly easy fix for the student indebtedness problem—get a job straight out of high school, save like crazy, and go to university later.[10]

In country after country, the rapid expansion of university systems and the number of degree holders have clashed with the needs of a stagnant and uncertain workforce. Much of this had little to do with universities, save for the expectations built up through personal and family investments in the education of young people. The serious economic problems in North Africa in recent years did not start with the universities. The same was true in Spain, Portugal, Greece, Italy, and other European countries, where broader economic forces wreaked havoc with national and regional economies.

In some nations, the dashed expectations sparked activist youth movements. Such was the case with the Arab Spring movement that swept across North Africa and the Middle East after 2010, the Occupy movement in the USA and Canada that attacked increasing inequality, and regional social and cultural protests against inequality and social injustice elsewhere in the world. Young adults in Greece, including those with and without university degrees, struggle with crushing rates of youth unemployment (around 50 percent officially) and declining wages. Not surprisingly, having been raised to expect better outcomes, many Greek youth joined the mass protests that spread across the country in the wake of Greece's cataclysmic debt crisis in 2015.

Most unemployed and underemployed young adults did not become revolutionaries, or even protestors. They struggled with their realities, continued to search for work and—following closely on the ideological foundations of the modern university, which linked outcome to individual effort and ability—largely blamed themselves for their inability to find work. In some instances, they were right. Decent jobs could be found in non-urban places—remote Indigenous reservations ("reserves" in Canada), the pre-2015 oil fields in North Dakota and Wyoming, and certainly for trained professionals in the poorer districts of the major cities —but these were not always attractive to college graduates raised to expect a more comfortable middle-class life.

Suffice it to say that many college and university graduates struggled—and so did those who started along the degree path and opted out. Those with large student loans carried a major burden into an adult life of low wages and uncertain employment prospects. As if it were not already difficult enough to find work, many of the new jobs were part-time and often with few or no benefits.

The harsh truth is that colleges and universities have been grossly oversold—most notably by the institutions themselves. The result has been that for some time now the dream has been in danger of dying, although governments have largely ignored the mounting evidence and the public seems blissfully unaware of it. Colleges and universities continue to promote the supposed advantages of a post-secondary education, arguing that they are not job factories, but institutes of higher learning, and that intellectual improvement should not be connected to crass questions of employment. Meanwhile the system undergoes a massive reorientation of its programming toward professional and technical fields of study.

Opening universities and colleges to women, minorities, Indigenous peoples, children from working-class families, and the disabled brought many thousands of talented and capable people into the advanced educational system. The world has been surely blessed by the perspectives, abilities, and contributions of young adults who, in earlier times, would have been locked out of career advancement through college educations. The same holds in the developing world, where university degrees had, for generations, been the exclusive preserve of the wealthy, the well-connected, and the highly gifted. To a point—imprecise and never examined—the opening of the university floodgates served a valuable personal, national, and global purpose.

But at some stage a tipping point was reached. Universities let in too many students for the employment market to absorb. The overemphasis on personal choice allowed young adults to select their own fields of study, skewing the skills of those graduating in favour of the educational interests of seventeen- to twenty-one-year-olds. A world desperate for highly skilled engineers got more psychology graduates. An economy eager for people with advanced technical skills got thousands of wildlife biologists. A national workforce that had space for a few hundred fine arts graduates a year could not absorb thousands of them. University education still worked for many, but not all, and increasingly not even most, of the first-year students who ventured, bright-eyed and more or less eager, onto the world's campuses each year.

Governments kept the floodgates open, and even expanded opportunities. American president Barack Obama urged more and more young people to go to college, apparently oblivious to the fact that sending more students into the system, not to mention weaker ones, watered down the quality of the country's skilled workforce. There was method in this seeming madness. With the global economy in dramatic flux, with financial crises building on massive technological change, there were not enough unfilled jobs in the economy to absorb the large number of young people graduating from high school. Governments faced a seemingly obvious choice: let the students enrol in a partially subsidized university system for four or more years, keeping them out of the labour market while they developed some saleable skills. Or, on the other hand, let them join the ranks of the idle and unemployed. Colleges and universities, if they did nothing else, served as a holding pen for a large reserve labour force that, if economic growth occurred as hoped, could capitalize on future job opportunities.

The college degree did not stop working as a route to prosperity and career progress, which should, in any case, be measured more in terms of job and life satisfaction than annual income. But it worked for fewer and fewer students all the time. With national dropout rates ranging from under 10 percent in nations like Germany to over 50 percent in the United States, millions of university students left the system each year without attaining the desired credential. Many of these, of course, found their feet through entrepreneurship, personal effort, family connections, or specialized training. But large numbers bore the mark of failure, of falling off the twenty-first-century career train, left to fend for themselves, degreeless, in a world awash in equally unqualified young people.

Always remember, though, that for a lucky and skilled minority, the college or university degree worked brilliantly. Without the opportunity for advanced study, these students might not have been able to secure the stable, high-paying jobs that launched them on a comfortable and productive life. Note in passing that the evidence is strong that students from wealthy backgrounds are far more likely to end up wealthy themselves. Perhaps the most assured route to a high income is having high-income parents and a stable family background. "Power couples" conceive bright children and bring them up in stable homes—only 9 percent of college-educated mothers who give birth each year are unmarried, compared with 61 percent of high school dropouts. They stimulate their children relentlessly: children of professionals hear thirty-two million more words by the age of four than those of parents on welfare.[11] Recognize, too, that many who did not go to college or graduate from university can also do well economically, largely because of hard work, personal qualities, technical skills and training, risk-taking, family support, pure luck, or specialized talent—think Bill Gates, LeBron James, and Taylor Swift. There are plumbers, pipefitters, real estate entrepreneurs, dealers at top casinos and hotels, franchise operators, building contractors, high-quality hairdressers, long-haul truckers, and many other working-class and technical personnel who earn upwards of $75,000 a year—or more than teachers in most states. In other words, not going to university can also be quite remunerative and personally satisfying, something that too many educators and politicians forget or ignore.

But here is the kicker. Americans spend billions each year on the world's largest and most impressive college and university system, with over several thousand degree-granting institutions. It's hard to say exactly how many billions of dollars are involved, but an article in *The Atlantic* estimated that the US federal government spent $69 billion in 2013 just on various grant programs to universities and colleges, not including loans.[12] Total outstanding student loans have now passed $1 trillion. Families spend billions each year, incurring sizable debts to capitalize on the perceived opportunities for their children. Young people devote at least four years and as much as a quarter of a million dollars in the hope that they will be able to convert their studies into a decent career. This is a staggering investment, one now being replicated around the world, based on uncertain and unspecified returns. This is gambling of the highest order.

WEIGHING PERSONAL QUALITIES AGAINST CREDENTIALS

There is a grand statistical debate taking place about the actual earnings of college and university graduates. On average, college graduates earn significantly more than non-college graduates. Is the college degree responsible for those increased earnings? Clearly "yes," in the case of accredited fields like Medicine and Accounting. No degree, no high-paying job. But consider these other elements. Smarter young people are more likely to go to college than people who are less intellectually gifted. Is it intelligence that produces the higher income or the credential? Hard-working, motivated, and conscientious young adults are more likely to succeed at university—and in the workforce. Should we credit the personal qualities or the college degree for their success as adults? People from wealthy families are much more likely to go to college and even more likely to graduate. Is income really the important dependent variable, rather than intelligence or education? After all, the non-college-educated children of wealthier parents tend to have higher incomes than the college-educated children of poorer parents.

So, how does one make sense of this statistical jumble? First, it is obvious that, *on average*, a college education carries real financial benefits. On average, college and university graduates do significantly better than nongraduates. Second, it is equally obvious that the field of study matters. The average income and career earnings of medical doctors greatly exceed those of film studies graduates, and electrical engineers make more money than wildlife biologists. Third, many of the career achievements are associated with the personal characteristics of the graduates. Before a single day at college, university students have set themselves apart from their high school classmates by being, on average, smarter, harder-working, more dependable, adaptable, and determined, as well as being significantly wealthier (in terms of family income). But heavy-duty mechanics and oil drillers can make more money than film studies graduates too.

What hangs over all of the averages and statistics is that they do not predict the outcomes for individual students. A mediocre high school graduate, attending a fourth-tier college, can soar to the top and become fabulously successful. A class valedictorian, accepted at all the top-five universities she applied to, can run into an intellectual brick wall during her first year at Harvard and skulk home in abject failure. An engineering graduate, entering the job market in the economic doldrums, can end up waiting on tables, just as a psychology student could turn into a world-class journalist and succeed magnificently. Students and parents plan for post-secondary education based on averages and stories of great successes, believing that each young woman or man can or will be the one who will achieve phenomenal results. Such is the naïveté of our age that people equate averages with individual outcomes, a risky venture at the best of times—and these are not the best of times.

Anecdotes do not pay the bills. College websites often have examples of Arts and Science graduates who went on to do great things. (See Yale's, for example.[13]) These stories—and some are truly inspirational—do not tell you what happens to an incoming high school graduate. The incoming student may be the next Steve Jobs, drop out quickly, and become a world-changing billionaire. He may be the next Malcolm Gladwell and become a truly impressive writer. She may follow in the footsteps of Oprah Winfrey (who did not quite finish her degree at Tennessee State University). But these are real longshots, offered up as part of the "You can be anything you want to be" mantra that dominates modern parenting in North America. While the individual stories are impressive—Kim Coates of raunchy *Sons of Anarchy* fame did graduate in drama from the University of Saskatchewan—but that in no way means that all USask drama graduates will follow his path from the Canadian prairie to Hollywood.

Nor, at the same time, do average incomes of university graduates tell incoming students what their employment and career outcomes will be, in large measure because all the statistics are backward-looking. Basing plans for an eighteen-year-old's future today on the basis of the career experiences of university graduates in the 1980s or even the 1990s is suspect at best. After all, the fundamental economic uncertainties attached to globalization and technological change have made predicting the future a mug's game.

The Dream Factories live on. There are thousands of stories each year of young people, including many from disadvantaged backgrounds, who make their way through university and launch themselves into wonderful jobs and enviable lifestyles. Modern society is populated by doctors, nurses, economists, university professors, accountants, financial officers, engineers, computer scientists, microbiologists, and many others who could not do their jobs without a high-quality advanced education, often requiring two or more degrees after high school. For many more, particularly those from poorer or marginalized populations, colleges and universities convert dreams into reality. These are the system's success stories and they deserve to be heard.

But colleges and universities also produce poor results, the numbers varying, based on the quality of the input (admission standards), the rigour of the programs (academic standards), and the nature of the field of study (professional standards). How often do these institutions publish accounts of the devastation of student and family dreams when young people are forced to withdraw because they lack the intellectual ability to complete an undergraduate degree? Do we hear about the international students with limited English-language ability, whose families saved for years and struggled to get them into a third-tier American or Canadian university only to have them fail to graduate and head home in despair, having used up the family's money? And is there much coverage, beyond the occasional obligatory story about English-literature graduates serving coffee at Starbucks, about the system-wide experiences with unemployment and underemployment? For many university students—no one knows the percentage, but it's much too high—the Dream Factories produce unhappiness. For a growing number, these factories produce outright nightmares.

There is a silver lining in this story. Many employers do favour college graduates, even if it is for work that does not require an advanced education, such a hotel clerk, rental-car sales associate, retail clerk, or the like. Fairly or not, many employers use the completion of an undergraduate degree as a sign of commitment to task, work ethic, and basic ability, and not any longer as a sign of excellence in such previously fundamental areas as writing and mathematical ability, basic understanding of political and legal systems, and general education. In other words, if you are hiring car-rental desk clerks, and of two hundred applicants, half have college degrees, there's no reason not to give them preference. So, in an economy with too few jobs of any variety, college and university graduates can usually find some sort of employment.

Using twenty-first century survival skills—marked by moving back in with their parents, getting regular contributions from Mum and Dad, sharing living accommodations with friends, holding down two or more jobs, postponing major life choices (marriage, children, buying a home), and getting by with less—young college graduates are generally making do. They may not enjoy the lives of the leisured and well-financed middle class that they and their parents anticipated, but neither are they on the streets. While aspiring to the upper middle class and beyond, many thousands of college graduates are settling into lives in the lower middle class, often enjoying lower standards of living than their parents and coping with ongoing uncertainty about the future. This, for the vast majority of young people in North America, was not the dream that they had been sold.

UPGRADING SKILLS AND CREDENTIALS

So, what are young people and their families doing about the growing crisis in the employment of university graduates? They are doing just what the Dream Factories and their government supporters want them to do: they are doubling down on their investments and continuing their studies in order to obtain a second or third degree. If graduates with a BA cannot find a job, continuing on to graduate school to obtain a MA should surely give them an advantage over the competition. To top it off, the best schools offer graduate stipends, research assistantships, and other support to help defray the cost of attending. There is not a great deal of evidence, however, that these educational gambles pay off in a major way. Less than a quarter of PhD holders end up with full-time faculty teaching positions. Instead, many wind up on short-term contracts. We won't get into the horrors of teaching at universities as an adjunct or sessional professor, but it's tough to argue that it's worth the cost in money and years that it takes to get a PhD. And, as in other fields, the production of MAs in Political Science, MScs in Biology, PhDs in English Literature, or Doctorates in Education is in no systematic way tied to evident market demand.

The steady and even growing enrolments belie the notion that there is a crisis in graduate school attendance. After all, if the number of people pursuing law degrees holds steady or dips only slightly, then surely that is an indication that the market has not yet discounted these degrees in any substantial way. But law is a good example. Changing technologies and the shift toward paralegals and outsourced research has reduced the demand for new lawyers. In many jurisdictions, finding a career-launching articling position has become a formidable challenge. Imagine completing a four-year undergraduate degree, fighting to get into a good law school, finishing a two- or three-year program, and then running into a brick wall when searching for the crucial first job.

Here, however, the signs of market awareness are becoming evident. The number of law school applications has indeed started to fall, particularly in the United States, where several small law schools have closed. But the law schools that remain need students to fill the classes and pay the bills. Faced with fewer applications for a fixed number of positions, the law schools simply go down the scale a little further—effectively lowering their standards of admission—in order to complete the incoming class. Lower-quality students likely mean higher failure rates, poorer performance at the bar examinations, and less-effective lawyers in the profession. This is hardly the outcome any country would want.

> ## CRISIS IN THE LAW SCHOOLS
>
> The USA is experiencing a decline in law school applicants, with 20% fewer applications this fall [2013], due to the slowly-recovering economy, staffing cuts at law firms, and the rising cost of a law degree. There are roughly 30,000 fewer applicants than there were just 3 years ago, says Wendy Margolis, an official from the Law School Admission Council, which tracks enrolment. Ohio State University's dean of the Moritz College of Law, Alan Michaels, explains that the recession caused a decreased demand for lawyer services. At the same time, he says, tuition at law school has risen; Ohio State's law tuition is currently $28,000 per year.[14]

Even here there are some oddities. The rush to graduate schools does not hold, incidentally, in the highest-demand areas, like engineering, the sciences, and accounting, where undergraduate-degree holders can usually still find good jobs. In these cases, international students make up the lion's share of the graduate enrolments, perhaps because of the lower math and science skills of domestic students. Some of these degrees are of value mostly to the incomes of those who hold them. The best example is the growth in Master of Education and PhD/Doctorate in Education programs. Most of these graduate students are practising teachers; the main attraction of the graduate programs is contractually fixed salary increases tied to the completion of an additional degree, even if the degree is not connected to their teaching duties. For the United States, the salary bill

PAYING THE BILLS

In order to manage student debt, some undergraduates have gone so far as to pay for their education by selling companionship and sex to older men. The usual income for "sugaring," as it's called, is between $3,000 and $5,000 a month, according to a Miami firm called "Sugardaddie." Allison, a twenty-three-old "sugar baby" in New York state, whose online name is Barbiewithabrain, has earned that much and more over the past five years from three successive sugar daddies.[15]

for these extra—and often irrelevant—degrees adds more than $5 billion a year to the education system's budget.

The situation in graduate schools raises the question about what else young adults can do in this job market to advance their interests and meet their aspirations. In the 1960s and 1970s, a high school diploma was sufficient to get the attention of most ordinary employers. By the 1980s and 1990s, an undergraduate degree was the key. By the 2000s and 2010s, the undergraduate degree, outside of specialized and technical programs, had started to run its course, providing access to entry-level jobs but rarely to desired careers. Now, graduate and professional degrees are deemed the key to entry into a successful economic future, although even here the shine has started to come off the advanced degrees. What a change this is from a generation or two earlier, when a college diploma was a sure ticket to the middle class.

The greater problem is that the doors are open so wide that the system is overwhelmed by students of minimal academic ability, motivation, and innate curiosity. Colleges and universities were not intended for the disengaged. Nor were they designed to be credential- and income-conferring organizations focused on students' short-term career needs. But this is what governments want them to be, what parents demand that they be, and what a growing percentage of the students expect them to be.

Universities were once bastions of achievement and meritocracy, although nowhere near what faded memories suggest. That still holds for the elite institutions, but many more now wallow in mediocrity. Here is a statement, alarming but true, that you won't hear from any government or university bureaucrat:

> For many of the world's university students, their attempts to get a degree will result in academic failure.

Graduates may experience minimal career benefits, be burdened with debt, will not have the expected job opportunities and income and may find they are not prepared for a successful career. For a minority—ironically largely in academic fields where the programs are regulated by outside professional agencies, like nursing, medicine, and engineering—university degrees produce superb career opportunities, high incomes, and a good chance at professional satisfaction. For many (but not all) of the rest, disappointment awaits.

Colleges and universities have never been perfect. Student thirst for learning was never as intense as nostalgia would have it, although we suggest (and experience reinforces) that it was demonstrably better than at present. The career outcomes for graduates were never perfect, but again better than at present. In over two generations, colleges have gone from being places to learn, as well as to mature and socialize, to places to prepare for a career. The tragedy of the Dream Factories is that, for a significant majority of the students in North America, they are also failing in this new role. What's more, with the surge of attempts to regulate sexual behaviour and freedom of speech, struggles over on-campus drinking, criticisms of college athletics, high levels of student debt, and many other expanding challenges, the colleges and universities in North America are slowly losing their special status as places to socialize, have fun, and discover one's future.

What conclusions can we draw from the many transformations of the past fifty or so years? First, there *are* career benefits, particularly for those who graduate. While much of this is accounted for by non-institutional elements, college graduates generally do reasonably well in the contemporary workforce. Second, there is still a college premium evident in the workforce,[16] and in most countries university graduates have considerably lower unemployment rates than those who do not have a degree. Our point, from the outset, is not to argue that there are no employment benefits from a college degree. Rather, we have emphasized the growing reality that colleges, which lose many of their admitted students enroute to graduation, produce uneven results that are not consistent with the promotional rhetoric and realities of the contemporary workforce.

While it is reassuring to note that college graduates usually do find work, it is depressing for many of them to discover that the work is insecure, low paid, and not connected to their expectations and what they feel are the promises of governments, institutions, and parents. Moreover, the college and university sector does not hold back in celebrating the accomplishments of their top graduates, using recruiting and promotional tactics that are more akin to late-night television weight-loss and hair-replacement advertisements than a realistic assessment of how college might change a young person's life.

But broader societal forces are at play as well, a fact that helps explain parental paranoia and youth anxiety about the future. Robert Putnam, an eminent American sociologist, documented the surge in inequality in the USA and described the rapid collapse of the American Dream. He put it bluntly:

> The causes of this increase in inequality during the past three to four decades are much debated—globalization, technological change and the consequent increase in "returns to education," deunionization, superstar compensation, changing social norms, and post-Reagan public policy—though the basic shift toward inequality occurred under both Republican and Democratic administrations. No serious observer doubts that the past 40 years have witnessed an almost unprecedented growth in inequality in America. Ordinary Americans, too, have gradually become aware of rising inequality, though they underestimate the extent of the shift.[17]

Putnam argued that unequal access to high-quality education is a significant contributor to the rise in inequality. But if advanced education were actually the panacea it is made out to be, economic inequality in the late twentieth- and early twenty-first century should have diminished because of the surge in enrolment. Instead it has grown.

3

OUT OF SYNC

What went wrong? While a college or university degree was never a guarantee of a great job, a high income, and a house with a two-car garage in the suburbs, it served as the closest thing North America had to offer as a guarantee of such an outcome—second only to being born into a wealthy family. That so many college and university graduates struggle to find good jobs is due, in part, to the over-enrolment and massive over-selling of the career benefits of a college degree. But the transformation of North American and global markets has played an equally important role in creating the gap between the dreams and aspirations of twenty-first-century youth and the realities of the world economy.

We can put this very simply. The massive effort to get as many people as possible to college or university is not matched by a comparable effort to create jobs for the increased population of young people and for those dislocated from the workforce as the result of various competitive forces. As James Clifton argues:

> The coming world war is an all-out global war for good jobs. As of 2008, the war for good jobs has trumped all other leadership activities because it's been the cause and the effect of everything else that countries have experienced. This will become even more real in the future as global competition intensifies. If countries fail at creating

jobs, their societies will fall apart. Countries, and more specifically cities, will experience suffering, instability, chaos and eventually revolution. This is the new world that leaders will confront.[1]

OUTSOURCING JOBS TO CHEAPER LABOUR MARKETS

With surprising speed, economic globalization and the rise of East Asia, India, and China have undercut some of the key foundations of the Western economy, displacing hundreds of thousands of workers and dashing the expectations of the young in many countries. What happened to the airline industry fifteen years ago serves as a good example. In the late 1990s, airlines found themselves facing a dilemma. They could continue to hire reservation agents in their own countries, paying a decent wage to get the college and university graduates that they preferred to hire. With benefits thrown in, they were paying more than $35,000 a year as a starting salary for what was, to North American youth, an entry-level and temporary job. But then improvements in telecommunications and computer systems provided access to huge pools of well-educated overseas talent. When India became readily accessible, the airlines (and other businesses) could hire from among tens of thousands of well-educated, highly motivated university graduates. The key differences? In India, these jobs carried an annual salary of $5,000—and any candidate fortunate enough to get one of the positions typically held on to it. The choice seemed obvious: one reluctant North American college graduate at $35,000 a year, or seven university graduates from India, the latter being more grateful for the jobs and often demonstrating a stronger work ethic and more commitment to the position. It makes sense that many telemarketing and reservation systems link phone calls to Bangalore or Mumbai, where staff from India are trained, with greater or lesser success, to speak with North American regional accents.

But that was only the beginning. Factory workers were laid off by the thousands throughout the early twenty-first century, with hundreds of North American factories shuttered and the jobs relocated to Mexico, China, Thailand, the Philippines, and India. The damage got worse during the 2008 global recession—brought to you by your friendly Wall Street subprime mortgage companies and their banking allies—a financial catastrophe that ended only when the United States government bailed out some of the most mismanaged and borderline corrupt institutions in the world. Things started to pick up in 2014–2015 at the macro-level, with "good news" circulating about the recovery of the American economy, although the crash in oil, natural gas, and commodity prices damaged the resource sector and Euro-instability, associated with the near-death experience in Greece and China's recent boom-and-bust cycle in the stock market, made it clear that a return to stability was a long way off.

Still, the much-ballyhooed recovery carried some ominous news. The jobs did not come back as expected. Much was made about a few promising developments. Apple, one of the world's richest corporations and one of the best American firms at hiding its profits overseas (Apple Luxembourg is fabulously wealthy, thanks to US tax laws), noisily congratulated itself on opening a new factory in California, primarily to offset growing criticism of the labour practices at its Foxconn and other Chinese manufacturing facilities. But the reality was that jobs did not follow the upsurge in manufacturing in America. Why? In large part because the country's impressive productivity gains and continued high level of investment in production-improving technologies increased manufacturing—but not manufacturing jobs. Economic recovery without a surge in employment seemed a partial victory, at best, and a worrisome sign about the economic future.

THE NEW ECONOMY VERSUS THE OLD ECONOMY

The new economy produced some high-tech jobs, but the much-hyped growth turned out to be a whimper rather than a roar. Google and Facebook do not employ as many people as General Motors and John Deere. Google, worth $365 billion as of August 2015, heading, apparently to $1 trillion[2] and one of the world's richest firms, had 53,600 employees in 2014, a drop of 200 from two years earlier. That same year,

General Motors had 216,000 workers worldwide, a drop of 3,000 from 2013. But let's get real here. Walmart—an impressive retailer with a fabulous high-tech backbone but not the dream employer of many young Americans—has 2.2 million employees worldwide and is the largest private-sector employer in the United States. It is a big drop back to the second-largest American employer, Yum! Brands, which has over 500,000 workers, mostly overseas. (Yum! operates Pizza Hut and Taco Bell.) UPS, a parcel delivery service and one of the best-automated firms in the USA, has almost 400,000 workers. There are high-tech or knowledge-based companies in the mix, with IBM (434,000), Hewlett-Packard (332,000), and General Electric (305,000) making the American top ten. The point is that Google is a drop in the employment bucket. Walmart has many times more employees.

For so-called "knowledge workers," the target of governments and universities around the world, an uncertain future lies ahead:

> ... there is really a double dose of bad news. For not only are their jobs potentially easier to automate than other job types because no investment in mechanical equipment is required; but also, the financial incentive for getting rid of that job is significantly higher. As a result, we can expect that, in the future, automation will fall heavily on knowledge workers and in particular on highly paid workers. In cases where technology is not yet sufficient to automate the job, offshoring is likely to be pursued as an interim solution.[3]

Much the same has occurred in the finance sector, remarkably one of the most desired career paths for young North Americans. Because of the appalling scandals and malfeasance that have wracked it in recent years, you'd think the young would avoid it like the plague, but such is not the case. The banking system has actually continued to grow, particularly in the United States, with the expansion of service outlets in a highly competitive market, but most of the growth has been in service or teller-type positions. In Canada, where an oligopoly of five large banks controls the majority of the financial market, job reductions have been more pronounced. It needs to be said that Canada has one of the world's most stable and dependable banking systems anywhere. While the USA was recovering from the collapse of Bear Stearns, Wells Fargo, Andersen Consulting, Fannie Mae, and many other financial institutions in the wake of the 2008 financial crisis, not a single Canadian bank closed down or was even seriously affected. Computerization has brought about sweeping changes, with work shifting from in-person support to online banking and heavily computerized systems. Banks hire many high-technology employees. The financial service and insurance industry remains a major employer—with close to six million employees (three times Walmart's workforce) in 2014. The securities sector, with almost 890,000 workers in 2014, is expected to grow by an additional 12 percent by 2018. Employment data shows that this remains a service sector, with over 500,000 tellers, 367,000 insurance sales agents, and almost 300,000 securities and financial services sales agents.[4] This is, of course, old-economy work, knowledge-based to be sure, but not exactly the exciting new jobs-of-the-future stuff that promoters of the new economy have been talking about for several decades.

The vaunted post–dot.com economy has produced fine jobs for high-tech wizards, entrepreneurs, and marketers, but far fewer jobs for ordinary graduates and other semi-skilled workers. According to the US Department of Labor, the animation industry—a key sector in the new digital economy—had only sixty-nine thousand jobs across the USA in 2012. What's more, this exciting sector, one that converted once-unemployable fine arts graduates into tech-stars, is notoriously fickle and cyclical, with companies expanding and contracting their workforce with distressing regularity and with many firms discovering that they can keep just the high-end design work in North America, although even that is facing competition from Japan and South Korea, with the more routine animation work—the digital equivalent of manufacturing assembly work—being automated or outsourced to China, India, and other countries.

Where is the work? Glassdoor, an American jobs and employment site, compiled a list of jobs in the United States for which there is the highest demand. Here are the top ten:[5]

JOB	DEGREE REQUIRED	AVERAGE BASE SALARY	OPENINGS
Physician	MD	$212,000	8,000
Pharmacy Manager	MPharm	$121,000	1,800
Software Architect	BCS	$131,000	3,200
Software Developer	ManBCom	$124,000	2,200
Finance Manager	MCom/MBA	$124,000	9,200
Solutions Architect		$122,000	3,500
Lawyer	LLB	$120,000	5,500
Analytics Manager		$116,000	1,400
IT Manager		$116,000	1,400
Tax Manager		$115,000	3,600

How does this match up with the experience of recent graduates? An estimate of the production of lawyers in the USA indicated that the profession expected to add almost two hundred thousand positions between 2012 and 2022. In that same time period, American law schools were expected to graduate more than three hundred thousand new lawyers. What are the other hundred thousand going to do? And remember that there are many unemployed and underemployed law school graduates already in the labour force, competing for one of the two hundred thousand new jobs.[6] To touch on a topic to be discussed at length later, major employers have increasingly discovered that four-year college graduates, especially in the high-technology sectors, are not necessarily a good match with job openings. They have turned to short-course providers, particularly in software related areas, who provide specially trained workers (many of whom already have a degree or two) with career-ready preparation.

These examples make several simple points. There are lots of jobs, and very good jobs, available in the North American economy. The jobs, however, do not align very well with the fields of study of American and Canadian college and university students. And even when there is a direct connection—law school and lawyers' jobs, computer science and software architect—there is often a mismatch between the size of the graduating class and the needs of the workplace. One starts to feel sorry for the university students and graduates of today, because the challenge of determining the right fields of study, the most promising fields of employment, and the best fit for a career is becoming extremely difficult, given the shifting realities of the North American workforce.

And for those who don't want to go to college for four years, there are still some surprisingly well-paid jobs that require training, but not a full degree. According to Nicholas Wyman's book *Job U*, these (presumably not the starting salaries) include:

Radiation therapist	$77,500
Elevator technician	$76,600
Nuclear medicine technologist	$70,180
Airline and commercial pilot	$98,410
Dental hygienist	$70,200
Medical sales	$85,000
Air traffic controller	$122,500

With a series of economic crises—including the 2008–2009 chaos created by the American subprime meltdown—piling on top of global workplace changes, job opportunities dried up quickly. College graduates got jobs—employers who had a chance to choose between a university or a high school graduate usually opted for the former—but few of the hirees expected that they would be working in Starbucks, a fire hall, at Home Depot, or a Walmart. What a difference in a few decades! In the 1970s, rental-car companies hired high school dropouts to staff their counters. By the 2010s, Enterprise Rent-A-Car in the USA declared with pride in its NCAA March Madness television commercials that it was the largest employer of college graduates in the country. Enterprise is a

successful and well-regarded company. Many of the graduates are hired
into management-stream positions and some do progress through the
ranks of the company. It's probably safe to say, however, that few parents
and college-bound students ever sat around the dining room table, college application forms and guidebooks at the ready, student loan forms
almost filled out, thinking that the end result of their studies would be
work as a clerk at a car-rental firm.

The scale of the transformation of the North American industrial
and professional workforce is not widely known. But tremors have been
rumbling under the labour force for decades, with surface cracks emerging during recessions as the cruel pressures of international competition
and technological change undermine such traditionally strong sectors
as automobile and technological manufacturing. Detroit has emerged
as the poster child for the continent-wide industrial meltdown, a city in
complete free fall, with blocks of abandoned homes, widespread African
American poverty, and near anarchy, surrounded by safe, comfortable,
and largely Caucasian suburbs of sustained prosperity. In Detroit, the
greatest increase in employment in the period 2008 to 2018 is estimated
to be in home health aides, not a well-paid occupation.[7]

The crisis was not limited to Detroit. In Cleveland, Ohio, and other
industrial cities in the Great Lakes and American Northeast, large companies shed hundreds of thousands of well-paid, unionized jobs. Recent
economic challenges have seen the problems spread throughout southern Ontario and into other northern-tier industrial states. Urban blight,
fuelled by a widespread flight of jobs and people from industrial areas,
became the hallmark of what had previously been the industrial heart-
land for the Western industrial world. It is as if, only forty years from now,
Silicon Valley were to become a wasteland of abandoned high-tech campuses, with the McMansions of former high-tech executives derelict, occu-
pied by squatters, or converted into crack dens in some form of apocalyptic
Detroit on the Pacific. What seems ridiculous and unimaginable for Silicon
Valley, or Austin, Texas, or San Diego, or Boston was just as far-fetched for
the Detroit of the 1970s. We are entering unfamiliar territory, with little
evidence that people are paying attention to the warning signs.

The story inside the numbers is particularly jarring. It turns out that
North America, the land of opportunity, is becoming decidedly less so.

The story is much broader than the Occupy movement's indictment of the One Percent and the endless—and partially deserved—critique of the richest people in the Americas. Few people realistically expect to rise up into the financial stratosphere, and, except for those who are obsessed by popular culture—fans of the Kardashians and their ilk—few intelligent people care much about the "uber-rich." Sensible people know that most of the One Percent, like the ever-fascinating Donald Trump, started rich, with boosts from their parents. Most people simply seek a reasonable income, with enough money for the basics and a few extras, a comfortable home, and health security. North Americans overwhelmingly aspire simply to the middle class, or at least to the package of financial outcomes and material well-being historically associated with that status.

LOSS OF INDUSTRIAL JOBS

One of the great success stories of post–World War II North America was that the rapidly expanding American consumer economy created conditions that propelled millions of otherwise average people from poverty into middle-class lifestyles. What stood out in this era was that, for the first time in human history, the Western industrial economy produced a large number of well-paid, wage-labour positions for people of average ability and skill. In previous generations, say before 1940, people of below average or of average ability struggled to find good work, and only a fortunate few earned enough money on a regular basis to enjoy a stable and comfortable life. The post–World War II period produced urban growth, fuelled the rapid expansion of suburbs, and raised expectations across society. The related development of the managerial class built an even broader foundation for national prosperity. This class included a large group of government workers in the rapidly expanding civil service, the staff of the expansive financial industry, the emergence of massive entertainment and media industries, and the stunning growth of the consumer retail trade, which included a large advertising sector. To top it off, the Cold War and the American adoption of the domino theory forced the USA to engage communism on many fronts, and that required a large standing military—and an even larger military-industrial complex to buttress America's international commitments.

The simultaneous rise of management, retail commerce, public administration, and high technology created intense demand for college- and university-trained graduates, while also offering decent incomes for armies of industrial workers who had minimal training and no particularly specialized skills. Opportunities for the well-educated were matched by prospects for hard-working and dependable workers of average ability. This was the America of the great postwar boom, a nation ascendant internationally, with an economy that dominated the world and social opportunities that were unmatched anywhere. Young people leaving America's high schools had a variety of good options, including a post-secondary education followed by entry into the burgeoning white-collar workforce, direct employment in any one of the thousands of manual and factory operations across the continent, or military service as a backup option. Not everything was rosy, of course, since it never is. African Americans had to surmount many barriers to opportunity, and immigrants often struggled to adjust. Women did not experience major employment and income gains until the 1970s. Even America at its height was no paradise. But the country worked better than almost all others on the planet.

The flood tide of American prosperity and social harmony began to ebb in the 1990s. Industrial closures swept across the United States, as companies fell victim to outdated technologies and intense Japanese, South Korean, and Chinese competition. The closures shifted to Canada and Mexico after the North American Free Trade Agreement came into effect in 1994. Women did find more jobs, but stagnant or declining incomes forced millions of families to have both parents working just to maintain their standard of living. Ethnic minorities, particularly African Americans, paid the greatest share of the cost, but so did poorly paid coal miners in the Appalachians and factory workers in uncompetitive industries. Impressions of prosperity lingered, buttressed by America's unrelenting confidence in the free market, a preposterously overhyped dot-com boom, and an explosion of home values and fraudulent mortgages. But underneath the façade of one of the world's least-regulated financial markets, the shiny possibilities of Silicon Valley adventurism, and hyperinflation in house prices, major cracks were emerging in the North American superstructure.

The most alarming change, with profound implications for youth prospects in the twenty-first century, was the rapid decline of opportunities for people of average ability and limited skill. With robots and mechanization replacing many factory workers, with global competition eliminating tens of thousands of jobs and crippling the effectiveness of most industrial trade unions, and with much of the country's economic growth occurring in high technology and finance, the general-purpose industrial labourer lost access to work, income, and opportunity. There were occasional bright spots—Alaska pipeline developments in the 1970s, North Dakota and Wyoming shale gas in the 2010s, Alaska and Texas oil plays, and artificially hyped housing construction—but the overall experience was distressing. Entire towns and regions, from Ohio and Illinois to rural Pennsylvania and upstate New York, suffered through prolonged collapse, urban decay, and a massive increase in poverty among the laid-off workers. In the twenty-first century, the pace of technological displacement accelerated. The current cost of replacing a worker with a machine in the industrial sector is around $100,000. If an industrial machine can be purchased for that sum, a regular position can be eliminated. For many companies, the resulting increase in efficiency and productivity is the only way to remain competitive.

THE LOSS OF MIDDLE-MANAGEMENT JOBS

Perhaps the great challenge for university graduates is one that has attracted little attention because it evolved slowly and with little fanfare. Starting with the rapid expansion of government, industry, and the service sector after World War II, North America created one of the most impressive middle-management cohorts in the world. The USA and Canada were not alone. Japan had—and still has—one of the most successful middle-management cultures anywhere. So does England, built around the financial and insurance industries. Germany's much-vaunted industrial establishment, like the banking sector in Switzerland, is likewise centred on a strong, educated, and conscientious middle-management layer. But consider the observation of Daniel Pink:

During the twentieth century, most work was algorithmic [described as "rules-based"]—and not just jobs where you turned the same screw the same way all day long. Even when we traded blue collars for white, the tasks we carried out were often routine. That is, we could reduce much of what we did—in accounting, law, computer programming, and other fields—to a script, a spec sheet, a formula, or a series of steps that produced a right answer. But today, in much of North America, Eastern Europe, Japan, South Korea, and Australia, routine white-collar work is disappearing; it's racing offshore to wherever it can be done the cheapest. In India, Bulgaria, the Philippines, and other countries, lower-paid workers essentially run the algorithm, figure out the correct answer and deliver it instantaneously from their computer to someone six thousand miles away.[8]

The transition had a major impact on the prospects for North American youth. In 2015, Robert Putnam published a brilliant but depressing book, *Our Kids: The American Dream in Crisis*, that documented the rapid division of USA society into "have" and "have not" populations. His monumental work makes it clear that college and employment affirmative action cannot overcome deeply entrenched poverty, marginalization, racism, and trauma at the family and community level. Putnam puts words and statistics to what is obvious across the United States and parts of Canada. African Americans are doing much more poorly and have little access to the American Dream. Hispanic Americans, legal or otherwise, have suffered egregiously in educational and employment outcomes. New immigrants, for years the source of much American energy and entrepreneurship, lag well behind. It's much the same in Canada, where immigrants struggle to have international credentials recognized and where Aboriginal peoples (as in the USA) often live with devastating poverty and community despair. Have-not regions—the Appalachians and Detroit in the USA, significant parts of the Maritimes and rural Quebec in Canada—rely on government transfers and make-work programs. The numbers are shocking: at the end of 2014, over forty-six million Americans relied on food stamps, and for three years in a row this figure included two hundred thousand people with Master's degrees and thirty-three thousand with PhDs.[9]

HIGHER EDUCATION AS THE ANSWER

The problems are deep and systemic, attached to advances in technology, the displacement of labour through globalization, and the shift away from heavy industry across North America. Consider the implications, according to Derek Thompson, writing in *The Atlantic*, who documented the growing number of nonworking men and young people without jobs.[10]

> The share of prime-age Americans (25 to 54 years old) who are working has been trending down since 2000. Among men, the decline began even earlier: the share of prime-age men who are neither working nor looking for work has doubled since the late 1970s, and has increased as much throughout the recovery as it did during the Great Recession itself. All in all, about one in six prime-age men today are either unemployed or out of the workforce altogether. This is what the economist Tyler Cowen calls "the key statistic" for understanding the spreading rot in the American workforce. Conventional wisdom has long held that under normal economic conditions, men in this age group—at the peak of their abilities and less likely than women to be primary caregivers for children—should almost all be working. Yet fewer and fewer are.

Starting in the 1980s, with industrial work eroding quickly, governments, parents, and high school counsellors turned to promoting college or university admission as the best path forward. The evidence was clear, displayed in the career and life experiences of those who opted for post-secondary education in the three postwar decades. The wage and income gap between high school graduates and those with college degrees was becoming steadily larger. What was missed in the celebration of the economic "success" of college graduates was the fact that, "The gap has increased mainly because of the collapse of wages for those who have less education, and not because of any dramatic increase in the earnings of college grads, especially new grads. The reason that fact about the gap matters is because it could well be that college grads do far better than high school grads and still do not earn enough to pay back the cost of their college degrees."[11] The bonus for spending three or four years in post-secondary education, forgoing income during that time, and paying tuition and living expenses was nonetheless impressive and well worth the effort. Get a Bachelor's degree and earn $1 million or more over a career than a community-college graduate, and much more than a mere high-school-diploma holder. Get a Master's or professional degree and add another impressive salary jump. Struggle through to the PhD and earn even more. The formula was so simple. Governments believed that the formula also applied to them: subsidize undergraduate and graduate education, consider these to be investments in people and society, and reap the benefits of much higher taxes in the future. Everyone wins. No one loses.

By happy chance, the *Learning = Earning* numbers worked out perfectly for the college and university sector. It turned out that, on average, a four-year degree produced $1 million in additional lifetime income for a university graduate over a nongraduate. The world's best marketing agency could not have found a better set of numbers. Even with the costs of going to school—and before the 1990s, tuition costs were reasonable and within reach for most middle-class families—and the delayed earnings, these young people enjoyed accelerated incomes, as well as cleaner and more attractive office environments.

College and university recruiters jumped to capitalize on the salary numbers. Sitting at dining room tables with prospective students or talking to an eager and earnest family at a recruiting fair, they could wipe out anxiety about high tuition costs and college living expenses with a simple reference to the million-dollar promise. Viewed this way, a degree was not simply an education. For parents, it was an investment, a financial commitment in their children's future. And as alternative pathways to comfort and prosperity dried up—often for the parents themselves, as they lost their jobs or struggled with a changing workforce—the college promise hung out there like a bright and compelling beacon. Come hither, it said, to jobs and opportunity.

But from the outset, these statistics had been misleading. Averages are averages, indicating what will happen across a broad population. The averages dealing with college graduates include the Harvard-educated doctor, the Wall Street financier from Princeton, the McGill graduate with a degree in neuropsychology, and the oil and gas engineer from Texas A&M, as well as the English literature specialist from Minot State, the psychology graduate from Cal State Northridge, and the film studies major from New York University. Even the most superficial analysis would suggest that the first four would have dramatically different career outcomes than the last three. But the average figures were undeniably true, as averages, and parents and high school graduates, eager for reassurance, accepted the idea, or, to put it baldly, the lie that a degree—any degree from any institution—would provide a ticket to the middle class.

Parents and prospective students were even more strongly seduced by the additional promise of high-quality institutions. If the promises of universities and colleges in general might be suspect, then at least the best institutions provided better prospects. Harvard, University of Southern California, and University of Texas-Austin were clearly going to offer greater hope than a third- or fourth-tier college. Ditto Stanford, Duke, Princeton, Duke, and Yale. The data seem to bear this out. The simple dominance of Ivy League graduates in the American finance sector provides seemingly irrefutable evidence of what many North Americans take to be an unassailable truth. If *Learning = Earning*, then *Learning at an Elite Institution = Even More Earning*. The result, of course, is intense competition for entrance to the elite schools, with the best institutions attracting many times more applicants than there are first-year spaces. In one of the many perversions of the United States' post-secondary education system, institutions are rated on the ratio of applicants to admissions. Clearly, a college that turns down more students is more selective and therefore more elite and more attractive. And so institutions seeking to position themselves as among the very best in an intense and overcrowded North American marketplace make a strong effort to recruit more applicants, even when they already have ten to fifteen times more would-be students than spaces.

THE JOBS CRISIS

But as the truth about graduate outcomes slowly became clear, the return on investment or ROI—an acronym that took over from a high-quality education as a primary goal for post-secondary education—started to decline. It also started to split between career-ready degrees and more general fields of study that lacked a precise career focus. Business schools, the weak cousin of colleges and universities in the 1960s, had become institutional superstars by the 1990s. Top business faculty members attracted rock-star salaries and attention. Students who had flooded into Arts and Science programs like lemmings in the 1970s and 1980s shifted gears in the 1990s and 2000s and headed for business schools. Even the prestigious American liberal-arts institutions—Colorado College, Middlebury College, and Swarthmore College—did the previously unthinkable and added business and economics degrees to what had once been the best Arts and Science undergraduate degree programs in the world.

The job crisis, which started in the low-skill industrial sectors, has started to infect the professional ranks. Law students, lured into degree programs by the prospect of high-profile and high-income jobs, have faced brutal job prospects across the United States and Canada in recent years. In the mid-2010s, thousands of new law graduates struggled to find articling positions, ringing up mountains of debt, and then failing to find the lucrative jobs they expected. The crisis here was driven higher by the out-of-sync career and salary expectations of aspiring lawyers who may have watched too many episodes of *Law and Order* or seen Michael Douglas's turn in *Wall Street* ("greed is good") as an enticement rather than an indictment against a failed financial system.

But you can't fool all of the people all of the time, as a self-educated American lawyer once said, and students eventually caught on and responded to the collapsing job market. In the United States in 2014, law school admissions fell by some 40 percent over the previous high. Law schools felt they had two choices: close their doors (several did) or lower their academic standards to fill their classrooms and pay the bills. The latter practice was particularly noticeable at the larger for-profit schools that had sprung up to meet the seemingly insatiable demand for legal careers. Canada, incidentally, followed a contrary track, with continued strong demand for spots in law schools—but equally severe difficulties for graduates looking for articling positions and full-time employment. In fact, two new law schools opened in Canada, both in smaller regional centres that had struggled to find lawyers willing to work in the areas.

In 2012, some American law schools, in desperation, reportedly gave in to the temptation to game the system.[12] After-graduation surveys are often pretty superficial and do not inquire deeply about the positions that former students hold. Surveyors simply want to know if the graduates have a job and if the position is related to their law degree. So, the solution must have seemed obvious. The law schools hired their own graduates and gave them quasi-legal jobs that were of long-enough duration to cover the survey period. The results improved, the law schools looked better, and no one complained; at least, not until the truth came out. When it was revealed that certain law schools responsible for training the nation's lawyers had betrayed the very principles they were teaching, many observers were disgusted, although the scandal did not get nearly as much attention as did the New England Patriots' "deflate-gate" scandal in the American Football Conference finals in January 2015.

Other law schools have become bottom-feeders. The classic example is Florida Coastal School of Law. In 2013 the median score of its entering class lay in the bottom quarter of everyone in the country who wrote the LSAT test, something that the LSAT administrators say makes it unlikely that these students will ever pass the bar exam. Nevertheless, the school charges nearly $45,000 a year in tuition. Ninety-three percent of the 2014 graduates had debt averaging $163,000—this for a degree they may well be unable to use, if they graduate.[13]

A substantial number of graduates in many disciplines, particularly in the Arts and Sciences, have had dismal job experiences. As a result, many students have chosen to continue their studies at graduate and professional schools in a search for careers and a decent salary. The continued pursuit of graduate qualifications has, for many aspiring students, proven disappointing as well. This is particularly true at the Master's level, where ROIs in certain Humanities fields have dropped below zero—a fancy way of saying that the cost of completing the degree plus the loss of deferred income is greater than any increase in earnings associated with the degree. So no million-dollar bonus here. This career calculus is fine if the motivation for completing the degree is learning and self-fulfillment. If the

FOUR BACKUP CAREERS FOR NEW TEACHERS

These are Canadian examples for teaching graduates who can't find jobs or want to delay their entry into the field, but the ideas are universal. For Royal Canadian Mounted Police, for instance, substitute FBI.

1. TEACHING ABROAD

There are many countries where English teachers are highly sought (e.g., South Korea, the Middle East, and Japan). If you're an adventure seeker, teaching abroad on a one- or two-year contract is a great option. The classroom experience could prove useful when you return.

2. PRIVATE TUTORING

You can work with tutoring companies such as Alliance or Kumon, or manage your own students. The rates are good—up to $30 per hour.

3. PRIVATE SCHOOLS

People shy away from teaching at them because of the stereotype about affluent students being entitled and unpleasant to teach. But this may not be true, and the classes are relatively small and teacher resources are abundant.

4. THE JUSTICE SYSTEM

Who says you have to stick to the classroom? The Royal Canadian Mounted Police has also been recruiting education graduates lately to work in civilian jobs as instructors, youth workers, or in victim services. Skills acquired in teacher's college— flexibility, planning, and multitasking—are useful in the justice system too.[14]

students (and the parents and governments that fund the system) select the degree in anticipation of a better job and higher income, then the outcome is a disaster.

The oversupply of people with undergraduate degrees has morphed, in short order, into an oversupply of people with graduate degrees. Where there were once too many people with Bachelor's degrees, there are now also too many with Master's. A good portion of this is artificial, though, since the largest field of graduate studies in North America— by a very significant degree—is in education. In the high-demand areas, where the continental economy truly needs highly skilled and well-trained people, like mathematics, computer science, and engineering, the vast majority of North American PhD students and graduates are international students. Not so in education. In this extremely inflated field, enrolment is driven by the immediate salary bump for teachers that follows graduation.

The evolving patterns of the modern workforce have destroyed dreams by the hundreds of thousands. Many Chinese families who borrowed heavily to get their children into a North American university have seen them struggle to find work when they returned home. Thousands of American young adults have lived in undergraduate-like poverty as they searched for work, and large numbers have moved back in with their parents. Failure to launch, much more than the title of a mediocre movie, became the hallmark of the Millennial generation. While many coped with long-term underemployment and unemployment, others ascribed failure to their own shortcomings. Few looked across a landscape of destroyed expectations and identified structural or fundamental flaws with the economic and educational order.

From about 2000 to the present, the experience of young adults has mirrored and contributed to the changing employment landscape across North America and around the world. Some succeeded and did extremely well. Ivy League graduates continued to land six-figure jobs on Wall Street. High-tech firms in Massachusetts, north Texas, and California scoured the graduation lists at MIT, Harvard, University of Texas–Austin, Stanford, and the University of Waterloo to find the highly skilled workers they needed for their new economy firms. In short, there was wealth and opportunity for the few; struggle and frustration for the many. More than the mantra of the Occupy movement, this described the real-life experience of college and university graduates in general.

4

THE DEATH OF AVERAGE

In August 2015, Democratic presidential candidate Hillary Clinton released a major statement on college and university education. It was a sweeping Obama-esque kind of transformative initiative aimed at public expectations, parental aspirations, and the dreams of millions of young Americans. Clinton promised that, if she were elected, her government would provide massive increases in funding for universities, free college tuition, and major changes and many billions of dollars' worth of other electoral goodies, all tied to the usual *Learning* = *Earning* formula of youth career preparation.

The Clinton plan is not simply unwise, but for a number of reasons it is counterproductive, reinforcing the false dream of millions of American young adults and putting increased national emphasis on one of the most narrow and uninformed public policy priorities of this generation: the idea that higher education always equals more income. America already has a college and university participation rate that is arguably too high, and now Clinton wants to expand it. In an interview, she said, "I want every parent to know that his or her child can get a degree or you can get one yourself."[1] One hopes that she meant every child or person sufficiently intelligent and motivated can get one.

If the United States somehow had an endless supply of jobs requiring a college degree—something that is clearly not the case —her statement would make sense. True, the plan will not fund students at private colleges, only at public ones, but the prospect of free tuition at state universities and colleges is bound to increase enrolment, especially in the absence of strong entrance requirements. Is a college degree or diploma really the answer to America's social and economic problems? Of course the United States has serious problems of social and economic equality, but higher education is not the panacea that by itself will cure them; certainly pouring more money into the system isn't the answer. As it is, there are some private colleges with relatively low tuition fees (Berea College in Kentucky charges $870 a year), and the Clinton plan doesn't pay for living expenses. There are a number of sources of money already available to needy students; notably, for Americans, the Pell Grant, which provides up to $5,700. There are a good number of public colleges with tuition fees lower than that.[2] And then there's the question of fraud. The rules to prevent this aren't clear, but you'd have to be naïve to doubt that fraudsters are already devising schemes to profit from Clinton's plan, should it be enacted. It's an all-round bad idea.

DISAPPEARING JOBS AND CAREERS

The obsession with the Dream Factories has become a serious American problem, and a global one too. While there are always improvements that can be made in the world's most complex, comprehensive, and diverse post-secondary system, the reality is that governments—and politicians like Hillary Clinton—are looking at the wrong end of the problem. As economist James Bessen wrote, "This is today's great paradox. Since the beginning of the personal computer revolution, the median wage in the United States has been stagnant. Information technology may even be hurting many white-collar workers, especially those with a college education. Voice mail systems have taken over from switchboard operators, automated teller machines do tasks of bank tellers, and computer systems have automated a whole range of routine clerical tasks. Workers in these occupations have to find new jobs or learn new skills to remain employed."[3] For a generation, hoping to reproduce the positive and career-building experiences of the 1960s and 1970s, North American politicians and government officials have expanded the university and college system, believing that preparing an infinite number of young people through undergraduate education was the key to national competitiveness and personal opportunity.

For the college and university dream to work, graduates have to find stable jobs with decent salaries and good career prospects. Students, parents, governments, and institutions can control the input—the number of enrollees and a considerably smaller number of graduates—but the second half of the equation—careers—is tied to the vagaries of the global economy. In a crucial study of the technological revolution, Rik Brynjolfsson and Andrew McAfee argued:

> [D]igitization is going to bring with it some thorny challenges. This in itself should not be too surprising or alarming; even the most beneficial developments have unpleasant consequences that must be managed. The Industrial Revolution was accompanied by soot-filled London skies and horrific exploitation of child labour. What will be their modern equivalents? Rapid and accelerating digitization is likely to bring economic rather than environmental disruption, stemming from the fact that as computers get more powerful, companies have less need for some kinds of workers. Technological progress is going to leave behind some people, perhaps even a lot people, as it races ahead ... [T]here's never been a better time to be a worker with special skills or the right education, because these people can use technology to create and capture value. However, there's never been a worse time to be a worker with only "ordinary" skills and abilities to offer, because computers, robots, and other digital technologies are acquiring these skills and abilities at an extraordinary rate.[4]

The evidence shows, in fact, that the North American drive for more and more tertiary education has outstripped the needs of the modern economy, and that the resulting underemployment and unemployment has caused serious difficulties for a large portion of the current generation.

And yet what passes for policy innovation in North America rests on doubling down on a failed and failing system. This is a gamble that the solutions of the 1970s, having fallen short of objectives for a generation, will somehow come right and solve the problems of the 2010s and 2020s.

NEW TECHNOLOGIES BUT FEWER JOBS

What is missing in Clinton's strategy—and what is missing from political and public-policy debate across North America—is a serious consideration of the transformations affecting the modern economy. Ultimately, the mismatch between the degrees and expectations of university graduates and the job market is only half the story. The first fifteen years of the twenty-first century have seen the worldwide transformation of work through technological change. In sector after sector, machines and digital technologies have replaced workers, initially in small numbers, but increasingly in the thousands. The changes happened first in industrial and resource industries, destroying thousands of jobs in forestry, pulp and paper, and manufacturing. The transformation spread into the service sector, with online banking changing the roles of bank clerks, and with e-commerce and other technological solutions undermining work in many other economic sectors.

Even though the transition remains in the early stages, the mass use of robots has undercut a great deal of industrial labour. Henry Ford would have loved the almost worker-free assembly lines of the modern automobile factory, but North American workers are less impressed with the mounting job losses, made worse by the shift of factories to Mexico and other low-wage countries. There are many other examples. The development of computer-based income tax forms and e-filing has disrupted the personal accounting profession. Amazon.com, famous the world over for its e-commerce operation, is truly impressive as a technologically enhanced retail company, with modern, computer-controlled and automated warehouses. But spare a thought or two for the thousands of former warehouse workers being displaced by these new technologies.

The world now faces the real prospect of continued accelerated change and rapid job loss. Autonomous oil rigs and remotely controlled mining operations promise to eliminate thousands of jobs. The first autonomous oil rig in the Arctic went into operation in 2015, and Australia's desert mines have been world leaders in remote-controlled extraction. The impact goes far beyond the miners and oil rig workers. Removing the front-line workers means immediate declines in on-site support staff, worker transportation, accommodation services, food and other delivery systems, and the related administrative activities. Companies wishing to stay competitive—particularly when working in high-cost remote regions, where extreme weather (e.g., 120°F in the Australian outback and -50°F in the Arctic) add to the difficulties of recruiting, retaining, and caring for workers—are strongly tempted to automate their operations as much as possible. But the job losses filter throughout the economy, cutting back on opportunities for young workers.

Outsourcing service and professional work to developing nations has eliminated many first-world jobs in recent years, and the advent of new technologies will likely accelerate the process. In the coming years, new technologies could conceivably overturn entire industries. Consider driverless cars. You thought Uber was bad for the taxi business: autonomous vehicles will eliminate the need for taxis altogether, along with the industry's expensive and cumbersome system of licences and government regulations. But individual car ownership will also be affected by the emergence of on-call services that will deliver a vehicle to your door and drop you off when you are done. Some experts claim—and this is where the transformative potential of new technologies becomes really fascinating—that driverless cars will result in a major decline in bodily injuries associated with auto accidents, which will in turn reduce the pressure on hospital emergency rooms, slash the number of specialized nurses and emergency physicians, reduce insurance premiums, and contribute to longer life expectancies. There is a lot of good news in there, as well as a good deal of futurist blather, but keep an eye on the number of jobs being lost and try to figure out what new forms of work and employment will emerge in their place.

Consider the transformative potential of 3-D printing. These new technologies, with applications ranging from the "production" of personalized candies to the "printing" of jet engines and massive sections of bridges, can stand traditional manufacturing and all of the related work on its head. The concept is simple. The 3-D printer downloads precise technical specifications over the Internet and, using extruded materials, produces the desired item. At present, home machines can be purchased for close to $1,500 and can pay for themselves in a year or two. The rapid innovations in the field will ensure that 3-D printers will be able to print complex machines, including circuit boards, fine art, engine components, human body parts (yes!), and many other things with a few clicks of a mouse. Again, follow the value chain in 3-D printing. The large-scale manufacturing plant becomes a thing of the past, but so does the warehouse, the trucking company, the retail store, and all of the employees associated with the intermediate steps.

Describing the advent of dispersed manufacturing, open innovation, and globally networked design, production, and marketing functions as the "New Industrial Revolution," Peter Marsh wrote, "The way companies switch their approach to suit the broader platform for global manufacturing will be central to their, and the world's future. 'Design-only' manufacturers will become a more substantial and dynamic group. Such businesses, predominantly located in the high-cost regions, will employ large numbers in product development. They will leave physical production to others, mainly in parts of the world with lower wages." Marsh also noted, in optimistic words filled with foreboding for people of average or below-average skills, "For the most talented, imaginative and technically qualified people, the new industrial revolution will create huge opportunities that will turn out no less exciting than those that changed the world during the original industrial revolution of the late eighteenth century."[5]

Advanced digital intelligence, based on expanding the power of the Jeopardy-winning Watson-type computer by a factor of several thousand or million times, could easily eliminate a great deal of the so-called "knowledge economy" work. Most mortgage approvals are already done by computer algorithms, and computers are better than most tax consultants at ferreting out the hidden assets of would-be tax avoiders. Research shows that computers can select the best short lists for job vacancies. But imagine how this applies to the so-called soft and human fields, such as clinical psychology, where studies have shown that computer programs can already outperform human analysts in terms of diagnosis. As two Stanford University psychiatry professors argue, "Computers and Internet-based programs have great potential to make psychological assessment and treatment more cost-effective. Computer-assisted therapy appears to be as effective as face-to-face treatment for treating anxiety disorders and depression. Internet support groups also may be effective and have advantages over face-to-face therapy."[6]

Older readers will remember "Lucy," the early mainframe computer program named after Charlie Brown's nemesis, that asked and answered questions: "What seems to be bothering you? You're sad? Why? Can you tell me about it?" It was fun, but now it seems to be a reality. Twenty years ago, society struggled to get people suffering with mental illness to visit a psychotherapist. Now, these patients are being directed, under clinical guidance, to put their mental well-being in the hands of a digital system.

One can only imagine how many low-level, repetitive government functions—and functionaries—could be replaced by well-designed computers. Look at Estonia, one of the world's most advanced e-countries, if you want to see the electronic future of government. Reducing cost and improving efficiency and productivity are the main reasons for investing in new technologies, but remember that each innovation has the potential to eliminate many jobs, although theoretically each one could also create an unknown number of spin-off opportunities. Science fiction writers have pondered the future of artificial intelligence for generations—and now it is staring the world in the face.

No sectors will be left untouched. For more than a generation, urban parking lots provided a common point of entry into the North American workforce for tens of thousands of immigrants who were drawn to the minimal requirements and the ability to work without English-language skills. There were a hundred and thirty thousand such workers in the USA in 2014. The work was straightforward: collecting receipts, running them through a time clock, and providing change. Many of these jobs are at risk. In their place are a variety of machines—for coins, bills, and credit cards—that provide access to customer-managed parking lots that are monitored remotely by video camera. More advanced systems alert drivers to the number of vacant spots in the garage and can even indicate where the vacancies can be found. Innovative systems allow drivers to reserve spots while en route to their destination, and direct the driver to the garage and specific space. Many automated systems send a text to the consumer when the allotted time is over, allowing the individuals to add extra time over their smartphones. So, better service, more information, more efficiency, and improved safety—but with fewer workers.

HIGH-PAY, HIGH-STATUS CAREERS

Consider the other end of the income scale—the well-compensated, deeply scientific, and high-status medical professions. This work is intensely personal, involving direct contact between patient and physician (or nurse or paramedical professional). These fields, despite global concerns about high costs and expanding medical needs, seem impervious to job loss, particularly given the health care needs of the industrial world's growing population of senior citizens. Medicine is also a profession with an intense appetite for innovation, ranging from nanomedicine (miniscule medical robots), personalized pharmaceuticals, remote surgery, implanted medical devices, highly specialized treatment techniques, and various other technical developments. These advances seem to be effective, as improvements in life expectancy attest.

But the scale, importance, and especially the cost of medical service is also a major incentive for labour-saving innovation. The most technologically optimistic specialists imagine a near future where smartphones and embedded technologies replace substantial portions of current evaluations and monitoring by medical professionals. High-technology solutions—contact lenses that alert patients via text messages of changes in blood sugar, digital tablets that provide remote and personalized assessments of various chronic diseases, embedded monitoring systems that alert both patients and their

JOB AUTOMATION

Jobs where the likelihood of automation approaches 100 percent: Telemarketers, Title Examiners, Sewers, Mathematical Technicians, Insurance Underwriters, Watch Repairers, Cargo and Freight Agents, Tax Preparers, Photographic Process Workers, New Account Clerks, Library Technicians, Data Entry Keyers.

Jobs where the likelihood of automation approaches zero: Fire Fighters, Oral Surgeons, Healthcare Social Workers, Prosthetists, Audiologists, Mental-Health Social Workers, Emergency Management Directors, First-Line Supervisors, Mechanics, Recreational Therapists.[7]

medical caregivers to changes in health indicators, nanotechnologies that attack diseases at the cellular level, sophisticated precision operating tools that allow complex surgeries at vast distances, and super-high-efficiency radiation systems that use synchrotron science to target radiation treatment at the smallest and least intrusive level possible—have already revolution-ized medical care in first-world countries. Helped by high-tech and cor-porate philanthropists such as Bill and Melinda Gates and Warren Buffett, companies have turned their attention to the developing world, looking for innovations that could address the health care needs of the "bottom billion," a global effort that has the potential to use new technologies to bring about major improvements in the life prospects for the world's poorest citizens.

All of this makes medical care one of the most dynamic and prom-ising fields of technological innovation—but it less clear what this means for the physicians, nurses, and paraprofessionals in the field, particularly in the industrialized world. Of course, there are many reasons for caution. Massive investments in e-health, particularly focused on the manage-ment of health records, have produced mixed results, at best, and several spectacular failures. Far from saving money, these efforts produced huge contracts for consultants and failed to deliver on the promise of massive labour and wage savings. If the technology works, however—and the passage of time suggests that it will, although perhaps not as currently anticipated—there could be a sharp reduction in the number of phys-icians, nurses, and other health care providers—although not, at least in the United States, an improvement in the staggeringly inefficient manage-ment of the nation's health insurance system.

The point of these examples is that an intense transformation is underway in the adult labour force in the present, and it will continue into the future. Researchers suggest that half of all of the jobs in the North American economy could be eliminated through technological change in less than twenty-five years. Half! Even if the figure is just futurist-babble, and the number is smaller, some changes are certainly coming, and even a 20- or 30-percent reduction will be catastrophic. Some of the remaining work will require high-end, science and technology-driven employees. These people will usually require advanced STEM (science, technology, engineering, and mathematical) skills, precisely the areas of study where North American students are at their worst and where the college and university system produces fewer graduates than the market requires. Some scenarios about future economic profiles foreshadow a world dominated even more dramatically by billionaires, with a small and wealthy tech-elite buttressed by global demand for their expertise, a large service sector that caters to the well-to-do, and alarmingly large groups of the unemployed and underemployed. While techno-enthusiasts claim that the technology-driven economy will both redefine work and create many new opportunities, the current trajectory of the "new economy" is far from promising for the majority of people who lack high-end skills. The American Bureau of Labor Statistics has made some interesting predictions on the future growth of STEM, as opposed to non-STEM, employment. Between 2000 and 2010, STEM growth increased 7.9 percent and non-STEM 2.6 percent. Between 2008 and 2018, these figures are projected to be 17 percent and 9.8 percent.

The creation of vast wealth in the digital sector has not been matched with a large and expanding workforce. The oft-cited example of Instagram—sold to Facebook for $1 billion at a time when it employed only twelve people—is emblematic of a fundamental disconnect between the prosperity of the elites and the reduced opportunities for the many. Even more dramatic is the case of Markus Frind, founder and for years the only employee of PlentyofFish (POF.com), an algorithm-based dating site. Frind sold his company in 2015 for $575 million, a pretty price for a firm with millions of dollars in annual revenue but only a tiny number of employees. The leading high-technology companies are small in terms of the total number of people who work for them. Some of the more dynamic sectors, such as animation, rely on a small, fluid workforce that struggles to cope with routine turnover and industry-wide instability. For those with the key technical skills—computer programmers, software engineers, software managers, and the like—the job market looks spectacular. Jobs are readily available. Salaries are high. And prospects, for now, look impressive. The field is not for everyone and certainly not for those with a generic college degree.

Companies compete for talent and offer handsome incentives to those with highly specialized skills, such as young professionals with knowledge of the semantic web (the "thinking" Internet). North American companies routinely cite labour shortages as a justification for hiring foreign workers to fill highly paid jobs. Indeed, international students are overrepresented in the STEM disciplines in colleges, particularly at the graduate level, and many use their expertise to move quickly into full-time employment and even permanent resident status in the USA or Canada. This creates some unique and creative solutions. The USA has been more reticent about allowing foreign workers into the country than Canada, frustrating American high-technology firms. Microsoft, eager to attract hundreds of workers for urgent projects, was blocked by American immigration rules. The company set up a satellite office in Vancouver, capitalized on Canada's more liberal immigration regulations, and got the workforce it wanted, operating only a hundred and fifty miles from the Microsoft headquarters in Redmond, Washington.

OUTSOURCING WORK AND FORECASTING THE FUTURE

But even in the IT sector, the present and the future of work are far from secure. For many American companies, it has been easier to move the work offshore. Starting in the late 1990s and following on the profitable lead established by outsourcing call-centre work, North American firms began shifting a lot of their high-technology work to Asia. Sun Computer Systems, once a leading American research powerhouse, currently has more than 90 percent of its high-technology workforce in Asia, with most of it in China. The Chinese firm Huawei, little known in North America, has a massive high-technology force—over a hundred and fifty thousand strong—and is a world leader in wireless technologies. Foxconn Technology in Taiwan, with over 1.5 million employees, is the world's largest high-technology firm, a title that for much of the postwar period belonged to American firms.

This new reality highlights the need for a highly specialized workforce, but it also suggests that the Western economy will require many fewer workers than at present. With China, India, the Middle East, Turkey, and other countries churning out hundreds of thousands of highly motivated, well-trained, and eager young STEM professionals, it is by no means certain that the current demand for workers in these fields will hold. This is where things get really unnerving. The economy is shifting—and certain highly skilled workers will have the best opportunities in the workforce of the twenty-first century. Logic clearly suggests that young adults should head to the STEM disciplines where assured employment awaits. But will it? It is equally possible that competitor countries will emerge to displace leading North American firms. To the degree that there are more jobs, they may well be in Taiwan, China, and South Korea (where most of the digital economy is based) or in emerging economies in India, Turkey, or Brazil. Or not. The reality is that no one knows for sure. And it is upon precisely these uncertainties and ambiguities that young people are expected to chart their educational paths and career aspirations.

Here is the dilemma that faces governments, parents, and young people when it comes to making sense of the evolving work environment. Everyone has no doubt heard—many times—about all of the new jobs, professions, and opportunities that will be available for young people in the future. It is easy to recall these optimistic and even enticing views. Futurist gurus predict that young people will have four, five, six, or more careers in their adult lives, so fast-changing will economic realities be in the coming years. Gone, they say, are the lifelong company careers, offering steady career progress, solid benefits, and security through to retirement. If the life of the company man or woman is disappearing, worry not, the story goes, for well-trained, flexible, and educated individuals will be able to adapt to an exciting, dynamic, and upwardly mobile workforce that is full of opportunity and adventure.

CST Careers 2030, a thoughtful exploration of the future of work completed by a company that helps parents save money for their children's college and university studies, provides an enticing view of what is in store. Old-economy jobs might be disappearing, but Careers 2030 paints a portrait of an economy moving, creatively and with dispatch, in exciting new directions. Consider some of these jobs of the future, according to CST: system tangilizer, integrated roofing systems designer, gamification designer, makeshift structure engineer, or robot counsellor. (Go to CST's website,[8] listed in the endnotes, if you would like to find out what a "system tangilizer" or a "gamification designer" is.)

In fairness, the future of work is as unknowable today as it was for any earlier generation, so CST's guess is as good as yours. Who in the 1930s could have fully imagined the world of work in the 1950s and 1960s?

Similarly, the comfort and optimism of the 1960s was no foundation for the employment possibilities of the twenty-first century. Current career forecasts show an interesting mix of traditional and new jobs, a focus on the persistence of work in the personal-service fields, and some quirky possibilities in the world of high technology. They also suggest that a good deal of employment in the future will be based on a client-contractor, rather than employer-employee, model.

THE END OF THE AMERICAN DREAM

But there are real problems with this view of the future of work. First, it turns out in fact that someone in 1930 could have guessed pretty accurately what the world of work would have been like in 2015, because, amazingly, 90 percent of people in the North American workforce are doing jobs that existed over a hundred years ago.[9] How is that for an employment world in rapid transition? Second, it's elitist: the largest employment categories are not computer scientists and medical technologists, let alone neuroscientists or mining engineers. Rather, the largest employment categories are retail clerks, cashiers, office clerks, food preparation workers and servers, registered nurses, and customer service representatives. Overall, it's a pretty traditional and unglamorous workforce, with the majority of workers doing low-skill, low-salary nineteenth- and twentieth-century work for the most part. There will be great, interesting, and lucrative jobs for some people in the future, but not for everyone, and not for all college graduates, either. It doesn't matter how many graduates are produced by all of the world's universities and colleges. Most of the jobs, even in the twenty-first century economy, will be basic, often menial, and with only a small percentage requiring highly specialized skills.

Unless technology really takes off, and unless companies produce waiter-robots, completely self-cleaning homes, digitally controlled hairdressing systems, self-driving trucks (whoops, those *are* on the way), total-technology fast-food restaurants, mechanized garbage collection, and nursing robots, there will continue to be a lot of very basic, service-oriented work in national and global economies. And it's hard to imagine that those jobs will ever pay very well or return the cost of a college degree.

In the West, the combination of globalization and technological change has begun to seriously undercut one of the most valuable elements of post–World War II prosperity and social success. For more than fifty years, the economy produced well-paid, stable work for millions of people with moderate skills or expertise. These jobs—in auto plants, government offices, manufacturing operations, mines, forestry, processing plants, and the like—were often unionized, with excellent wages, benefits, and job security. Across North America, a stable and prosperous society emerged, based on middle-class opportunity and the stability of relatively low-skilled and reliable employment.

This was the magic of post–World War II America. Average people—high school graduates with reasonable work habits, but no particular entrepreneurial instincts or specialized skills—found that the economic order worked quite well for them and their families. The jobs were not necessarily personally fulfilling—few workers truly loved factory work for General Motors, the line in a Milwaukee sausage plant, or a regular shift in a Kraft food-processing operation. These were not the careers of the superstars and the exceptionally talented. But they provided decent opportunities for hundreds of thousands of people. Based on the nature of the late-twentieth-century North American economy, these industrial and white-collar workers could buy a house, provide for their families, and enjoy a comfortable life. This became the new normal—the realization of the American Dream, which offered a reasonable level of prosperity for millions of North Americans of average ability.

College graduates had it even better. The burgeoning middle class found a wealth of opportunities for those young people who completed their degrees. Nothing was assured, but on the whole most college graduates did well, entering middle management or the professions, or using their skills to launch one of the hundreds of thousands of new businesses and franchises that marked the expanding Western economy. For college graduates, this was the perfection of the American Dream, and the source of the belief that the Dream Factories had truly created personal opportunity and growth prospects.

Throughout the postwar years of economic expansion and prosperity, North America offered two major career paths for young people. Unskilled unionized work served a large portion of the workforce while college-educated graduates self-selected into largely white-collar employment and had a similarly great run through the 1960s and 1970s. Not everyone made it into one of these two paths. (The United States also had a third option—the military—that attracted thousands of young adults each year.) A considerable segment of labour was not unionized, notably coal mining, which persisted into this period. The unemployable struggled, as they always have done. The lesser-skilled young men and women found jobs in the growing low-end service sector, either using these positions as a launching pad into a life of work or hanging on to the lower rungs of the American career ladder.

But imagine if one changed the qualification from a college degree to a union card in the mid-1960s. The standard university data indicates that college degrees provide much more substantial earnings over the course of a career. Yet income data also show that unionized workers in key sectors, like the auto sector, also secured much higher wages over their adult lives than the North American average. In other words, getting the right union card, even in areas of relatively low skill, was just as much of a path to prosperity as a university degree. Politicians don't say this much—even Hillary Clinton, a friend of trade unions, has no grand plan to increase their membership—even though the causal relationship between membership and high earnings was once just as strong as it was for a college education.

Unfortunately the union advantage—a critical part of the creation of a largely unskilled middle class in North America—has mostly disappeared. The serious contraction of the steel and auto sector, along with global competition and technological change, has undermined the strength of the unions. Membership crashed in the private sector in the 1990s, and the long-standing wage advantage quickly evaporated. What had once been a near guarantee of middle-class prosperity—a unionized job in an auto plant, steel mill, or manufacturing plant—eroded quickly. Within twenty years, the private-sector union card went from a path to a comfortable life into something of an anachronism. By the beginning of 2014, private-sector union membership in the United States had fallen to less than 7 percent.

There was an exception to this pattern. Members of public-sector unions went in the opposite direction, earning higher-than-average incomes, greater job security, superior benefits—whether or not the job was an unskilled security officer at an airport, a clerk in a government agency, or a unionized functionary in a Washington office. Nearly 37 percent of the public sector is unionized. The public-sector union card, it seems, is an equally important means of securing middle-class opportunities and incomes for a group of workers whose actual work skills and responsibilities do not necessarily warrant above-average pay.

UNCERTAINTY FOR THE NORTH AMERICAN WORKFORCE

It is not clear how the average North American worker will flourish in the technology-enabled economy of the twenty-first century. Email has undermined postal work. E-commerce is replacing tens of thousands of retail workers. Computers can process applications and documentation faster and more accurately than humans. Robots replace factory and industrial plant operators. Advanced machinery can cut more trees, haul more coal, drill deeper wells, handle more parcels, and otherwise surpass the outcome, cost, and effectiveness of human-based processes. In the emerging economy, lower-paying jobs for the unskilled remain, but they are in hotels, restaurants, coffee shops, airports, car-rental operations, and the like. There are high-paying jobs—for a small number of workers—in the high-salary, high-energy, and technologically rich design, development, marketing, and related digital sectors. What is missing—what used to be the "guts" of the North American economy—is low-skilled, well-paid, and stable employment for people of average or even below-average ability and accomplishment.

The shift to a technology-enabled economy and the requirements for an up-skilled workforce has altered the fundamentals and created new challenges for young adults seeking to replicate the success of their parents and grandparents. The vast majority of the high-paying jobs and expansive career opportunities require advanced technological and scientific skills, high levels of motivation, curiosity, and inventiveness. Only a small portion of the student population is suited to positions of this type and is capable of meeting the educational and training needs of the advanced workforce. Furthermore, the college and university system is not well placed to respond to these twenty-first century realities. Finding a way forward for the average student and worker is one of the greatest challenges of the coming generation.

This is the cornerstone of the new American economy: excellent opportunities for those with the best and most relevant credentials, uncertain prospects for the generalists, and significant challenges for those without the basic skills needed in the high-tech era. Over the next twenty years current trends are likely to accelerate, with greater technological displacement of work, increased specialization, major shifts in the nature of employment, career preparation, and lifelong work. Many—but not all—of the best paid and most secure posts will go to college graduates, as they have in the past few decades. But if the best jobs do go to college grads, it doesn't follow that all college graduates are assured of excellent opportunities, particularly if the colleges and universities continue to flood the employment market with hundreds of thousands of non-specialist graduates who are not properly prepared for a workforce that is already dramatically different than that of their parents and grandparents.

The nature of the evolving economy shows both halves of the Dream Factory reality. For those who select the right fields of study and have the right mix of motivation, intelligence, work ethic, and entrepreneurship colleges will continue to produce "dream" results. The new high-technology economy will require thousands of highly skilled and well-trained individuals—and the best schools and the best programs will deliver superb results for their graduates. Some areas of study will struggle—will accounting continue to lead to career success for graduates in the face of mass digitization?—while others will produce remarkable results. Watch for digital design and design generally to maintain their current trajectory. Colleges attract the best and brightest within contemporary society, including some students who are brilliant and have remarkable analytical, writing, and research skills. These graduates, who enter brilliant and leave brilliant, will make fine employees or entrepreneurs, as they have always done. Each year, the colleges will find recent graduates who have had great results after leaving university. The message will be that Dream Factories work.

But they do not work for everyone. If advocates of college expansion have their day—Clintonesque visions of universal post-secondary education abound in the modern world—there will be many more weak students attending university. Weak students become weak graduates, and weak graduates make poor employees. Moreover, poorly prepared and underskilled high school graduates rarely succeed in the math- and science-rich, technologically sophisticated fields, the ones that have real and sustained employment possibilities. The overproduction of graduates in prominent fields, such as law and business, reduces the career prospects and income levels of the whole sector. That the wage premium for college graduates has largely disappeared is a classic illustration of the basic operation of supply and demand. But in the emerging tech-driven twenty-first-century economy, these graduates will be even further removed from the employment mainstream.

A post-graduation experience of unemployment and underemployment is not the career trajectory touted by the college recruiting offices and post-secondary advocates preaching about the benefits of university degrees. The life of the average American, counting on a college degree to put him or her on a higher-income path, has shifted dramatically. So, too, has technology ravaged the employment and income prospects for unskilled industrial workers. The reality is that the twentieth century is gone, the twenty-first century is here, and the pace of technological change in the workforce is accelerating. Those institutions and individuals that understand the transitions and seek education and training accordingly have the potential to flourish in the modern economy. They will make their parents and colleges proud and will find eager employers. But the current college and university model is far from ideally suited to the new tech-based economy.

There is a brass ring in America, and the number of billionaires continues to grow. But the trajectory is less dramatic and far more personal than the standard American narrative has it. Hard work, sacrifice, saving, and risk-taking are the skills needed for financial success.

5

UNPREPARED FOR WORK

Over the past twenty years or so the gulf between employers' expectations and those of young job hunters has widened dramatically. Not only do many Millennials not have the specific skills and abilities that they need in order to be hired, but psychologists tell us that often they have a set of attitudes and traits that put them at odds with prospective employers in terms of work ethic, salary increases, and promotion.

Here is a simple test, one that we have never seen applied systematically or professionally. We freely confess that this is anecdote masquerading as research—something no academic should do. But the results, as a conversation starter if nothing else, have been interesting. For the past few years, we have been asking college professors a simple question: reflecting on the graduating year or senior students you have taught in the past few years, how many would you hire if you were using your own money? We were not asking them about writing a reference or using up a research grant. We wanted to know how many they would select if they were dipping into their own pockets to cover the salary.

What started off as a casual discussion starter turned more serious as the comments arrived. One senior colleague, who taught advanced courses at one of the world's best business schools, was troubled by the question. He said he would report back. He called three days later and said, "At best, four or five." So, two courses a year, over five years (the time frame he set for himself), forty students per class. Four hundred students in total and, by his admittedly exacting standards, he could identify only a handful of students—one percent or so—that he would be willing to hire and pay himself. He was deeply troubled by this realization and by what it said about his program and the quality of the students. Interestingly, his primary criticisms of his students related to work effort and reliability, not to intellectual ability or formal learning outcomes. Conversations with other faculty members have produced similar, although not so dire, results, but no one we have spoken to was willing to hire more than one-quarter of their senior students. It is a sad, albeit unscientific fact that professionals who know these young adults the best are not impressed with what they have seen and who they have trained.

> ACCESS OR QUALITY—OUR UNIVERSITIES CAN'T HAVE BOTH
>
> The misalignment of higher education with the job market is now acute, [critics] argue. Universities are more focused on what professors want to teach than on what students need to know to land good jobs. We churn out far too many graduates in some areas (humanities, basic sciences) and far too few in others (applied science and technology).
>
> In academia, this is heresy. Academics insist that universities must not become job factories. Their mission is to guide students to cultivate the life of the mind. But there's a big disconnect between what academics want and what students want. For students, higher education is all about the job. Yet, they get virtually no counselling about what returns they can expect for their investment, or what their job prospects might be.[1]

UNREALISTIC AND UNPREPARED

Employers, it turns out, have similar feelings. By a wide margin, they are unhappy with the work ethic, abilities, and expectations of college and university graduates. Overall, they say that new hires have unrealistic expectations, want the jobs to adapt to fit their needs and interests, refuse to take the long view on employment and career development, and often fall far short in terms of basic skills. Companies are worried about the suitability of new workers and about their ability to remain competitive in the face of growing worker demands for higher pay, more generous working arrangements, and more employee-centric environments.

There's a good deal of evidence that senior college students, in North America at least, have unrealistic ideas of what their salaries will be in their first jobs. Perhaps most delusional are graduating MBAs, who apparently expect their first positions to pay a salary of around $140,000. The actual figure for those with four years or less of experience is $55,700, and $72,000 for those with five to nine years.[2]

These expectations are a creation more of popular culture than of workplace realities and reflect a generational infatuation with Google and Apple. But the workers recruited by the most prominent high-tech and cutting-edge firms are top-of-class graduates, with superb track records, top-notch abilities, and prodigious work ethics. Anyone who is not in this class need not apply—unless you are Owen Wilson and Vince Vaughan in *The Internship*, where they parlay street smarts and basic creativity into an internship with Google; another example of Hollywood fantasy straying a long way from reality. Nonetheless, the mythology has emerged that good employers offer free lunches, fooze-ball tables, some variation of Google's open time to work on world-saving initiatives, and the option of coming to work in baggy shorts and a T-shirt.

The attitudes of Millennials came into sharp focus about five years ago, during a private working session involving post-secondary institutions and some leading technology firms. The company hired a social scientist to study student attitudes toward work, corporate loyalty, and life expectations. The results—drawing on more than twenty-five thousand completed surveys—were striking: high expectations for starting salaries ($53,000 a year to start), rapid promotion (within eighteen months), respect for work-life balance, insistence on a respectful and supportive workplace, and limited overtime work, with time off in compensation. When asked about the first question they would ask a prospective employer, the number one answer was "When am I eligible for a vacation?"

The analyst then offered a thoughtful commentary on how companies had to adjust to fit with the new realities and how hiring and retaining young people required an adaptation to the social realities and career expectations of young people. A corporate vice-president interjected, with a simple message: "We cannot compete globally if our newest workers have these expectations." When the analyst started defending the rigour of the analysis and the reliability of the conclusion, the VP jumped in again.

"You don't understand," he retorted. "You have just given my company the best evidence yet about why we should relocate more of our white-collar work outside of the country."

Colleges are contributing to the cult of high expectations and self-esteem, bending over backwards to support students and ease their transition through their studies. Institutional commitments to "retention" give the impression that colleges are shifting responsibility from the individual—"perform or leave"—to the faculty and staff. At the same time, though they do not mean to do so, colleges are taking measures that lessen the relevance of a university degree as something that can toughen students, allowing them to demonstrate that they can handle the pressure and stress of difficult, time-sensitive, and demanding work; in other words, what employers expect of them in the workplace.

Within the volatile mix, prestige and excellence matter, likely much more than they should. As Alison Wolf, author of *Does Education Matter?*, wrote before rapid economic changes put even a stronger priority on elite students and institutions:

> [E]mployers are perfectly aware that not all the brightest, most capable young people went to the top universities, or vice versa. But they do feel that the probability of finding "the best" is higher if they hire graduates of selective institutions with a global brand. For all the occasional rhetoric of politicians, no one in the post-war West has been sacked for habitually hiring graduates of Tokyo or Cambridge, or picking MBAs from INSED, London Business School or Harvard. On the contrary, what boards of large companies habitually request from their human-resources department are profiles of the universities that recruits attended—and what they want are plenty of recruits from the top.[3]

This, in turn, produces more pressure to attend elite schools and ramps up the competitive advantage of the top universities in the world. It also puts a significant cap on the career experiences of young adults from lesser-known colleges.

Universities have in fact made many changes, some long overdue, to accommodate students and make their lives easier. Some, like recognizing the special challenges associated with learning disabilities and the real difficulties of coping with stress, are obviously good ideas. Less so are pet centres for students during exam period (places where they can stroke puppies and kittens), easing off on firm deadlines, reducing reading lists and writing assignments, lowering standards, removing mandatory attendance in many courses and programs, and many other developments designed to ensure academic "success," by which most institutions mean getting a degree.

The result of changing standards has been many students who skip classes, few who do extra reading outside of class assignments (or even for class assignments), and many who show a limited commitment to their studies. This, in turn, has produced growing evidence that students are gaining few demonstrable skills through their undergraduate studies, such evidence in itself being one of the greatest indictments of the modern college system. The evidence—though colleges would strongly disagree— is that the actual development of skills has fallen dramatically because college campuses have been swamped, often with mediocre students; the demands on instructors' time are pressing; and the cult of recognition and reward—the celebration of various kinds of minor student achievements—is beginning to infiltrate the university system. This, ironically, may seem hard to reconcile with the remarkably high failure rate across the American college system, which shows that many do, indeed, fail, especially at junior and for-profit colleges. This distressing phenomenon should be the focal point for urgent government action. Similar situations have attracted the attention of the British and Australian governments, but the US government has focused its efforts on encouraging retention as opposed to improving high-quality outcomes.

Much the same applies to the intellectual life of the academy. In the idealized (and to some extent imaginary) world of the past, colleges were places of great intellectual ferment and productive debate. Indeed, many of the great intellectual innovations of the modern age—women's rights, the recognition of the special challenges of minorities, the plight of the poor in North America and globally, gay and lesbian rights, and the environmental movement—have had strong connections to the university system and found many recruits on the nation's campuses. In recent years, universities have become more timid, but they are not, as many critics like to suggest, shamelessly politically correct, afraid to deviate from the left-wing, pro-feminist, urgently environmental agenda. This stereotype is simply inaccurate; campuses tilt toward the left, or their administrations do, but business schools and science faculties are no left-wing breeding grounds. And there is greater diversity in the arts disciplines than one would think from the public debate.

But with these caveats, there are emerging signs of intellectual caution, of trying to ensure that students do not stray into difficult territory. A legitimate concern about the incidence of rape (much lower than the media coverage would suggest) on university campuses has produced sexual conduct codes, and the emergence of relationship permission forms. A growing number of course syllabi come with "trigger warnings" to alert students to potentially offensive or troubling material within the readings and lectures. In journalism, the think-tanks of all political persuasions and the blogosphere have replaced the academy as the focal point for many of the most original ideas and much of the critical commentary about contemporary North American and global society. While there are great and even provocative thinkers on college campuses, they are outnumbered by a much larger number of people who conform to the new consensus of soft-liberal political controversy.

GETTING THE CREDENTIAL, NOT THE LEARNING

Throughout all of this, securing the credential—rather than the learning historically attached to the degree—has assumed top priority on campus. The result has been the graduation of many degree holders with unimpressive abilities. Many studies demonstrate that a shocking number of college graduates have weak writing skills, analytical abilities, command of content, and few of the attributes that people have traditionally associated with college studies. That many international students graduate with inadequate English-language skills has become something of a scandal in Australia and should be so in the United States and Canada as well.

THE CONSEQUENCES OF ACADEMIC ENTITLEMENT

Academically entitled students are those who, for example, might believe it's acceptable if they leave class early, that exams should be rescheduled if they conflict with
their personal plans, or believe they should get marks simply if they demonstrate that
they're trying hard, according to Katrina van Wieirngen, one of the group of students
who analyzed the data ...

   Students with higher levels of academic entitlement reported earning lower grade
point averages

   Students with lower academic entitlement attitudes were less likely to engage in
academically dishonest behaviours like cheating on a test or plagiarizing on an essay
compared to those who scored higher

   Students with consumerist attitudes who believe they deserve good grades because
they "bought" their education also tend to have lower GPAs and higher levels of academic entitlement.

   Higher levels of academic entitlement were a strong predictor of higher levels of
workplace entitlement, or unrealistic expectations about salaries and workplace conditions, rapid promotions and regular bonuses.[4]

Not so long ago, the equation *Learning = Earning* defined the college
system. The current approach—*Learning = Expectations and the Possibility
of Earning*—is dramatically different and far less compelling. But it makes
sense. Mediocre university graduates are unlikely to make stellar employees although, ironically, there are excellent examples of college dropouts
who do well career-wise. Bill Gates, Steve Jobs, Harrison Ford, Mark
Zuckerberg, and the other members of the elite college dropout list are
the exceptions that prove the rule. But this list is overwhelmed by a massively larger group of people who probably should never have gone to
university in the first place. The sad reality is that employers are right to be
skeptical of the current generation of college graduates and are right to be
cautious in using the college degree as an assurance of real and sustained
accomplishment, proven work ethic, critical skills, and discipline knowledge. It is a tragedy that the generic value of the degree has been devalued
so dramatically, for there are many degree holders who have enormous
potential and have demonstrated real and sustained accomplishment.

   Most students are blissfully unaware of their collective shortcomings, and mediocre effort and commitment have not stopped graduates
from believing that they deserve great rewards. A recent American study

made it clear that most students want, and expect, a good benefit package, opportunities for personal growth (this is the era of self-actualization), friendly co-workers, and job security. A high starting salary, interestingly, was tenth on the list. More students than ever were interested in working for a company committed to ethnic diversity, wanted to work close to home (those apron strings—and the appeal of free room and board with Mom and Dad—are very strong), and preferred a casual work environment. The report highlighted the general inflexibility of young workers and the growing expectation that work should conform to them rather than the other way around.[5]

There are many explanations for these supposed shortcomings. Colleges and universities are doing a lousy job, it is said, and the faculty members' retort that they are not intended to be job-trainers falls on unsympathetic ears. It is the elementary and secondary school teachers' fault, parents declare, for the decline in standards, along with educational experimentation. Educators have overpraised and pandered to their students, thus eroding the quality of learning. Society is to blame, say others, for permissiveness, promiscuity, the Kardashians, social media, and rampant consumerism. High school teachers privately blame problems on parents who don't back up the schools' efforts and who are relentless in their defence of their precious and ill-mannered children. How else do you account for one author, Mark Bauerlein, describing today's youth as "*The Dumbest Generation*," and see many nod their heads in agreement? More seasoned analysts underscore the changing nature of the continental economy, which has eliminated many early-life employment opportunities for young people.

More problematic is the overriding commitment to self-esteem, to a nation-wide effort to build confidence, to reward the mere existence of life, and to convince young people that they are talented and capable of "being whatever they want to be." This is a wonderful sentiment, and music to the ears of many parents. The cult of self-esteem, now thoroughly built into the elementary and high school system and adopted unconsciously by many millions of parents, emphasizes several key elements: praise over criticism; recognition for the smallest achievements; acceptance of each person's unique characteristics; avoidance of pressure, criticism, or assertive behaviour by adults; pedagogy that recognizes achievement rather than routine or taxing work; constant celebration; and the removal of negative influence. For parents, this means the avoidance of corporal punishment or time out for bad behaviour, family praise, and child-centric approaches to family responsibilities. These concepts have been widely accepted by teachers and school systems, except in high-performance private schools where the older system has been retained. And, most notably, the cult of self-esteem has been rejected almost uniformly by those responsible for producing true high-performers, including sports coaches, dance instructors, and music teachers. Authoritarian, demanding, aggressive guidance lives on, but only at the periphery of the North American child-rearing environment.

Turn the equation around and focus on the challenges facing the most disadvantaged young people: impoverished African Americans, newly arrived immigrants, and children raised in conditions of extreme poverty. Robert Putnam, in *Our Kids*, produced a searing indictment of North America's inability to protect the present and future of poor children. He makes it clear, as others have also suggested, that the vast majority of these young people have, from birth, little prospect of receiving a good education, being properly prepared for adulthood, or finding a rewarding career. Putnam has made addressing this issue the highest priority in his distinguished career as a sociologist, but his study emphasizes that too many of these young people are doomed by the oppressive weight of poverty, neighbourhood despair, and racism.

Amy Chua, who loves to provoke debate with her sharply written commentaries on youth and family (*Tiger Mum* was a humdinger in this regard), also does not buy into the self-esteem idea. In *The Triple Package*, she and co-author Jed Rubenfeld identified groups that are enjoying singular success within America. The groups are diverse: Mormons, Cuban exiles, Nigerian immigrants, Iranian and Lebanese Americans, Asian Americans, and Jews. In turn, these groups demonstrate what Chua views as the three major reasons for success: a superiority complex, fundamental insecurity, and impulse control. These traits might also be described as a belief in personal and collective destiny, a realization that the odds are stacked against them, and the ability to postpone gratification in the short term in anticipation of having it in the longer term. The foundations of personal success, according to Chua, rest on resilience, self-reliance, collective action, and personal responsibility. She certainly did not emphasize efforts by parents and teachers to tell young people that they were good, if not excellent, at everything that they did.

Paul Tough also does not accept the mantra of self-esteem. In *How Children Succeed*, a Malcolm Gladwell-esque exploration of the preconditions for personal success, Tough doesn't focus on formal education and standard performance indicators as measures of personal potential. Instead, he identifies three key characteristics that he argues are crucial for long-term personal success. He highlights the surprising importance of curiosity and an innate interest in the oddities, structures, and processes of the human and natural condition. Tough talks a great deal about "grit," or the ability to work hard, persist, and see projects through to completion. His third personality trait is "character" itself, a combination of reliability, integrity, trustworthiness, and honesty. What stands out about Tough's list is that these are not standard elements in elementary and high school curricula, but they speak to the fundamental importance of parenting and family circumstance. Importantly, they have an inverse relationship with the mantra of self-esteem. For Tough, personal qualities are what matter in terms of career and life success, traits that speak to people's ability to work through adversity, maintain a deep and abiding interest in the world, and demonstrate both resilience and integrity in everything that they do.

While curious people are generally both more interested and interesting, there is a direct connection as well between curiosity and success in the twenty-first-century economy. As he argues:

> Curious learners go deep, and they go wide. They are the people best-equipped for the kind of knowledge-rich, cognitively challenging work required in industries like finance or software engineering. They are also the ones most likely to make creative connections between different fields, of the kind that leads to new ideas, and the ones best suited to working in multi-disciplinary teams. Consequently, they are the ones whose jobs are least likely to be taken by intelligent machines; in a world where technology is rapidly replacing humans even in

white collar jobs, it is no longer enough to be merely smart. Computers are smart. But no computer, however sophisticated, can yet be said to be curious.[6]

For Chua, Putnam, and Tough—and there are many others trying to figure out how to anticipate and identify individuals of real promise and ability—the standard approach of emphasizing educational outcomes and lavishing undeserved praise on young people is not the key to personal success. Chua argues that certain cultural groups have, through adversity, self-control, and an inbred sense of cultural superiority or destiny, the drive and ambition necessary to succeed. Putnam, less optimistically, uses extensive statistical analysis to show what always makes us uncomfortable: that the realities of birth, upbringing, and socio-economic circumstances put barriers in front of individual prospects. Tough leaves more room for personal characteristics, the drive, interest, and integrity that help explain individuals who move beyond their social and economic class and who succeed because they have the qualities needed to prosper and advance. What all three agree about is that telling young people that they are exceptional and destined to succeed is the wrong way to prepare them for success.

Similarly, scientific studies of self-esteem show that it is not well-correlated with academic or career success. Put simply, children raised with an inflated sense of their abilities and competencies are ill prepared for the realities of life—where the workforce and adult life have much harsher standards and expectations than in the world of the self-esteem gurus.

DIGITAL NATIVES OR ANALYTICAL NOVICES?

That young people are increasingly becoming what Don Tapscott calls "digital natives" further complicates the situation. The people now entering college and university have spent their entire lives under the spell of the Internet and related social media. They have, on the average smartphone, instant access to billions of page-equivalents of information, much larger and more multilingual and comprehensive than any of the world's great university libraries. They operate in Google and

Wikipedia space, where an answer to almost any imaginable question can be found within seconds. The ideal of filling one's head with information through advanced study seems, to someone reared in the digital age, absurd and unnecessary. This has led Tapscott and others to reject the notion that this is the "dumbest generation" and to argue that these young people are tech-savvy, digitally sophisticated, and able to navigate the world of mass information with speed and ease.

The "digital natives" idea is attractive, even compelling. Google, after all, does make mass information readily available. But the emerging idea that there is no reason for students at Texas Tech to learn that the North won the Civil War, or that the roots of anti-Semitism in Germany predated the rise of Nazism by centuries, or that there are various streams of Islam, often at odds with each other, or that economic recessions have attracted a wide variety of responses from national governments over the decades, and so on, completely warps the nature of intelligence, knowledge, and analysis. To argue that having access to digital information is the same as having useful knowledge would be like suggesting thirty years ago that anyone who owned a set of the *Encyclopedia Britannica* should be granted a PhD automatically because they had the core details of the human and natural world at their fingertips.

Access to information bears only a tangential relationship to the ability to analyze, interpret, use, critique, and evaluate it. Young adults, born digital as Tapscott says, have precious little understanding of the world at large. The majority are disengaged from politics, spend much more time on Facebook and Snapchat than reading the *New York Times* online or *The Economist,* and use the Internet for social rather than

HACKING YOUR EDUCATION

Going to college is like joining a gym. It's effective only if you put in the work. If you join a gym and never work out, you'll stay weak. If you pay for college but never deeply engage, you'll stay ignorant. You should go to college only if you have the self-control to actually learn, just as you should only join a gym if you have the self-control to actually work out. People ask me all the time: who should and shouldn't go to college? There is only one definitive answer of who shouldn't go to college: those who don't want to go to college. The converse of that statement is also true. You should go to college only if you want to go to college and know exactly why you are going to college.[7]

learning purposes. All surveys show that young adults are largely disengaged from the realities of contemporary world affairs, have less interest than ever in national or international politics, and only a superficial understanding of major contemporary issues. Add to this the growing evidence that they do not read much in the traditional media—newspapers, magazines, and books—and we have a generation, with the greatest access to information in world history, that is curiously disengaged from the world around them.

Again, we add our standard caveat. There is a subset of this generation, smaller than we would like to admit, that is truly digitally enabled, that uses YouTube libraries, e-magazines, blogs, and other new media to be more connected to the world than any group of young adults in human history. They were the ones who followed the Occupy movement, the remarkable events of the Arab Spring, Canada's Idle No More Indigenous demonstrations, and the Syrian refugee crisis. They are also the ones with the best understanding of societal trends, emerging commercial opportunities, the realities of the global marketplace and workplace, and the diversity of the human condition. These young people are at the vanguard of the climate change debate and are aware of the long-term consequences of contemporary choices.

To be around these young adults is to be amazed and impressed with their global awareness, their engagement, and their commitment to active participation. Digital technologies shape lives and empower those who choose to capitalize on the information explosion in ways that would have been previously unimaginable. But there aren't enough of these young people. Perhaps 5 percent or 10 percent of youth understand the power of the Internet and appreciate the opportunity and responsibility to engage with the broader world.

The members of this group are the exceptions, the ones with a strong likelihood of life and career success. The prevailing view is that they are not as financially driven as their "greed is good" predecessors. Let's hope this is true. But the idea that the current generation, whose teenage years have been shaped by the optimism and intervention of President Obama, is motivated to fight climate change, battle inequality, promote diversity, and so on, does not hold up well. Among the truly gifted, such as the graduates from the world's elite Ivy League colleges, economics is the most popular major and working for leading financial firms is the top career objective. So much for optimism and social change. While self-actualization and world service may be how the current generation wishes to be seen, the reality is that the top graduates are still focused on income and career opportunities.

AN UNPREDICTABLE PATH FORWARD

It is too early to determine the accuracy of these descriptions of North American youth. They may surprise us. That certainly happened with Baby Boomers, the graduates from the era of sex, drugs, and rock and roll, dismissed by the adults of their day as shameful hedonists. The young adults of the 1960s turned into the middle-class professionals of the 1980s and 1990s, the excesses of their generation forgotten during the boom times of the late twentieth century. Of course, they were lucky to be around during a period of expanding economies, a shortage of trained managers, rapid population growth, and the opportunities created by rapid globalization and technological change. It was these things, rather than the career preparation opportunities presented by anti–Vietnam War protests, sexual and pharmaceutical experimentation, and anti-establishment moralizing that accounted for their success as adults. What did stand out—and this reality shapes and defines the contemporary debate about preparing young people for their careers—is that the rapid growth of the Western economy created excellent opportunities for those with an advanced education, a group comparatively small in number and eager to capitalize on the material prospects of the last quarter of the twentieth century.

For the current generation seeking to make their way in a rapidly changing and unpredictable world, the path forward is determined by an unknowable mix of personal qualities and economic realities. To use Paul Tough's scenario, individuals can have grit, curiosity, and stellar character, they can be a member of one of Chua's exemplary groups, and they can have all of the socio-economic benefits of being raised in a favoured family and neighbourhood, yet they can still find themselves unemployed or underemployed if no good jobs are on offer. This is what we see happening at present. While the smartest and best-positioned young people will continue to do well—a 15 percent unemployment rate still means an 85 percent employment rate—the nature of the contemporary economy is curtailing opportunities for many Millennials.

We see this even when it comes to first jobs. For generations, preteens and teenagers eased into the world of work. Neighbours hired kids to baby-sit, cut their lawns, or paint their fences. Tens of thousands of kids had paper routes. Before the advent of online and preauthorized billings, young paper boys and girls canvassed for subscriptions, delivered papers, collected payments, maintained books, and bore financial responsibility for any unpaid accounts. For teenagers, and those even younger, a newspaper route was an impressive and often intensive introduction to the world of work, business, and entrepreneurship. This kind of early-life work experience introduced young people to the world of savings, personally paid purchases, deadbeat clients, and a modicum of financial independence from parents.

This world of low-paid work is changing as well. A growing number of adults are moving in on what was once youth work, particularly in the fast-food and service sectors. Recent immigrants are finding it more difficult to find better-paid employment, and so they are settling for entry-level jobs. With the uncertainty of pensions and old age security, and with longer life expectancies changing long-term planning for retirement, thousands of older people have also been pushed back into the workforce, and many of them are willing to take part-time jobs as retail clerks or servers, jobs that once went to the young.

More cheerful news is the fact that a substantial group of young people do not fit into the pattern of entitled youth. This is particularly the case with Millennials from lower-income families, and particularly, recent immigrants, who are foremost in the effort to climb at least a rung or two on the financial ladder. The North American economy has thousands of family-owned businesses, staffed by young family members who work hard through their high school and college years. These people, who often struggle with their families' high scholastic expectations as well, learn the relationship between work and income, effort, and independence early. Far from being the spoiled children of privilege that dominate popular culture—the lately famous Paris Hilton comes to mind—these Millennials are the embodiment of the Western industrial spirit: hard-working, ambitious, and determined. There is an important message here. Employers looking to find solid and promising entry-level employees, knowing that there are many aspirants for decent positions, will typically be able to identify individuals with a solid work ethic and experience. These people, of course, make the others—the spoiled and unchallenged—look much weaker and less attractive by way of comparison.

Many young adults do not do a great deal to help their case, throughout their college years. Students, regardless of academic specialization, can help themselves by finding career-relevant work, by volunteering in constructive and resumé-building ways, and by connecting their university studies to future or desired work. They can seek out work experience or internship programs, get involved in student government, or otherwise find ways to build and demonstrate their employability.

Some youth do this, intentionally working toward a career and looking for ways to make themselves attractive to prospective employees. Some institutions, of course, make the alternation of work and study terms a key element of their undergraduate training. But North American colleges generally emphasize coursework and pay insufficient attention to preparation for the world of work. Equally, institutions and faculty members generally pay little attention to the needs of employers and industry—few see skills training as their role—with the result that many students are generally ill-prepared for the transition to employment.

There is a mistaken belief that the selection of the right major and a strong performance in the classroom translate into good career prospects. They don't. Few employers (only about 15 percent) pay attention to student grades as a means of selecting new employees. Even the choice of institution is significantly less important than graduating students and their parents believe. The graduates of the truly elite schools, which use exceptionally refined selection procedures to identify gifted applicants, have a strong chance of an excellent career, but, significantly, not appreciably better than if the same students had gone to a less prestigious school. It is the quality and character of the young adult, it appears, and not the degree or institution that sets them on a track to real success. It must be tough for families that paid a quarter of a million dollars to get their children through an Ivy League School to discover that their sons and daughters likely would have had a similar career outcome if they had attended the local state university.

That so many North American children avoid math and science contributes to the problem of employability. There are reasons why so many of the tech rock stars are immigrants or the children of immigrants. Other cultures, particularly in East and South Asia and also in Eastern Europe, value the rigour and challenge of math and science more than Canadian and American students and families. These subjects are hard, even with a calculator at hand, and they are ones that a distressing number of young people are permitted to avoid. As a consequence, many of the high-end careers, in the technology fields, finance, accounting, medicine, and engineering, are closed off at the end of high school, before the young even reach college.

For much of the twentieth century, North America retained a large and seemingly insurmountable educational advantage, even as the characteristics of its young adults became more evident. Youth in other countries lacked the advanced training that was increasingly standard in the USA and Canada as well as the English-language skills to work easily in the dominant economic system on the planet. Their high schools and universities were ill-equipped to prepare them for the realities of the increasingly technology-driven world. Complacency became the norm and, in an extraordinary burst of global citizenship, the USA took the lead in exporting its college/university model internationally and bringing the best and the brightest (and the wealthiest) from around the world to study at American institutions.

By the twenty-first century, however, nations the world over had caught up and even surpassed North America. They could not touch the elite universities—the top fifty in the world, fifteen of which were in the United States, three in Britain and one each in Canada and Switzerland.[8] But they certainly became competitive with the lower-tiered institutions. Within a generation, North American youth went from having sporadic competition at the elite level—from the UK, Germany, Sweden, and Japan—to facing resurgent institutions and millions of competitive graduates from countries as diverse as Saudi Arabia and Taiwan, China and India, Turkey and Finland. Preparedness for work, innovation, and twenty-first-century competitiveness is, in the end, a comparative issue. While we would argue that the bottom two-thirds of college and university graduates have fallen substantially in quality against their 1960s and

1970s counterparts, the reality is that there are more smart ones than ever, because the pool of global graduates has grown dramatically, surpassing their predecessors in quality and, in many institutions, exceeding the quality and workforce preparedness of the average American college graduate at a non-elite institution.

Employers voice their disapproval of this cohort's attitudes to work, pay, responsibility, and career development. The misalignment of program choices with the needs of the workforce means that there are a large number of job vacancies and an ever-greater number of degree-holding university graduates without a regular career. North America does not pay much attention to global comparisons and has failed to notice the marked improvement of educational outcomes and career preparation in countries around the world. Being competitive in the modern age requires preparedness for the global, high-intensity, and fast-changing realities of the high-technology world. It does not require student-centred, solicitous college programming and young adults who shy away from difficult subjects, demonstrate a mediocre work ethic, and carry high salary and career expectations with them into the interview room.

6

ADJUSTING TO REALITY

Today the world of work, employment, and career-building is changing, with the shifts coming faster and in more complex ways than most people would have guessed a generation ago. While young people fear for their futures, there is tremendous uncertainty, individually and collectively, about the best way to approach the future. Colleges and universities are more than ever at the centre of the search for a path that leads to opportunities, job security, and the prospect of a reasonable income. But the existing model—of traditional, four-year undergraduate degrees in traditional subjects—is a risky gamble based on twentieth-century assumptions. The world is changing, more rapidly than most people believe. It remains to be seen how much and how quickly colleges and universities will be able and willing to adapt as well.

Universities are conservative by nature, and their commitment to core principles and traditional approaches remains an institutional strength. Nevertheless, they have slowly been transforming themselves. The rise of "studies" programs, shifting away from the standard disciplines and focusing on new theoretical approaches, emerged out of purely intellectual and political processes that had nothing to do with the job market. Academically innovative, these new degree programs—gender studies, ethnic studies, queer studies, and the like—make no pretense of being tied to employment outcomes, save for generalized bromides about the value of a liberal-arts education. These new programs are largely attracting students already within the Humanities and Social Sciences, though these fields of study have been declining as a percentage of the overall student population as young people vote with their feet and turn to programs designed to make them career-ready.

It is evident, not least to those in charge of colleges and universities, that these institutions must change—and the sooner the better. But, like giant ocean-going tankers, they are anything but nimble, and do not do well when they have to change direction quickly. The major question—of fundamental importance to young people and to the institutions—is whether or not colleges and universities will hold on to their primary role in youth preparation and whether or not high school graduates will find an alternative to the Dream Factories. Remember that the last twenty-five years have been hard on many traditional institutions: everything from video, book, and record stores to the post office have had to transform themselves or else close down. The rise of Massive Open Online Courses, Totally Open Online Courses, for-profit colleges, international educational competition, and, perhaps the greatest threat to the status quo—work-based education and training—have brought the transformative technologies of the twenty-first century to bear on post-secondary education.

Rapid and dramatic change is never easy, and it often claims some victims. Think of this from the perspective of institutional flexibility and responsiveness: North America has a massive investment in what is an increasingly outdated model of post-secondary education. Consider the investment in physical plant alone. A medium-sized non-elite university, say a state college with twenty thousand students, has a billion dollars invested in buildings, which are, from an efficiency perspective, massively underutilized, but that's another issue. Harvard has twenty-six million square feet of space, more than five times the size of the Mall of the Americas in Minneapolis, the USA's largest shopping centre (4.87 million square feet), or Canada's West Edmonton Mall, the largest in North America (5.3 million square feet). Add to that hundreds of faculty members, several times as many staff members, often several generations of entrenched ways of doing things, a central role in the regional economy, and you have an institution that is difficult to budge at all, let alone move dramatically. The nature of university tenure-stream contracts, which make it difficult for institutions to dismiss faculty members, is a severe restriction on college flexibility. The problem has been addressed by shifting hiring practices from full-time appointments to contingent con-tracts, the so-called "adjuncts." These short-term, non-tenured arrange-ments, which now cover more than half of all the instructors in the American college system, give greater institutional flexibility, but at severe cost to the incomes and career stability of PhD-qualified faculty members.

STUDENT DEMANDS, INSTITUTIONAL INERTIA

There is simply no way that these institutions can back away from their massive investment in post-secondary infrastructure. It is extremely dif-ficult for colleges and universities to drop existing programs and repos-ition faculty from social justice, peace studies, human sexuality, and puppeteering to digital animation, neuropsychology, and nanotechnol-ogy. And, to speak a truth that some shy away from, many of those who currently populate arts courses lack the background and ability needed for success in the math- and science-based programs that are among the best-connected to employment possibilities.

Colleges are conservative by nature, preserving and representing values and practices that have endured, in one form or another, for cen-turies. But when universities evoke the "traditional role" of the institu-tion, typically citing the brilliant work of Cardinal Henry Newman, the nineteenth-century Anglican turned Catholic whose thoughts on the meaning of the academy have been long admired by proponents of college learning, they are summoning the spirit of a long-abandoned institutional model. Comparing the university system of the twenty-first century to the college life admired by Newman is akin to justifying and celebrating the achievements of Walmart by calling on the tradition of the small-town storekeeper who kept his pickles and crackers in barrels and maintained his records on a piece of slate. There are similarities—both are retailers, serving customers, just as Newman's college and the modern ones edu-cate students and produce scholarship—but the scale, manner, assump-tions, class composition, role of faculty, and many other characteristics are wildly disparate. If colleges and universities are to flourish, they must respond to the challenges of the present and not rest on the laurels of this past, much as it pains the traditionalist in us to say so.

It is here, in institutional responsiveness to the realities of the twenty-first century, that universities and colleges have stumbled most badly. The best colleges and universities deliver what they want to deliver in the form of research and teaching. (The worst ones generally do poorly on both accounts.) But it is an altogether different matter to produce what students and society say they want—jobs and careers. In this context—responsiveness to contemporary expectations and requirements—even the best are less than successful. Remember, as you contemplate the defensive public relations pronouncements of the academy, citing average graduate incomes and rates of employment, that they conveniently leave out the life experiences of students who entrusted their futures to these institutions and then failed to complete their studies. Given that there are more young American adults in the dropout group than the graduation cohort—a stunning indictment of the American system—the omission is egregious.

So what is the solution? Perhaps it helps to begin by speaking a plain truth: people who are hard-working, conscientious, and intelligent are generally likely to do well regardless of their field of study, or, in fact, whether they choose to go to college or not. The corollary, alas, is also true: people who are unfocused, undependable, and of below-average intelligence will face difficulties, and enrolling in college will not change this, regardless of what politicians may say. College is an answer, but it is not everyone's answer.

What university is prepared to say the following: "Those of you in specialized, professional fields will likely find good work, while those of you who drop out or who fail to gain specific technical skills may well discover you have wasted your time and money here"? What politician, apart from Democratic presidential candidate Bernie Sanders, will speak this harsh truth: "Young adults from wealthy families, who are the beneficiaries of better education, parental role modeling, and family support will on the whole substantially outperform equally smart and ambitious minority or poor students in the workforce"? Which analyst, risking credibility with bold forecasts, will say, "The coming technological transformation will undercut the career relevance and viability of many post-secondary education programs, while eliminating many of the jobs to which young people currently aspire"? Or, "While demographic and economic realities will ensure that most university graduates find work of some kind, the reality is that the number finding a comfortable and secure future in relatively short order is declining rapidly"? Or, more sobering still, "The real challenge is not finding employment for the talented and motivated, but rather creating jobs that pay a living wage for young adults of average or below-average intellectual ability and mediocre work ethic"? What *Bloomberg* magazine calls "routine" jobs have declined by more than 10 percent since 1982, while "non-routine" jobs have increased by about the same amount.[1]

At this point, it's fair to comment that we've pointed a good many fingers of blame, without offering much by way of constructive suggestions. The situation, though grim in general, certainly is not without hope for individuals. Thus, as a response to the realities of twenty-first century education and work, we offer the following ideas. First, parental and youth expectations need to be reined in—not everyone is going to be a rich professional. Second, the fixation on colleges and universities as the focus for youth aspirations must be drastically reduced. Third, these institutions must be reformed to make them more responsive to public needs. And fourth, the debate about the future of youth must be reoriented away from colleges and universities toward a more realistic view of twenty-first-century job creation.

CONSTRUCTIVE IDEAS FOR THE FUTURE

As nations worldwide try to refocus their educational and training systems, the hardest part will be convincing parents to reorient their priorities. The cult of university is staggeringly powerful in the United States, and getting more so, and it is being exported around the world. This is particularly true for new Americans—and especially recent immigrants from Asia—who place an extraordinary priority on university education.

It doesn't help that prominent politicians—from President Barack Obama's constant cheerleading for universities to Democratic presidential candidate Hillary Clinton's ambitious plan for college support—only reinforce the false idea that there is only one real way to get ahead in life. As a first priority, let's face the reality of twenty-first-century education, career preparation, and work. Parents need to focus less on their children's self-actualization and the dangerous ideology that all young people can be whatever they want to be. In this environment, it is crucial that parents be honest about their children's abilities, aptitudes, and motivation. Few parents can will their children to be successful in academic studies. Young adults have to make their own way, and no helicopter parents can really replace the need to stand alone, both academically and in career terms.

We will know that something has changed when the bookshelves full of publications that rate, promote, evaluate, list, describe, and analyze colleges and universities and that fuel the seemingly insatiable demand for guides to university begin to empty out. An entire industry has evolved around the *Earning = Learning* formula—shorter than Einstein's and a lot easier to understand, but, alas, not nearly as sound.

As a second priority, let's work to persuade the public to stop fetishizing colleges and universities and take a more realistic approach to post-secondary education. There are other opportunities for high school graduates that get far too little attention. Many new high school graduates should not go to college immediately. They should consider getting a job, if only to prove to themselves that they really do need an advanced education. Or they should spend a year volunteering, nationally or internationally, to assist others. In New Zealand and Australia, a year abroad is a rite of passage for thousands of young people, providing an opportunity to experience the world and "find themselves." In other words, there is no great rush to head off to college or university. This is the "gap year," and more young people should consider it.

There are other educational opportunities open to high school graduates. Community colleges, which offer a combination of adult upgrading, short courses, job training, and technological instruction, are sadly underrated as career-launching pads. These colleges are usually well connected to the regional economy and often have tight relationships with major local employers. Many colleges offer high-end, high-technology programs that are academically rigorous and professionally challenging. This is equally true for technical institutions, which have become increasingly important with the emergence of a science-based economy. The technical institutes are underdeveloped in the United States, but are better established in Canada, which has a number of high-quality polytechnics. High school counsellors need to do a much better job of promoting community colleges and technical institutes as an educational alternative, equal in value and impact when matched with the abilities and employment aspirations of young people.

A rebalancing of the post-secondary system is a third priority. The best universities must stay—and their role could be expanded and improved—but other institutions should probably close. Admission should be restricted to those who have demonstrated the ability to succeed and who have the appropriate level of motivation, intelligence, work ethic, and curiosity. Using colleges as a holding ground for the unmotivated and the incurious is a massive waste of students' time and money—not to mention the money of their parents and the governments.

There is no precise target here, either in the total number of students and the number of institutions, but colleges that fail to graduate more than three-quarters of their first-year students should be considered for closure. If closure for those places were a requirement, though, in four years the American college system would almost disappear. According to *U.S. News & World Report*, only 107 US colleges graduated three-quarters or more of their 2008 starting undergraduates in the traditional four years[2] (though many more, presumably, graduated in five, six, or more years, and some students transferred from one college to another). That is a breathtaking statistic.

Approaching the problem differently, students who fail to secure high school grades of 85 percent or more would not be permitted to go directly to college or university and would have to prepare for advanced study through attendance at community college or another upgrading facility for one or two years. Of course there would have to be some independent body to prevent grade fraud at both college and high school levels. Otherwise, no college whose faculty wanted to keep their jobs would graduate fewer than three-quarters of its students, and high school grades would be subject to even more inflation. If the politicians' promises of increased access and lower or free tuition come true, the possibilities of institutional dishonesty will be even greater. More and more students will crowd into the mass-market colleges on all that lovely tuition money provided by the government. Why not? It's a pleasant way to spend some time, and it would be free. The opportunities for fraud would be colossal.

A mass closure of institutions is simply not going to happen, however. Colleges and universities protect their autonomy vigorously—and many portray the admission of underqualified students as a commitment to equity, second-chances, and ethnic rebalancing (a line of argument that actually is true in the case of several remarkable institutions that have reputations for giving weak students a chance to capitalize on their potential). But for the rest, the fact that they are exploiting marginal students, burdening them with debt, and filling their heads with unrealistic dreams—a particular weakness of the for-profit university system—is papered over with self-serving appeals to higher social causes. Regions that are dependent on college spending and employment do not want institutions to close, either, no matter how mediocre their performance. Governments and politicians have shown themselves to be more devoted to access than to achievement, to providing post-secondary opportunities than to focusing on true accomplishment and the preparation of a smaller but more talented cohort of college graduates.

Closing a college is as painful and rife with controversy as closing a military base, though not nearly as common. The United States closed 350 military bases between 1988 and 2005. Of course, each base was a major contributor to the local economy, and politicians fought against closures in their districts. Faced with a perpetual gridlock, Congress punted the issue to an arm's-length committee and gave it the power to make binding decisions. The result was controversial and devastating for those communities that lost millions of dollars a year in annual spending. But the government was able to authorize a systematic and evidence-based process for eliminating redundant and unnecessary bases.

There is no such option available on the college front. In the USA, about a hundred and thirty colleges have closed since 1990,[3] often denominational colleges in underpopulated rural areas. Some years none closed, other years there were as many as ten. Six closed in 2014. These tiny institutions usually close when they run out of enough students to keep the bills paid. Small public institutions are safer, proof of government generosity and caring in keeping them alive, even in the face of declining enrolments, admission standards in free fall, and dismal graduation and employment rates. But with governments clinging to the belief that accessibility is the key to personal and societal progress, they cannot bring themselves to admit that any public institution is ill-suited to the challenges of communities and regions. Canada, whose university system is almost entirely government funded, has seen virtually no closures (a small college, Notre Dame, in the middle of British Columbia, being the oft-cited exception, but that was forty years ago).

Moody's Investor Service has bad news for small colleges. A report it issued in September 2015 warned that the inability of many small colleges to increase revenue will lead to more closures, perhaps as many as fifteen a year by 2017.[4] These colleges are victims of "an iron triangle of doom," involving fewer students in the pool and increased costs to provide financial aid to them—the average discount on fees is now 48 percent, something that is deadly to the revenue stream. Still, fifteen annual closures would be far less than one percent of the total of the USA's colleges and universities.

One recent American example—the attempted closure of Sweet Briar College in Lynchburg, Virginia—demonstrates the challenge of facing up to fiscal realities. Sweet Briar is a highly regarded liberal-arts college for young women. It has a long and distinguished history, having been founded in 1906, and has a ferociously loyal alumni. With costs rising, enrolment stagnant, and a sizable but insufficient endowment, the president and board shocked the academic community by announcing in March 2015 that the college would close before a substantial financial collapse occurred. The response from students, past and present, was immediate and intense. In the end, alumni formed an organization, "Saving Sweet Briar," to head off the closure. The president and board stepped down and the college was saved, at least temporarily. While the effort was admirable and the enthusiasm impressive, Sweet Briar is a victim of broader societal forces that will be difficult to defeat, even with the very best of intentions.

Most institutions cope with severe financial pressures in traditional ways: raising tuition fees, which is harder to do as demand declines; shifting from full-time faculty members to part-time, adjunct lecturers; and launching fund-raising drives. Larger institutions rake in the money— Yale University makes $2.4 million per year on application fees alone ($80 from each of the nearly thirty thousand young people competing for one of the coveted two thousand spots), donations to Harvard ran to $1.16 billion in 2013–2014, New York University raises well over $1 million a day, and even a small, elite, liberal-arts college like Williams College has stockpiled a $1.7 billion endowment. In keeping with the pattern of inequality that is so ingrained in American society, 2 percent of the USA's colleges gathered in almost 30 percent of the money raised. Put simply, the colleges that need help the most—open-access institutions serving poor and marginalized populations—receive little external support, while those that cater to elite students and well-to-do families wallow in donations.

Then there are the outliers, institutions that forge their own paths. An example is a new campus, "Mountaintop Project," founded with a $20 million grant from Scott Belair, co-founder of Urban Outfitters. Affiliated with Lehigh University in Pennsylvania, it has no lecture halls and no lectures. The students will spend their time innovating and thinking up solutions to the world's problems at a campus "where the ideas never stop coming."[5]

Some institutions, therefore, are sheltered from the urgent need to change by a combination of high status, high tuition fees, global demand for elite schools, massive endowments, and a strongly loyal alumni base. These top-ranked institutions—CalTech, McGill, Swarthmore, Duke, and about a hundred or so others across North America—are fully protected from external pressures. They attract many of the continent's brightest students (often with the wealthiest parents), students preselected for career success and prosperity. No wonder students clamor to get into the golden institutions: Stanford has 42,000 applications for 2,100 first-year seats, William and Mary has 14,500 for 1,500 enrolled students, and elite public institutions like the University of Michigan get 52,000 applications for 6,300 enrolled first-year students. Compare these American numbers to McGill University, in Montreal, Quebec, where 48 percent of applicants are successful, even though McGill is a top-one-hundred-ranked, globally competitive university, easily of a comparable academic standard to the Ivy League institutions.

While these institutions shape parental expectations about getting their children into college, the reality is that most American colleges accept the majority of those who apply to them. This means, in turn, that these colleges and universities are vulnerable to declines in applications, have little chance to raise tuition rates much, and cannot always draw on a deep well of alumni support, although a good football team can help here. They have one option—and it has been taken by many—which is to lower admission standards. But this is the start of a downward spiral. Lower entrance requirements produce a weaker student body. Institutions can then fail more students, resulting in reduced revenue from fees, or keep them and lower the graduation expectations. Weaker graduates, without the basic abilities, work ethic, and drive of graduates from the elite schools, are typically less attractive as employees and, when hired, will not perform at the highest standard. It is these struggling institutions—the below-standard ones that will never self-identify as such in their promotional materials— that are under the most urgent pressure to adapt to the new realities.

But financially weak institutions, with faculty and staff worried about their jobs, students and parents concerned about the status of their degrees, and governments urging institutions to take more and weaker students, are not in a good position to adapt rapidly to complex and little-understood workforce dynamics. This is particularly difficult when the institutions, many faculty-centric rather than student-focused, reject the widely held expectation that their primary purpose is to prepare students for a quick and successful integration into the world of work.

It is important to know the nature of the challenges. One of the most serious changes has been the erosion of the "arts bump." This phenomenon is captured in the old Arts Faculty joke. Question: "What does the engineering graduate say to the arts graduate every morning?" Answer: "Hi, boss!" A couple of generations ago there was a substantial truth underlying this jest. The best way to describe the arts bump was "starting low, finishing high." Arts graduates, for much of the last half of the twentieth century, entered companies in low-level positions but demonstrated their creative and critical thinking skills and earned steady promotions. In time, typically by their forties, many arts graduates caught up and passed the professional graduates, moving into supervisory and management positions. But the arts bump has eroded in recent years, particularly as companies recruit for specific skills and experience. It's not quite as bad as the current iteration of that joke, where the positions are reversed, and the arts graduate asks the engineer, "Do you want fries with that?" A better way to describe the situation now is the "arts progression," where graduates start low, stay low longer, move up slowly (save for the surging prospects of the occasional star), and finish in the middle. As John Goyder, a leading sociologist who studied this arts bump phenomenon in Canada, wrote:

> For these people, university program planners and course instructors in the humanities and social scientists need to be mindful of the unsympathetic job market waiting for their students ... When liberal arts catch-up was detectible within surveys ... that was nice evidence that

humanities and social science education indeed fosters
generic workplace skills of long shelf-life. The catch-up
has now been washed out by over-supply.[6]

Equally important, colleges and universities that speak sententiously about shunning the market and focusing on "real" learning have in fact enthusiastically capitalized on the unrelenting demand for a college degree. From the shameless overpromotion of the elite universities, eager to pad their admission statistics and artificially inflate their rejection rates, to the callous recruitment of obviously underqualified students into high-cost private universities, the college system has taken a high-demand market, flooded it with expensive and highly competitive advertising, and encouraged millions of students to launch a university career for which many are ill-suited. The flood of students paid the bills for faculty and staff, justified increased government investments, attracted large bequests and donations, covered the costs of impressive new buildings, and supported spending on everything from new residences to the ridiculously high salaries of football coaches. Students were willing to pay, and universities were happy to take their money, even from obviously mediocre students who were doomed to fail. But the students kept coming.

The market was, from the 1960s on, a marvelous, rocket-powered driving force for colleges and universities. Colleges assumed that the attraction lay in their intellectual brilliance and, a little less so, their capacity to cultivate character, social responsibility, and citizenship. That was true, the polls tell us (and how did we know anything before polling?), since students in the late 1960s and early 1970s reported that they attended university in order to pursue social justice, personal development, and to improve the world. Or they attended just because that was what young people from their social class did after high school. They could indulge or cultivate these interests because of the all-but-assured jobs that awaited them after graduation.

By the 1990s, the balance had shifted. The vast majority of students—85 percent or higher in most polls—indicated that they attended college or university to find a decent career and to earn a higher income. They had, in other words, internalized the evidence from the 1960s and 1970s—college graduates earned higher incomes and had better career

choices than non-college grads—
and from the promotional materials from universities and their
supporters. In an uncertain economy, these messages rebounded
with extra power in the early
twenty-first century, sending millions more students around the
world to university and convincing
hundreds of thousands of families
to spend large sums of money to
dispatch one or more children
overseas to attend a foreign school.

In the case of law, long-term
oversupply produced declining
employment results and lower
income for graduates. Most of those
from the highest-quality institutions—Yale, Harvard, Stanford,

COLLEGE DEBT DELINQUENCY
AMONG THE MIDDLE-AGED

A new report in the *Wall Street Journal*
details how delinquency on student
loan debt is actually highest among the
middle-aged, defined roughly as adults
between 40 and 60. Delinquencies for
those in their 40s stand at an alarming
11.9 percent. Meanwhile, over the past
seven years debt rates for those in their
50s and 60s have doubled and tripled.

Many parents—no longer able to
tap home equity to pay for their children's education—are taking out new
student loans to do so. An Education
Department program that provides
loans to parents to fund their kids'
education is among the fastest-growing of the government's education
loan programs.[8]

and Toronto—continued to do well. Top-flight firms still wanted the best
talent. But the second- and third-tier schools, sending graduates into
an overcrowded job market, discovered much poorer prospects. In the
2010s, applications to law school dropped dramatically.[7] Not only are
smaller stand-alone law schools in serious danger, but even the top-tier
ones are getting nervous. Paul Campos, a law professor at the University
of Colorado, author of *Don't Go to Law School (Unless)* points to the high
tuition and the bleak job prospects for law graduates even from the better
schools. Huge unsecured government loans that can't be discharged in
bankruptcy have created "an indentured class of people," he says.[9]

RELYING ON MARKET FORCES TO RESHAPE PROGRAMS

In the end market forces do work, even in relatively market-insensitive
places like universities. As disgruntled students and their cash-strapped
parents push back, reeling from poor or uneven work experiences after

graduation, these institutions are forced to take notice. Unsustainable patterns emerged during the 1990s and 2000s. Business schools exploded in status and attractiveness, part of the widespread search for professional opportunities. Students applied in the thousands for the most competitive programs, especially in engineering, architecture, and design. New programs—animation, digital media, anything computer-oriented—provided alternatives to the traditional majors. Preprofessional programs—prelaw and premedicine (a holding ground for the perennially optimistic and status-conscious parents)—grew in importance.

If markets produce winners, they also produce losers. For every Google and Apple there are companies like Kodak, a former industrial giant crushed by new technology, and Hewlett-Packard, a long-time star that has fallen on hard times. Liberal-arts institutions struggled to find students. Many of the world's best liberal-arts colleges responded to changing markets by adding business and other professional programs to a curriculum long dominated by the study of traditional disciplines. Colorado College, built around a brilliant and bold block program (one course at a time), added economics and business to their offerings. Union College offers business and finance. Even small Sterling College allows students to study accounting, social entrepreneurship, capitalism, real estate, economics, marketing, entrepreneurship, leadership, and international business, all at a comparatively cheap price of $18,000 a year. But at least these colleges are trying to respond, albeit by copying programs and fields of study that have become as ubiquitous in colleges and universities in the 2010s as English and biology were in the 1970s. But imitations are not innovative. It is ironic that institutions staffed by some of the brightest people on the planet are obsessed with reproducing standard programs rather than responding to the needs of the economy and the expectations of parents and students. Business programs, a useful innovation in the 1980s and 1990s, had become so commonplace as to be unexceptional by the 2010s. Business graduates will, in less than a decade if not already in some areas, become the arts graduates of the 2020s, with far too many of them chasing far too few jobs.

In comparison to the rapidly expanding business programs, enrolments in the Humanities declined dramatically, a victim of unkind—and sometimes unfair—criticism of the quality and effectiveness of their programs, particularly in terms of career preparation. The number of Humanities degrees granted rose substantially from the 1940s to the 1960s, but have fallen to half of all what they once were, as a percentage of overall college degrees granted. Once-dominant fields, such as English literature, lost tens of thousands of students across Canada and the United States—along with the faculty positions and funding associated with them. The basic sciences lost ground to the applied sciences, amidst criticism from faculty members that universities were being transformed into training institutes and had lost their intellectual integrity.

It is fair to anticipate further enrolment declines in coming years if the colleges and universities do not adjust to market realities. Even if the Dream Factories have lost some of their cachet, though, the reality is that society has not yet produced a clear and successful alternative to them. Building long-term institutional futures on the present-day absence of a new-order Dream Factory is a shaky proposition at best. To put it simply, colleges and universities have few options. They can stick to the status quo and experience a slow and painful decline in institutional fortunes for all but the highest-quality institutions. This is the most likely scenario for most colleges and universities, as the internal cost of change is too great and institutional resistance considerable. Without a major institutional threat—such as a sharp decline in applications—major change is unlikely. Colleges and universities respond to inputs (i.e., student demand for places) and not to long-term outcomes (i.e., employment and future salaries).

Another option would be to sharply reduce the total number of students, starting with the academically weak and putting greater emphasis on getting high school graduates into the right career track, training institute, or college. This is unlikely at the state or provincial level until parental expectations shift, and there are currently few signs of this happening. Reorienting students from colleges and universities to technical schools and other training options has to be made more attractive and higher status before such a shift can be made.

Alternatively, colleges could dramatically reduce the number of students in career-insensitive undergraduate programs, emphasizing the intellectual quality and rigour of the courses for those who remain, while producing career-ready programs for the displaced students. This is underway on many campuses. But progress is slow and resistance considerable. This issue is being presented as a battle to the death for the academy. A September 2015 report said that Japan was planning to close many Humanities and Social Science programs in preference to more practical fields of study. The response to this news—which highlighted the antediluvian nature of Japan's educational policy, led to a *Wall Street Journal* story, and spread like wildfire across cyberspace—demonstrates how quickly defenders of the *ancien régime* will run to the barricades. There was one problem with the hysteria about Japan. It was not true, with the clamor resulting from a misreading of one small portion of a government document.

Yet another option would be for colleges and universities to adjust, however reluctantly, to a more career-focused orientation to undergraduate and graduate programs and to accept the need to be responsive to job market conditions. Some institutions, particularly those with declining admissions, have shifted in this direction already, with uneven results. Colleges, hamstrung with tenure-stream faculty members who are difficult to remove or reorient, change slowly and often with considerable internal foot-dragging. A half-hearted shift that is resisted within the institution is unlikely to produce dramatic or positive results.

If these institutions are wise, they will adapt, creatively and enthusiastically, to the changing economic environment, and develop experimental programs in close collaboration with industry. For-profit institutions need to demonstrate employability and have both first-mover advantage and internal cultures predisposed to flexibility. Some not-for-profit colleges, often with corporate encouragement and support, have undertaken such shifts. Technical institutions (called polytechnics internationally) are set up for this transition and have made significant transformations by creating innovative new programs.

This frank assessment of the current situation produces unpromising conclusions. There are simply too many college and university graduates, and they are often in the wrong fields as they attempt to find the constantly moving target that is the twenty-first-century world of work. Even excellent students in the nonprofessional fields are better trained for the economy of the 1990s than for the prospects of the 2020s and 2030s, a brutal reality that everyone, from governments and universities on down to parents and students, is having real trouble recognizing.

But, remarkably, expectations remain sky-high, despite the obvious warning signs, and here is the main reason for inaction. There is no widely shared answer to a simple question: "If not university, then what?" Right now, the best one can offer is to focus on the most market-ready of the college degrees—finance, computer science, engineering, design, nursing, and medicine—and try to find a niche in the competitive job market. The rush to the most career-ready fields will overwhelm the employment prospects in short order unless, as with medicine and, formerly, law, the profession works with the institutions to constrain the number of entrants. This approach, though, tends to be anathema in countries committed to freedom of choice, even if the surplus applicants are attending state-funded institutions or supported by government student loans and bursaries.

In a market economy, there are always workarounds. Can't get into a top American medical school or law school? There are always options in other countries that will prepare you for American licencing examinations. Remember, too, that the American invasion of the supposedly evil fortress empire of Grenada involved the rescue of medical students studying there. They were the real winners in the inconsequential conflict, securing positions in the American medical schools that they had been unable to enter in the first place.

So, the question still holds. What should students and their parents do? If colleges and universities controlled enrolments to better match the needs of the economy, opportunities for graduates would spike. If they raised their admission standards, marginal students would be compelled to make more realistic career choices. In the absence of such institutional or governmental self-control—an exceptionally unlikely event, save for a handful for expensive technical and professional fields—students have to proceed knowing that the colleges and universities will continue to overproduce graduates, in some markets at a furious, opportunity-killing pace. Students have to find other ways to distinguish themselves. If they want to get into a good program at a good university, they need to consider extensive volunteer activities, carefully selected summer jobs, the aggressive pursuit of leadership positions, and relentless networking (capitalizing on the benefits of hobnobbing with the well-to-do in residence, at the fraternity/sorority, or on sports teams). Resumé-building has become almost equal with academic performance in shaping the career prospects of college graduates, taking the intensity of the Grade 11 and 12 application frenzy and extending it through four or more years of university study. In short, young adults *can* prepare, seriously and systematically, for career opportunities and to make themselves attractive to potential employers.

Right now, one of the major defaults for recent college graduates is to double down, returning to school for a professional degree (MBAs and education degrees are the favourites) or for graduate studies—even though the career prospects for graduates in the Humanities, Social Sciences, and core sciences are often dismal. An increasingly attractive alternative is to head, degree in hand, to a community college or technical institute, often for a diploma. With a reasonable number of jobs available in specific technicalities—dental technicians, heavy-duty mechanics, app designers, and the like—university graduates can demonstrate their career-readiness. Of course, they could have done this straight out of high school, saved a lot of money, and reduced the study time by two or three years. Hundreds of thousands of university graduates have gone down this track, often regretting the lost money and years. More studying and career preparation, on top of a four-year degree, carries a real cost to the economy, families, and individuals, a burden that the young are increasingly appreciating.

Watching young adults flail around looking for a real career and real opportunity is tragic. The (not so) young woman interviewed recently who had a Bachelor of Arts, Bachelor of Education, Master of Business Administration, and Master of Education and was now registered in a PhD in Education because she wanted career opportunities beyond her $45,000-a-year job is emblematic of a generation lost on the high seas of contemporary employment. She will clearly do whatever it takes to prepare herself for a job. She just doesn't know what to do.

Governments, working with the institutions, could do much better. One common response, other than pointing to the success of the German and Scandinavian post-secondary education systems and wondering why governments, institutions, and students cannot produce comparable outcomes, is to point to the continued strength of the trades. As the author of the *Higher Education Bubble* observed, "[T]he Bureau of Labor Statistics predicts that 7 of the 10 fastest-growing jobs in the next decade will be based on on-the-job training rather than higher education. (And they'll be hands-on jobs that are hard to outsource to foreigners: If you want your toilet fixed, it can't be done by somebody in Bangalore.) If the [Washington] *Post* is right about this trend, a bursting of the bubble is growing likelier." While low-skill, high-wage industrial work—such as unionized assembly plant operations— has fallen on hard times, skilled tradespeople remain in high demand. From the medical technologies—have you checked out the high-tech equipment in the average optometrist's office?—to pipefitting, welding, and power engineering, the skilled trades remain the cornerstone of a great deal of industrial, resource, and medical work.

It is here that the shortcomings of contemporary assumptions about college and university are most painfully evident. While an Arts and Science education provides the opportunity for fine intellectual growth, such a degree is less successful in guaranteeing a pathway to a new job and a lifelong career than it was two generations ago. Polytechnic and technical institutes have, in contrast, proven far more responsive and creative in adjusting to the new economy. In fact, these schools have at their core a commitment to staying at the cutting edge of contemporary industry and to aligning instructional activities and programs with marketplace needs. The high-profile universities have become the stars of the twenty-first century market and innovation economy, seen as driving forces in competitiveness and productivity. But while their technical-institute counterparts—for example the highly-ranked Rensselaer Polytechnic Institute—are well regarded by industry and intelligent students interested in technical fields, they are less well known to liberal-arts students. The admission statistics are instructive, with fourteen thousand applicants, over four thousand acceptances, and a jaw-dropping total cost for undergraduates at Rensselaer of over $60,000 a year in tuition, board, and fees.

What the polytechnics have failed to do in North America is to capture the public's imagination in the way that they have in Europe. Technical education is held in high esteem in Germany and other European countries. But in much of the rest of the world, parents and young adults remain obsessed about a college or university education and about the white-collar jobs that they assume await after graduation. That many graduates are now cycling back to polytechnics and community colleges in order to become career-ready has still not changed the mindset of most families about the desirability of a university education.

HIGHLY SKILLED WORKERS ARE IN HIGH DEMAND

Colleges and universities currently produce too few highly specialized workers and too many general education graduates. The finance sector no longer needs thousands of entry-level customer service agents; what it requires is people with combined financial and computing skills to run high-speed trading systems. The mines and industrial plants will need many fewer semi-skilled employees and more technology-savvy professionals. Today very few "average" individuals—whether college trained or not, with "average" defined to include intellectual ability, motivation, work ethic, and reliability—can make the transition to the high-paying, new-economy jobs. Meanwhile, high-tech and other specialist companies are forced to import the advanced technological personnel they need from overseas.

There is, however, a large part of the post-secondary system that is more responsive to the marketplace. For-profit colleges and universities have received bad press in recent years, deserved by some—say, the ill-managed firms that exploited the naïveté of the poor and ill-educated and turned the US Pell Grant system into a corporate bank. But the for-profit system, particularly at the level of diplomas and short courses, lives and dies on

> "AVERAGE" IS OVER
>
> Average is over is the catchphrase of our age, and it is likely to apply all the more to our future. This maxim will apply to the quality of your job, to your earnings, to where you live, to your education and to the education of your children, and maybe even to our most intimate relationships. Marriages, families, business, countries, cities, and regions all will see a greater split in material outcomes; namely, they will either rise to the top in terms of quality or make do with unimpressive results ... This imbalance in technological growth will have some surprising implications. For instance, workers more and more will come to be classified into two categories. The key questions will be: Are you good at working with intelligent machines or not? Are your skills a complement to the skills of the computer, or is the computer doing better without you? Worst of all, are you competing against the computer? Are computers helping people in China and India compete against you? If you and your skills are a complement to the computer, your wage and market prospects are likely to be cheery. If your skills do not complement the computer, you may want to address that mismatch. Ever more people are starting to fall on one side of the divide or the other. That's why *average is over*.[10]

US INSTITUTIONS MARKETING
SECOND BACHELOR'S AS
WAY TO IMPROVE GRADUATE
EMPLOYABILITY

A growing number of US PSE institutions are marketing second bachelor's degrees to graduates looking to improve their employability in a tough labour market. While many institutions have long offered post-baccalaureate training, these new programs distinguish themselves by offering students complete degrees in a reduced time period. Oregon State University, for instance, has since 2012 offered a computer science degree that can be completed in just one year. The courses are being touted as a way for graduates to build complementary skills to their previous degrees, and present an alternative to a master's degree, which may require a previous degree in the field; moreover, many employers do not require the higher credential. They also present an alternative to postgraduate diploma programs, which may not provide the credential that some employers are looking for. However, pursuing a second degree—even in an abbreviated time period—can be costly, especially for the kind of underemployed graduates for whom these programs are being designed.[11]

its ability to move students through programs quickly and into appropriate jobs. By 2012, for-profit institutions represented nearly 12 percent of the American undergraduate market. Yet they only get about 1 percent of the attention, and most of that through the activities of businesses like the University of Phoenix (it's a company) and Corinthian Colleges (the industry's biggest failure). The numbers are not impressive. Only 37 percent of students attending for-profit colleges graduate, and they have much higher student debt loads (and default rates—13 percent of America's enrolment, 47 percent of America's student loan defaults) than in the not-for-profit sector. But the actions of the worst institutions should not be allowed to distort the image of all of them.

The best of these colleges are particularly good at market-sensitive, short-course training in everything from hairdressing to computer repair. They open and close programs as the market demands and work hard to place their graduates—knowing, as they do, that employment rates are among their best recruiting tools. The full for-profit university model, led by the University of Phoenix, has fallen victim to that institution's monumental fall from grace that included—in the wake of scandals about student loans and admission policies—a decline by half in admissions over five years, a sharp drop in revenues, company-wide layoffs, and the closure of dozens of small offices across the United States. It is not yet clear how quickly—if at all—the sector will rebound.

Taken as a system, the colleges and universities of North America have considerable resilience. While the core disciplines are conservative and losing market share (to use a commercial phrase they despise), the professional schools are proving to be more creative. Business schools have fragmented the once iconic MBA into dozens of sub-fields, from Sports Management and International Business to Non-Profit Organizations and even Social Enterprises. North American schools have branches around the world, primarily through their business schools but they are showing a growing interest in other professional degrees. In the case of New York University's controversial campuses in Singapore and Dubai, they are also exporting high-quality liberal-arts education. Psychology-based institutions, such as the Adler School of Professional Psychology (a not-for-profit) and Pacifica Graduate Institute (also a non-profit), offer intensive and highly regarded professional degrees, focusing on people active in the field. The field of professional education offers a nearly endless variety of career- and income-enhancing graduate degrees, the attraction lying as much in union contracts that pay for extra degrees as in the teachers' intellectual curiosity. Colleges and universities are not moribund, but it is the lethargy of their core operations and their willingness to admit too many underqualified and unmotivated students that contributes to their difficulties.

WORK-LEARN PROGRAMS, BOOT CAMPS, AND UNSCHOOLING

If your company was well-established, prosperous, and committed to excellence, how would you recruit? Would you head for the elite campuses and fight Wall Street and Google for the best graduates? Would you hold an open competition, counting on digital evaluation systems to cull through a mountain of applications to find a handful of potential candidates? Would you focus on the graduates of specific programs that appear to be preparing students well for the kind of work you have in your company? Or would you look for a new way of identifying and preparing the precise kind of employees that you wanted and invest in their preparation for working with you? Maybe you would hire promising high school graduates and have them combine work and education during their early years?

The first three options fit with the current college and university system—and with the manner in which parents and students think that the employment market works. The fourth option is on the rise and stands to become increasingly prominent as companies retake control of the training and employment system. The final option—which challenges colleges to place themselves in a subordinate position vis-à-vis employers—currently operates through cooperative education programs that allow students to follow semesters of study with work terms.

Until recently, the majority of employers used colleges and universities to filter out the best possible employees for their companies. This was an efficient system, because it produced many consistently capable graduates with high exit standards for the selection pool. Companies trained them for firm-specific jobs and moved them about within the company until they found their career niche. While this model is still followed in some sectors, including banking and finance, the reality is that companies now want to hire new employees who are specifically trained for the jobs that need to be filled.

Companies have now found a new system that combines employee selection and early-stage training for the corporate environment. This approach allows open competition for potential employees, without establishing a preference for graduates from any specific post-secondary programs; identifies the specific job responsibilities associated with the position; uses advanced assessment techniques, focusing both on resumés and psychological evaluation, to select a small number of candidates; brings the top candidates together (and pays them) to participate in a training session, which could be an extended boot camp (a one-day introduction to corporate culture) or a multi-week, highly specialized training program that tests the candidates' suitability for the job on offer and allows the employer to hire the best participants while thanking the others for coming.

Where this has been used, the group of participants included high school dropouts, experienced workers, and university graduates (right up to the PhD level); the selection of candidates focused on their performance in the boot camp exercises and not on their prior jobs, resumés, or educations. The participating companies want to find workers who have the right aptitude, an obvious work ethic, collegiality, and trainability. This system—which focuses on specific jobs and which does not use college degrees as a filter—has the potential to undermine the central role of universities in the career development process. It does not take much imagination to see this system changing from company-specific training programs to multi-firm selection boot camps, operating for smaller employers.

This approach to credentialling, workplace preparation, and employment is not a distant fantasy. Leading and creative firms have already started down this path. In a fascinating report, *Education to Employment: Designing a System that Works*, Mona Mourshed and her colleagues at McKinsey & Company put forward a new system for workplace preparation. Perhaps the most revolutionary steps they describe involve the assessment of the specific skills and abilities that applicants might bring to an employer. Consider two evaluation systems that are already operational.

The first system is WorkKeys Assessment (ACT, or American College Testing, USA), which selects candidates who have the highest potential to adapt to a specific corporation setting. The WorkKeys evaluation tests basic and core competencies and specialized skills (tied to over eighteen thousand different jobs) required within specific companies. In many ways, the presence of such a system is an indictment of the existing post-secondary system, which produces graduates who do not necessarily have the required skills and aptitudes for employment success. WorkKeys stands between applicants and employers, providing a National Career Readiness Certificate that allows companies to identify those candidates who are best able to fit with the firm's needs.

The second system is Mozilla Open Badges. The idea of an additional credential—essentially a credential that provides detailed information on candidates' abilities—has spread to the Internet. Mozilla's Open Badges allows individuals to demonstrate their specific competencies and abilities for potential employers and permits firms to develop tests or standards suitable for their company or organization.

While the availability of these testing tools allows degree holders to confirm, explain, or build upon formal education, they also permit people without a college, university, or community college degree or diploma to demonstrate that they have the exact skills needed by the company. This system is already allowing non-degree-holders to demonstrate their advanced competency in cutting-edge technical skills. In earlier times, companies might hire someone who, because of his or her formal education, looked closest to being their ideal candidate. This approach placed a high value on a college or university degree and provided degree-holders with a clear advantage in the employment marketplace. Assessment tools trump that advantage, allowing companies to select individuals who have the precise competencies and abilities that they require, taking the guesswork out of the recruitment process.

Education to Employment also described a variety of work-learn programs designed to prepare employees for work at specific companies. These programs are based on curricula derived from inside each company. One of the most ambitious programs was developed by the Automotive Manufacturing Training and Education Collective (AMTEC). The partners in AMTEC developed a list of core competencies required of their employees, based on the specific needs of automotive manufacturing. Then they transformed the list of competencies into a set of sixty modules, each lasting from three to eight weeks. Companies can use the modular program to train new hires, as part of the selection process, or to test existing employees to identify areas in need of upgrading. This approach is used on a national scale in Australia as part of that country's vocational education and training program, with the modules often integrated into diploma and degree programs as a way of demonstrating competence in areas of workplace need.

Another innovative work-learn program is Apprenticeship 2000 (USA). When Blum and Daetwyler, two partnered German firms, established factories in the USA, they needed workers for very specific mechatronics work, something that existing college programs did not provide. The firms collaborated with Central Piedmont Community College, offering to pay college tuition fees and provide a regular salary, to produce the specialized workers wanted by a growing number of participating companies. Participants are tested for aptitude and suitability before they are officially entered, and those who complete the program get their journeyman's certification and a college credential. But they do so through direct work on the factory floor, and combine "book learning" with practical experience. Job readiness is not an issue for their graduates, who also earn a small salary as they complete their studies. The companies can spend more than $175,000 per graduate—a substantial corporate cost that is made up through easier transitions into the workforce.

In India, Wipro hires thousands of university graduates, and works in-house to retrain them as computer programmers. The company has developed its own training operation—three or four months in length—with the training, which is closely integrated with operations, focusing on specific company needs.

Back in America, Newport News Shipbuilding had encountered considerable difficulty finding college and technical graduates with the ability to make a smooth transition into company operations. Their answer was a long-running apprenticeship program that builds an introduction to corporate culture and company operations within its specially developed shipbuilder curriculum.

The initiatives defined by Mourshed and her colleagues demonstrate a fundamental failing of the post-secondary system. The programs she describes are focused on the candidate and the employer, rely on personal assessments to determine suitability, and provide training in the specific job skills required by the firms.

Creating work-learn programs, rather than the current (and under-utilized) learn-work model of the cooperative education system, would also put the employer and the employee/trainee in the forefront. The core elements of the model are straightforward. Companies would select promising and hard-working high school graduates (recognizing that most of the things a firm needs to know about a young person in terms of basic abilities, writing skills, integrity, work ethic, and ambition are readily apparent among many senior high school students) and hire them at a decent starting salary. This could be, for the sake of the argument, $25,000 a year. The candidates would work in the firm, perhaps moving through various departments as they learn about the company and as the employer identifies the most appropriate place for them. The young employees would take two courses a semester at a college or university (in person if the campus is close, or online) and two courses in an intensive summer semester. One of the courses would be counted as part of work hours. The courses would be selected to suit the aptitudes of the student-employees and the needs and interests of the company.

Over five or six years, the students would gain a complete college degree in a field of interest and employment relevance, as well as five or six years of work experience, with responsibility and duties improving over time, based on appropriate performance, a steady and gradually rising income with little or no student debt, and a long-term and secure position, if work performance was satisfactory.

This model would work well for employers, particularly those having difficulty attracting candidates for specific positions at the firm's worksites. A company based in a small town or isolated location could use this system to select, train, and retain employees, including those raised in the surrounding area. Compare it with the increasingly standard experience of university graduates: a college degree, likely of interest, but with untested employment impact; limited work experience; and small and stagnant income, typically tied to standard summer jobs and part-time employment at college; a sizable if not crippling debt; and the challenge of finding a good position in a very tight job market.

But consider this approach also from the company's perspective. The company could sweeten the employment pot by covering the tuition fees for program participants. If the system were managed properly, the companies would have their pick of elite high school graduates, often with local knowledge and contacts; they would have a chance to find the right employment niche within the firm for the individual; the company would get a hard worker and determined individual at comparatively low cost, with specific education and training tied to their workplace needs; the firm would engender strong loyalty among employees, who would contrast their work-learning experience with that of their high school friends who took the standard approach. We know that high school students go to college and university to enhance their career prospects. This model, which gives a high priority to the learning experience at college, responds to two of the greatest pressures in the contemporary economy: finding good jobs for young adults and training high school graduates for the demands of the twenty-first century workplace. What better place to learn the latter than inside a company?

There is a simple message in these last two options: companies do not need colleges and universities to identify, hire, and train top-flight employees. Modern evaluation techniques—easily and cheaply done online—can identify many promising candidates. Adaptable training programs, focusing on the work needs of the firm, can be developed in-house, provided by a for-profit company or, when institutions are flexible and responsive, delivered by a community college, technical institute, college, or university. The environment in post–high school education is changing and, if these two options—Work-Learn and Boot Camp Training—take hold, traditional employers could find themselves losing out in the competition for the best and most promising students. This could, in turn, hurt the college-university brand and force a widespread reconsideration of the place of post-secondary education in the preparation of young people for the world of work.

There is also the "unschooling" or "uncollege" option—the avoidance of college or advanced training all together. Popularized by Peter Thiel, a founder of PayPal, unschooling involves resisting the clarion call to college and university and the search for personal opportunities for advancement. Thiel himself offers well-paid fellowships—$100,000 for one year—to convince talented people to bypass university in favour of self-employment. Others, like current high-tech superstar, Elon Musk, also promote the avoidance of traditional educational models for various alternatives, including through the Ad Astra initiative that replaces formal education with inspired and curiosity-driven exploration, and unCollege. org, which encourages young adults to launch a program of self-discovery. As Dale Stephens, the founder of UnCollege.org declared, "I am not arguing against school, I am writing in favor of choices. You—we—must learn that we can make our own decisions. We can take data, evaluate them, and come up with a solution. We don't need teachers to tell us the answer. We don't need parents to give us hints. We, as individuals, have the power and capacity to make our own decisions. Hacking your education is a lifelong commitment. A lifelong commitment to forge your own path and define your own values. Not accepting what others want for you, but figuring it out for yourself."[12] Author and educator Blake Boles agrees:

> We spend big bucks on college because we've confused receiving a college degree with getting a higher education. They're two different things. A college degree proves that you can survive four years at an institution. It's a piece of paper that says, "I followed a prescribed path to success." A higher education, though, is first and foremost the capacity to self-direct your life. Someone who has a higher education can define her own vision of success and pursue it, even in the face of

difficulty. College is one path to a higher education, but it's not the only one. Sometimes college graduates lead self-directed lives, but sometimes they don't; a college degree does not guarantee a higher education.[13]

The unschooling movement rejects the automatic acceptance of traditional education, including college, celebrates individual initiative, and offers a biting critique of what is often described by the strongest critics as the mind-numbing and soul-destroying ethos of contemporary schools and universities. These models hold particular appeal for the highly talented, but they do not offer significant opportunities for the large mass of young people seeking to enter the workforce.

The advantage of supporting colleges and universities is that they are simple to understand, iconic, and have sufficient track records to present themselves as a truly credible preparation for those entering the workforce. And they do work for the right students in the right programs at the right time. The problem with the alternatives to college is that they lack the history, contemporary culture, and demonstrated salary outcomes to back their claims to suitability and impact for young adults. People will, for good and understandable reasons, continue to invest in the old system, even in the face of mounting evidence of its limitations. Colleges and universities have the added advantage, from an institutional point of view, that the employment failures of entering students (including dropouts and those who fail to move easily and quickly into good careers) are easily blamed on the students themselves, rather than the system. Poor program selection, opting for a low-status institution, getting low grades, or failing to prepare adequately for the jump to the world of work are all described as personal errors of judgement or execution, absolving the institutions or those who support them from any responsibility for the poor outcomes.

REORIENTING THE DEBATE TO FOCUS ON JOB CREATION

The angst about colleges and the training of young people is ill-founded. We readily admit that we believe sending ill-prepared and unmotivated young people to universities, under the false and misleading impression that learning inevitably leads to more earning, is wrongheaded. It is also clear to us, however, that universities have been resistant to change and are not adequately focused on the career-readiness of their graduates.

We are convinced, however, that the underlying and fundamental problem is not the educational institutions, however much they obviously need reforming, but the steady loss of high-paying jobs, particularly for people of average or below-average ability. Colleges and universities didn't cause this problem, but their inability to adapt exacerbates it.

Right now, however, there is a global obsession with getting young adults into places of higher learning, although, interestingly, not as much concern about getting them out successfully. The strong belief continues that a credential, even more than the learning, knowledge, and skills supposedly associated with that credential, is sufficient to pave the way to opportunity, despite mounting evidence that that is not the case. With half of all entering students in America leaving before graduation and with many students opting for non-work-related fields of study, it is clear that the current system is not closely aligned with the priorities of young adults (high-paying jobs, preferably in a Google-type office environment), government and business (employment-ready young people ready to fill industry's needs for trained employees), or society at large (launching young people comfortably into careers and adulthood).

In our view, the focus is on the wrong end of the equation. Follow the debate about student debt, which is usually carried on with little thought about how young people are spending the money that they have borrowed, lowering or abolishing tuition fees (a massive benefit to well-to-do families), and ensuring access to all who want to pursue advanced study (without considering that people of lower ability are likely to be ill-suited for college work). The discussion is all about the input factors—young people, tuition subsidies, student loans, seats in classes—and not about the other end of the tunnel, the job market. We know that there are jobs in the modern economy; despite efforts to promote youth unemployment as being at near-crisis proportions, the reality is that those students who want or need to find work can generally find employment. What is at issue are crucial factors. Is it part-time or full-time work? High-paying or entry-level? Career building or basic employment? Related to their fields of study or unrelated?

The focus for the college and university debate is on factors that governments and families can actually address. Families can save for their children's education. They can co-sign for a student loan. They can let their children stay at home while they are students. This, they can handle, with greater or lesser degrees of ease. But unless they own a substantial business, they probably cannot create a job for their son or daughter. They cannot force an employer to offer a higher salary, with excellent benefits, and long-term security. Governments, on their side, can underwrite an expansion of a public school or offer tax breaks for university tuition and make more money available for student loans. They can build more university classrooms and fund career-advising officers. They cannot (at least not in North America) order employers to create more jobs for recent graduates. They cannot dictate pay scales or guarantee the long-term future of work. Governments and families have combined to do what they can for young people, believing that education will provide a buffer against economic and technological change, buying into the *Learning = Earning* equation, and encouraging students to be more career-focused in their preparations.

But another side of the question is also critical. Where are the well-paid jobs? We can identify the high-wage, high-skill positions, because employers are often lamenting the shortage of specialized, highly trained, and hard-working graduates for emerging firms. We can often see the even larger number of entry-level jobs that are on offer, largely in the service and retail sectors. We can see the high-profile job losses due to technological change or international competition. But crucial phenomena, such as the slow receding of the middle-management world, are almost impossible for the average observer to track.

There have been many technologically driven transitions in the past, and economists are quick to point out that the workforce adapted to them. Millions of agricultural positions have been lost, just as many manufacturing jobs are now disappearing. But where are the new ones? They may be coming, but the number of job-killing innovations seems to be much larger than the newly created positions that are suitable for people of average skill and ability. Computer programmers working on the semantic web? Yes, there is a real shortage. Jobs offering $40 an hour plus benefits at a unionized automotive plant are easy to spot when they disappear, but it is hard to see the low-skill, high-wage positions that will provide a living for the displaced workers and those coming behind them.

The modern industrial world needs to reorient the conversation. We know what universities and colleges can do—and we even know most of what should be done to make them better, more efficient, and more focused on the career outcomes for young people.

Colleges and universities have a key role to play in the transition to the emerging "new economy." It is unlikely that they will ever recapture the glory of the 1950–1980 period, when they served, for too short a time, as true Dream Factories for young adults. Those days are gone, although colleges and universities will continue to produce often impressive results for the smartest, most capable, and hardest-working of their students. What has also gone is the expectation that a college degree is a golden ticket that will lift a young adult straight toward the middle class. It is hardly surprising that in the complex, technologically advanced, and globalized twenty-first century that a nineteenth- and twentieth-century institution would not be able to continue unscathed. It is also not surprising that institutions that served their main beneficiaries—faculty, staff, and governments/donors—very nicely for several generations would be resistant to radical and sustained change.

But colleges and universities, even though they may have a diminished and different role in the future, are here to stay. Their first and obvious role is to preserve the best of what they do in academic terms, stop trying to be "everything to everybody," and transform their training and education systems to allow young adults to adjust more readily to emerging twenty-first-century realities. They can expand the positive side of their function as Dream Factories by being responsive to the world of work and the needs of graduates and employers and by cutting back on overenrolment, faculty-centric operations, and the destruction of ambitions through the mass failure of students. And yes, someone has to teach Latin and classical Greek; these languages and culture are integral to the roots of our civilization.

Colleges and universities also have a major role to play in creating the "next economy." The world of work c. 2050 will be different than that of today and not likely in the way that most people think. Stripping away jobs from those of average skills will lead to a growing and disenchanted underclass—marginally employed and poor people—on one hand and an *uber*-class of highly skilled specialists with the ability to capitalize on real opportunities on the other. But there is no simple path to the new economic order, one that holds possibilities for people across the spectrum of ability, preparation, and motivation. Most of the commentators on the evolving world of work in the age of advanced technologies speak optimistically of income-redistribution systems that will enable the unemployed and underemployed to keep their heads above water financially—a centre-left fantasy that is, sadly, highly unlikely to emerge. And even if the job situation comes right over time—a decade? two decades?—workers, companies, and the overall economy will experience dramatic dislocations and hardship in the process.

Adjusting to the new realities will take an enormous amount of work and creativity. Researchers, thinkers, planners, and policy-makers, working closely with the entire post-secondary education system, have to come up with strategies that create jobs, opportunities, and good futures for the youth of today and tomorrow. North America has done well at producing jobs and protecting many—but not all—of its citizens from penury. But we have ignored the warning signs for years. From the 1960s to the twenty-first century, family incomes were protected primarily by the conversion of one-income families into two-income families. Save for a return to nineteenth-century child labour or the widespread adoption of polygamy, adding more family members to the employment pool is not going to happen. The rise of underemployment, the "gig" workforce, contingent or short-term labour, multiple part-time jobs, returning to live at home with parents, and other strategies have papered over the public awareness of the fundamental shifts that are occurring.

Like addicts hooked on never-ending enrolment growth and seemingly limitless public adoration, colleges and universities will have to adjust to the new economic and employment conditions. There is enough evidence of young people, parents, and companies using alternative strategies that it seems clear that major changes are underway. Foot-dragging is common among these institutions, if only because so many see a focus on career-readiness as an attack on their central mandate. Come the revolution, as our left-leaning colleagues say, the prospect looms that universities could find themselves marginalized, looking in on the rapid and global transformation of learning, training, and employment.

7

STRATEGIES FOR YOUTH SUCCESS

We return to a vital question: "What do we tell our kids?" Families face the prospect of adjusting to rapidly changing educational, employment, and economic realities, while still being bombarded with old-economy messages about the *Earning = Learning* model and the primacy of universities as the universal pathway to prosperity. For the rest—and we argue that that cohort is close to 75 percent of young people—college is not the best choice, even in a strong economic environment. Three-quarters! It hardly seems possible, but remember that at least half who start don't finish, and a significant part of those who do finish don't get the result they hoped for.

What makes this issue so difficult is that as a society we reach into the past for lessons and strategies and are much less aware of future dangers and possibilities. Parents who went through university or college in the 1970s and 1980s, who found middle-class opportunities and discovered the "good life," are reluctant to criticize the system that brought them such opportunity. As they canvass their social network, however, they learn of friends and colleagues who have been downsized or who have had to opt for multiple, contingent jobs. Everyone knows someone—perhaps many people—who are now earning less than they did a decade ago because of the economic fallout from the financial collapse, the devastation of the housing fiasco in the USA, the 2008 recession, and subsequent economic challenges. The belief continues to grow that the current generation of young people is likely to have a lower standard of living than their parents—surely a fundamental family nightmare. In these times of great uncertainty, parents are far more likely to support their Dream Factory— which produced good results in the past—rather than what they see as fanciful and flaky initiatives, allegedly adapted to the possibilities for the twenty-first-century economy. But they are wrong to do so.

North America's growing college obsession, including a sharp increase in the number of parents setting aside money for their children's education, is evident in a recent pre-movie advertisement for a college savings plan shown in theaters in the fall of 2015. Great visuals, ominous anticipatory music, attractive actors. The message was direct. Lily, off screen, was studying hard, determined, and talented. But she needed help. Fortunately, she had wise and thoughtful parents who understood the importance of planning financially for her future. In the last scene, the camera pulls back to show Lily on the couch, reading on her iPad, alert, bright, and attractive. Lily, heaven help us, is about eight years old. Apparently it's never too soon to start obsessing about Dream Factories.

Enough already. Lily and millions like her have lives to lead before they start worrying about college. While super-bright children can be readily identified early on, we know far too little about work ethic, curiosity, emotional abilities, and specific talents to think we can determine at that age who is college material and who isn't. We do know that not all students can handle even the basic requirements of a rigorous university, highly technical or professional program of study, even if the challenge rests more with upbringing, education, and work ethic than basic intelligence. Of course, almost all parents think that their children can and should go to university, producing a self-replicating cycle that feeds on itself and that generates endless preoccupation with university attendance. You won't have much luck finding an advertisement that speaks positively about community colleges, apprenticeship programs, entrepreneurship, or other post–high school options, except those put out by those institutions themselves.

The problem is that the relentless beat of institutional messaging (if you love your child, you will bankrupt yourself to get her into an elite school), government pronouncements (the fate of Western civilization and the economy appears to be tied to the number of young adults who go to university), and parental aspirations (your children have to go to college if you want them to get ahead). Look what this has produced: too many students in the wrong programs, too many dropping out, too many having difficulty finding decent jobs, mounting student debt, millions of "failures to launch," and a generation suffering from a widespread disconnect from the workforce. Families need new strategies for the twenty-first century, ones that place university and college in their right perspective and that focus on the emerging and long-term possibilities for education, training, work, and prosperity in a rapidly changing world.

As we were writing this book, the following news flash was circulated by *Inside Higher Education*, an excellent online source for the latest developments in post-secondary education:

80 Colleges Plan Major Reforms in Admissions

Eighty leading colleges and universities are today announcing a plan to reverse a decades-long process by which colleges have—largely through the Common Application—made their applications increasingly similar.

Further, the colleges and universities are creating new online portfolios for high school students, designed to have ninth graders begin thinking more deeply about what they are learning or accomplishing in high school, to create new ways for college admissions officers, community organizations and others to coach them, and to emerge in their senior years with a body of work that could be used to help identify appropriate colleges and apply to them. Organizers of the new effort hope it will minimize some of the disadvantages faced by high school students without access to well-staffed guidance offices or private counselors.

While the goals of the effort are ambitious, so are the resources and clout of the colleges today announcing this campaign. These colleges include every Ivy League university, Stanford University and the University of Chicago; liberal arts colleges such as Amherst, Swarthmore and Williams Colleges; and leading public institutions such as the Universities of Michigan, North

Carolina at Chapel Hill and Virginia. The 80 members expect more institutions to join.

While they aim to create a new way for students to apply, they also hope that the portfolio system they create prods changes in high school education that could have an impact beyond those who apply to these institutions.

This initiative, while worthy at some levels, is symptomatic of everything that is wrong with our college-obsessed environment. These elite institutions, which already reject 85 to 95 percent of applicants, are asking parents, teenagers, teachers, and counsellors to institutionalize their efforts to get young people into an elite school. The idea that kids in grade nine should be "thinking more deeply about what they are learning or accomplishing in high school" is unhelpful and more than a little dispiriting. They should be studying the periodic table, developing math skills, and learning to write properly. They should not be focusing on how they can prepare an application to one of the world's elite schools—a goal that only a tiny percentage of them will ever realistically reach and, even more important, one that is not necessarily the best educational and career preparation choice for the vast majority of students.

Here is the headline and story that we would like to see—but don't hold your breath:

Governments, Employers, and Post-Secondary Institutions Combine to Provide Real-World Educational, Training, and Employment Advice

In a stunning reversal of existing educational trends and processes, a consortium of government agencies, major employers, and post-secondary institutions have combined to create an online, user-friendly tool that will help young people and their families make educated decisions about their high school and post-secondary options.

"We have come to realize," states the prospectus for *Career-Ready for the Twenty-first Century* (CR21C), "that the national preoccupation with colleges and universities is not preparing young people adequately for the challenges of the modern workforce. We realize that employers are not happy with the skills of many newly hired graduates and that young people and their parents are increasingly apprehensive and obsessive about the transition to an uncertain and unfriendly job market."

The new online service is based on a frank assessment of individual abilities, preferences, and career-readiness. It matches a young person's educational track record, core competencies, residential preferences, and career expectations (including salary) to real-world job opportunities and the employment standards of major companies. The service focuses on meeting the needs of young people, in a clear and unvarnished manner, and is not designed as a recruiting tool for educational institutions.

As Donald Trumpetter, a leading advocate for educational reform and a spokesperson for the five thousand largest employers in North America, said, "Employers find that young people, regardless of degree, have unrealistic and inaccurate notions about the world of work. To the degree that the pursuit of employment is an objective, the students need to be much more aware of the competitive and rapidly changing nature of work."

While CR21C provides educational and employment advice for students, it goes much further. The online program provides a comprehensive assessment of basic core competencies; mini-tests imbedded in the system provide alerts to young people, parents, and teachers of serious deficiencies. For example, students whose answers to questions betray significant writing problems will not be able to proceed with the system, but will instead be strongly urged to seek remedial writing help. Participating companies have worked with the system designers to integrate employment-specific questions for students who have indicated an interest in their field of work. Students who do particularly well on these

imbedded and hidden tests may be offered training positions with the companies, even before they graduate
from high school.

We will not see this approach to career-readiness, but we should—or
at least something like it. The current over-promotion of college admission has blurred the vision of several generations. The new system pro-
posed by the eighty elite colleges is worse than what we have now: it will
tie the dreams of tens of thousands of young people and their parents
to universities that are already overflowing with well-qualified students.
But *nihil desperandum*, as the surprisingly large number of American
high school students who study Latin will tell you. (One hundred and
forty-nine thousand took the National Latin Exam in 2007.) Given the
unlikelihood of a coordinated approach to student preparation and
career-focused education, there are still strategies and opportunities for
young people looking to find their personal Dream Factory and to avoid
following the swarm into a system that, whatever its many strengths, has
serious deficiencies.

KNOW YOUR CHILDREN AND BE HONEST WITH THEM

In the age of social media, helicopter parents, the self-esteem obsession,
parental overload, career angst, and educational chaos, parents have lost
their critical faculties when it comes to their children. Put aside families
mired in poverty, who struggle to provide basic support for their children,
and focus on the majority, who are seeking positive futures for their teenagers. With the celebration of youth achievements and the formal education system's abandonment of excellence as a priority and competition as
a means of achieving excellence, the challenge of preparing teenagers for
the future falls back on the parents' shoulders. It is hard to remember that,
only thirty years ago, families left the effort to push teenagers to succeed
to the school system, typically to the teachers and administrators, who
believed firmly in excellence. With the pursuit of collective mediocrity
overtaking the commitment to demonstrable achievement, families now
have to make the decisions and do the planning themselves.

Parents need to be serious about evaluating their children's potential. By definition, half of all children are below average; not all of them can achieve great things. Certainly, they are unlikely to succeed as adults if they are not expected to make real commitments to learning and personal development at an early time. Parents actually know, if they are honest, how their kids are doing. They know if their teenagers are reading (and reading something more serious than the *Hunger Games* books). They know if they have good study habits, if they have truly applied themselves, and if they are capable of hard work.

CONSIDER EDUCATIONAL ALTERNATIVES

The wide-ranging critique of public education in the United States (and, to a much lesser extent, so far, in Canada) is founded on both the failure to provide proper educational opportunities to the poor and marginalized and the inability to challenge the best students to achieve their very best. The mediocre performance of American teenagers in the global Programme for International Student Assessment (PISA) educational rankings is an indictment of the US education system.[1]

Consider what the 2012 PISA report said of the USA, which outspends many nations that do considerably better on the tests given to fifteeen-year-olds in the OECD countries:

> Among the 34 OECD countries, the United States performed below average in mathematics in 2012 and is ranked 27th (this is the best estimate, although the rank could be between 23 and 29 due to sampling and measurement error). Performance in reading and science are both close to the OECD average. The United States ranks 17 in reading (range of ranks: 14 to 20) and 20 in science (range of ranks: 17 to 25). There has been no significant change in these performances over time.[2]

This is a miserable performance, well below the achievements of Japan, Finland, South Korea, Shanghai (which is best seen as a country-equivalent rather than being buried in China's massive student population), and other leading educational countries.

Let down by an education system that seems to obsess more about teachers' rights than educational achievement—although, to be fair, governments are constantly debating educational outcomes instead of taking steps to address the shortcomings of the current classrooms—parents are on their own. Many are finding other educational avenues, often at considerable expense. For the well-to-do, many of whom fight for places in the best preschools, the best kindergartens, and the best elementary and high schools, the financial challenge is simply a precursor to planned expenditures on college and university. Children have become a major expense item for parents, more so than in the past, with education seen as a significant investment.

One result has been a rapid expansion in private-school education. According to the Council for American Private Education—the "Voice of America's Private Schools"—privately operated schools accounted for almost a quarter of all schools in the USA, with almost 5.3 million students in 2011–2012. Equally important, the fastest-growing sector of the private-school system were nonreligious schools, representing almost 20 percent of the total.[3] This means there are more than thirty thousand private schools across the country, many advertising their commitment to school discipline and higher educational standards. This option is, of course, not available to people of modest means, but the fact of its growth shows how desperate parents can be. Other parents have gone further, removing their children from organized schools and providing home-schooling instead. By 2011 over 1.77 million students were educated at home—over 3 percent of the total school-age enrolment—under the supervision of their parents. Current estimates put the figure at about 2.2 million.

There are many reasons parents send their children to private institutions or teach them at home. The issues are often religious and social in nature: recently, in Ontario, Islamic students were withdrawn when public schools introduced a sex-education course. Public schools can be strained, occasionally even unsafe, environments. But for a significant percentage of the parents, educational quality is a key motive, even though the cost of an elite elementary and high school can equal college tuition. At one level, however, parents paying attention to educational standards and encouraging their children to succeed academically is a sign that some parents are taking extra steps to ensure their teenagers are properly prepared for the future.

ADAPT TO THE WORLD OF DIGITAL LEARNING

In a provocative and balanced book called *The End of College: Creating the Future of Learning and the University of Everywhere*, Kevin Carey highlighted the growing importance of digital education as an alternative to standard and expensive college experience. With digital delivery systems, learners could take short up-skilling courses, maintain constant contact with advanced education, combine work and education, and otherwise adapt learning to the person rather than forcing the individual to respond to institutional priorities, structures, and programs. Students have an opportunity to develop digital learning skills—which are different from standard learning styles and require more self-discipline and focus—while in high school and to refine these abilities over the rest of their lifetimes. While the digital education system is uneven and still somewhat experimental, the reality is that continued improvements, greater choice, delivery refinements, and the further integration of learning and employment will give digital learning a major boost. As Carey suggests, "Enrolment in the University of Everywhere will be lifelong, a fundamental aspect of modern living. Instead of checking into a single college for a few years on the cusp of adulthood, people will form relationships with learning organizations that last decades based on their personal preferences, circumstances, and needs. Unlike today, belonging to a learning organization will not involve massive expenses and crippling amounts of debt."[4]

At present, the preoccupation of parents, students, and governments is with credentials—evidence of the completion of a program of studies: the credential is more important than the students' actual learning. (In professionally accredited programs, the credential does demonstrate that a certain skill set has been acquired.) To the degree that the focus is on learning/knowledge and skills/competency, certainly these can be achieved outside the formal university environment. It is also clear that new digital systems do enhance learning opportunities and do allow for maximum flexibility. Of course, there is an old technology—called the book—that also allows for independent learning and the development of impressive skills and abilities, albeit without the interactivity and technological assistance available through computer-assisted learning systems.

AVOID THE COLLEGE OBSESSION

Dinner-table conversations play a crucial role in young adults' educational preparation and planning. When parents obsess about colleges—going beyond reminiscing about their youthful experiences and talking about what the family is sacrificing to save for the children's college tuition, discussing the application experiences of neighbouring kids, and debating the admission standards of various elite schools—they establish a clear baseline for their teenagers' educational planning.

Our suggestions here run counter to standard American practice, which emphasizes college to the detriment of all other alternatives. The net effect is to put college or university on a pedestal and to turn other choices—community college, apprenticeships, entrepreneurship, and so on—into lower-quality options. Parents can support their children by attending job fairs and focusing on the outcomes of advanced training rather than the educational inputs. They can explore, ideally together, the quirky and complicated world of work.

Focusing on the future of work rather than college, which is after all only a way-station on the path to adult life, will get both teenagers and parents emphasizing what is important. Students who become convinced and excited about a specific job or career are likely to pay greater attention to their academic preparation and, if appropriate, their college studies.

LEARN WHAT WORKS

In individualized North American society, conversation focuses far more on personal attributes than on group performance. That focus strips away valuable and important facts about what works in terms of preparation for the future. We know, for example, that teenagers raised in poverty struggle to succeed academically and encounter difficulties making the transition to the world of work. As Robert Putnam has shown in *Our Kids*, the odds are stacked against young people who experience trauma, live in difficult circumstances, attend substandard schools, or otherwise come from the large and growing American underclass.

But what works on the downside also works at the other end of the spectrum. There are certain groups who show extraordinary levels of achievement, not because of who they are, but because, like the underclass, of where they come from. Without taking anything away from the individual effort involved, the collective experience of certain subgroups of American society suggests that there are other characteristics that are important to determining success. The remarkable academic achievements of Asian Americans are a case in point: if enrolment at the University of California-Berkeley was based entirely on high school performance instead of partly on racial quotas, the percentage of Asian Americans in the incoming class would rise substantially. Their experience, in turn, reflects the commitment of Asian families to academic achievement, the sharp focus on mathematics and science, and a parent-sustained work ethic that underpins the drive to succeed.

Members of the target group do not need to be reminded of the key values and human characteristics of high achievers. These crucial

ACT'S ANNUAL SCORE REPORT SHOWS RACIAL GAPS, MEDIOCRE SCORES

A record 1.84 million high school students who graduated in 2014 took the college readiness test—suggesting that more young people have college in their sights. But for many test-takers, succeeding in postsecondary education might be an empty hope. Average scores remain stagnant. Only 39 percent of test-takers met three or more of the ACT's college readiness benchmarks in English, math, reading and science—a percentage that's unchanged from last year. And striking racial gaps persist. As in previous years, African Americans and Latinos scored much lower, on average, than their Asian-American and white peers …

On the benchmarks, Asian-American test-takers did best, with 57 percent meeting three or more. Forty-nine percent of white test-takers met three or more standards—compared to 23 percent of Latino test-takers and 11 percent of African-American test-takers. African Americans scored lowest on the test. Just 10 percent of African-American students who were tested met the science benchmark.[5]

elements are inculcated at a young age and sustained throughout their lives by group pressure and encouragement. In *The Triple Package,* Amy Chua and Jed Rubenfeld argue that the there is a darker side to the pattern of success, including extreme pressure to succeed that can strip the joy from childhood, a desire to break out of the group consensus, psychological challenges associated with exceptional personal demands, distrust of nonmembers, and a preoccupation with being socially conventional.

People who are not members of a Triple Package group can, at an individual and family level, still have the characteristic sense of superiority, insecurity, and impulse control. The sense of superiority, while entrenched within select cultural groups, can be individual in nature. Insecurity, in contrast to the beliefs of the educational establishment, is a strong motivation to work hard and improve one's achievements. High achievers know how to defer gratification in the interest of long-term success. These characteristics can occur, equally, within a family that promotes achievement while highlighting vulnerability and the need to suppress unproductive urges. But when an individual or family share these qualities—and there are many that do and that achieve impressive results—they do so without collective support and group pressure. If nothing else, however, it should help nongroup members to appreciate the qualities that drive other people—their competitors for the best educational places and best career opportunities.

PURSUE EXCELLENCE

It is clear that the achievement of excellence in one area of life can carry over to another. Given the importance of young people learning the relationship between effort and personal outcome, and given that this basic formula is no longer prominent or assured in the school system, it is vital that families find opportunities for excellence in other pursuits. Of course, the hard-driving, often intense promotion of high achievement that was once part of general education still survives other fields. Sports coaches, music teachers, and dance instructors, among others (try a martial arts class if you want real intensity), produce intense learning experiences. They insist on extensive practice and repetition and have extremely high expectations for top performers. They push their charges into competitive situations and make it clear that success is the primary or only option.

ENSURE COMPETENCE

Parents by the millions have come to realize the challenges of personal achievement and educational preparation. Many are not waiting for the school system to adapt and modernize—and to produce outcomes comparable to those of Finland, Taiwan, and South Korea—or are taking matters into their own hands. After-school programming is nothing new. Japan's impressive educational outcomes have long been tied to the *juku* (cram) schools, which students attend religiously throughout their school years. There are comparable services across Asia, with millions of Chinese students attending after-hours English classes and other forms of academic or university preparation.

For generations, the excellent North American education system provided enough preparation to ensure continued academic and professional success. But the weakening of American schools, and to a lesser degree Canadian ones, has forced some parents to seek extracurricular help for their children. Knowing that competence underlies all plans for long-term success, and knowing that the school system in many communities is failing to provide adequate preparation, parents opt for private-sector competence-building programs. Commercial ventures such as Kumon, Sylvan Learning Centres, and Oxford Learning Centres have attracted millions of participants, with the number of centres and enrolled students skyrocketing alongside dissatisfaction with public education and the perceived competition to get into top schools.

Deciding to use the extra learning services represents a deliberate family response—certainly not the kids'—to the challenges of competition in the modern age. It is hardly surprising that Asian American families are significantly overrepresented in the learning centre classes, reinforcing the reality that certain socio-cultural groups are predisposed to make an extra effort to get their children a head start on the competitions of adulthood. In this instance, the extra homework is designed to ensure that young people have the basic skills sought by employers and top schools, giving them a leg up on the competition.

UNDERSTAND THE CHANGING NATURE OF WORK

While much parental effort focuses on getting children into the right schools, achieving the highest marks, and securing a place in the best colleges or specialized programs, much less effort is devoted to exploring the uncertain future of work and the economy. The average family should take at least half of the effort that they currently expend on planning for college admissions and devote it to understanding the evolution of employment. Right now, there is a massive industry in college guides, application manuals, college and university ratings systems, and the overproduction of materials designed to help students and families select the best institution for their children. Parents have a huge amount of information at their fingertips, plus counsellors, guides, and advisors to help navigate the byzantine world of college admissions, all because of the facile and oversold *Learning = Earning* formula.

It is vital that families, with young people fully engaged, pay more attention instead to the evolving North American and global economy. Unless families have a good sense of the contemporary economy and a reasonable appreciation of the future prospects, it is difficult to plan properly for their children's education, training, and career strategies. The future is a complicated place, filled with uncertainty. The certainties of the present evaporate with shocking speed, spoiling the best plans of thousands of young people.

Five years ago, every guidance counsellor in North American would have confidently advised a science-based student to consider a career in petroleum engineering or a related field. With surging global demand and prices, and the opening of massive continental oil and gas fields, jobs in oil, gas, and infrastructure were readily available. Tens of thousands of young people, learning of the high-paying and readily available jobs, headed off to college, university, community college, or technical institutes, preparing themselves for good careers. This was a classic example of how best to prepare for the future: check the economy, look where jobs are readily available, get the right education or training, and be flexible as to work location. Young people who followed this strategy appeared to be headed for carefully planned, well-deserved career success, including a high income, steady work, and long-term prospects.

Look what happened next. Prices and demand collapsed because of a surge in global supply, alternative energy supplies, and conservation efforts. President Obama, after protracted waffling, killed the Keystone Pipeline and with it thousands of jobs. Oil and gas field projects slowed dramatically, eliminating thousands of additional positions. Service and supply companies followed suit, further eroding the employment base in what had been a dynamic and expanding field of work. Students who graduated after 2010 hoping for oil and gas work were bitterly disappointed, as opportunities and high wages dried up with shocking speed. Remember that these were the students who did everything right—looking forward, planning carefully, and being career-focused and academically careful.

This was not the first time a generation of college graduates and well-trained young people aimed for work in a specialized field, only to have the proverbial rug pulled out from underneath them. A wave of computer science and computer technicians, drawn to the industry by the excitement and euphoria of the dot.com boom, found themselves scrambling for jobs in the spectacular bust that followed. Only a few years later, the grotesque and uncontrolled expansion of the American financial sector during the subprime fraud drew thousands of young people into the industry, looking for the six-figure jobs that had been dangled in front of them by high-risk financial firms looking for an advantage. Here, too, the plans were awry. The paper-thin underpinnings of the real estate market, propped up on a fraudulent pastiche of self-delusion and institutional excess, destroyed several of the world's largest financial firms, many smaller companies, and tens of thousands of high-paying jobs.

In both of these cases, and in many other local or regional examples, young people had the opportunity to monitor the expansion of a particular sector. They could see the opportunities—high-wage, quick-hire jobs on offer—and could see the route to career success: get out of high school, secure a proper training in a related firm, send out resumés, and settle in quickly to a high-pressure, high-income career. The media celebrated the employment tsunami, telling endless stories of college recruiting manias, high starting salaries, salubrious working conditions, and constant job jumping. The computer science explosion and the financial euphoria provided proof positive of the *Learning = Earning* college promise, with universities promoting the wonderful career prospects that awaited.

Given all this, parents and young adults have to do the best that they can to prepare themselves for future uncertainty. There is no magic bullet. Learning does not automatically equal earning. Lining up for current opportunities is no assurance that the jobs will be there in a few years' time, as many have learned to their bitter disappointment. New technologies are ravaging the world of work, creating some new openings, and eliminating many existing jobs. Making sense of it all is difficult, and the search for an easy and simple answer is going to prove elusive. The short answer about the future is that no one knows what lies ahead. Is it really possible that technology will eliminate thousands of medical jobs? Will remote surgery replace surgeons? And what about law and accounting? It is happening in retail. Will it come to the transportation sector? What new jobs will emerge?

Parents should follow market trends as best they can, realizing that there are no easy answers and no easy assurances of what lies ahead. Families trying to identify an easy road forward for their children will find the task elusive and fraught with confusing messages and misunderstandings. Two recent books—*The Second Machine Age: Work, Progress, and Prosperity in a Time of Brilliant Technologies* by Andrew McAfee and Erik Brynjolfsson and *The Coming Jobs War* by Jim Clifton—explore the uncertainty but, distressingly, provide little in the way of a prescription for young adults charting their future. These books—like *Dream Factories*, perhaps—do a better job of identifying the problem than of offering sage advice and certainty. Families must become future-watchers if they want to help their children prepare for the uncertain prospects that lie ahead, for young adults, college graduates, and society as a whole.

CAREER PLANNING FOR DISADVANTAGED FAMILIES

It goes without saying that the path to success is much easier for the wealthy and privileged—and even for the middle class—than for people of lower socio-economic background. Although North America remains a land of some opportunity, particularly for immigrants, the reality is that millions of Americans and Canadians are locked in place, seemingly doomed by the circumstances of their parents to live lives of poverty and marginalization. It seems grossly unfair that so many young adults—African Americans, Hispanic Americans, Indigenous peoples, and others—having been raised in harsh circumstances must face so many challenges in breaking out of the cycle of poverty.

There are, of course, more than a few individual success stories, typically celebrating a remarkable parent (often a single mother) or parents who propel their children forward by sheer love and willpower, or in some cases, young people who do pull themselves up by their proverbial bootstraps. The impressiveness of these accomplishments masks the fact that the vast majority do not climb the class ladder. They lack the basic skills to capitalize on higher educational and training opportunities; family wealth to protect against despair and fund ambitions; and are constrained by the structural limitations of race, ethnicity, and social class.

In these situations, disadvantaged families have to capitalize on every opportunity in order to create future success. Aligning themselves with a sympathetic teacher, a coach, a music instructor, or some other agent of excellence and achievement is an excellent route out. There is nothing better than a mentor to help teenagers in a disadvantaged setting overcome their circumstances. There are programs available for young people at risk, but the challenges of overcoming economic and family circumstances are very real. Unless our governments put social welfare supports in place to help poor and disadvantaged young people, the economic uncertainty and coming workplace changes will fall disproportionately on them alone.

GUIDING THE YOUNG IN AN UNCERTAIN WORLD

There are no easy solutions for the workplace dilemmas that face today's young adults. There are promising elements, to be sure. The ongoing retirement of the Baby Boomers—the oldest are about to turn seventy—has the potential to unlock hundreds of thousands of rewarding careers and middle-management jobs. The Boomers are holding on longer than people expected, as they struggle with their own uncertainties, but they will go one way or another, and sooner rather than later. The shift from an industrial to a service economy, with mushrooming growth in the care of the elderly, creates many openings. If the current situation holds into the future, it seems likely that job prospects for young adults whose specialized skills align with specific workforce needs will remain strong. Professional graduates will do much better than general Arts and Science students, particularly in the academic fields that are regulated by external agencies and that regulate enrolment. It is also likely that college graduates will do better, statistically, than those without a degree. The extent to which a college degree is responsible for the difference remains a matter of dispute, because family advantages count for a lot as do higher intelligence and work effort. But, when an employer is faced with a choice between a college graduate and a high school graduate, the former will generally win, even if the work does not require a university degree. Families will respond to uncertainty by doubling down on their investments in education, college preparation and selection, and university tuition. Complexity and uncertainty generate conservative responses, not creativity. It is vital that families examine opportunities more broadly, based on a realistic appraisal of what their teenagers are capable of achieving.

Blue-collar work—including the trades—holds continuing promise. At present, parents and families generally have discouraged young people from considering the full range of opportunities, just as certainly as the exaggeration of teenagers' academic abilities and the downplaying of practical and technical skills blinds them to their realistic prospects.

With this in mind, parents need to provide a consistent introduction, inside and outside their family, to the value of work and the importance of paying one's own way. The current pattern of insulating teenagers from the realities of life, financial and employment-related, only hurts them in the long run. Developing a solid track record of reliability, steadily increasing opportunities, and a strong work ethic is crucial to long-term success in the workplace. Employers do not want to teach young people how to work. Parents should also ensure that their children develop math and science skills to the highest level that fits with their capabilities. We know that technology, digitalization, and computers will drive the future; we are not likely to return to a future driven by manual labour and skilled craftspeople. Young adults who hide behind a smartphone or a video terminal but who do not develop more advanced technical and scientific skills will find themselves at a severe disadvantage in the workplace of the 2020s and 2030s. Technological literacy, based on keeping a watching brief on emerging and evolving systems, is going be seen as a key employment skill.

And while thinking of all this, you might want to keep in mind what one source calls the "five most over-rated degrees." These are:

1. Psychology

Because "helping people is exhausting," and you may spend your career helping others for very little pay. This seems awfully selfish, doesn't it?

2. Studio Art

In 2012, the unemployment rate for recent grads with fine arts degrees was 12.6%, and recent graduates make about $30,000 a year. But if you love art, perhaps you won't care, and good for you.

3. Education

Teaching is stressful, and American teachers are woefully underpaid. Like #1, it's a labour of love.

4. Hospitality

Hospitality management has an unemployment rate of 9.1% for recent grads and 5.7% for experienced grads. Yearly earnings for recent grads average at $32,000 and $53,000 for experienced grads. Hospitality is certainly not the worst choice, but it's also not as solid a career path as you may think.

5. Fashion Design

Fashion design is another degree option that sounds fun and exciting. As with studio art, everyone has a passion for it, and almost no one is getting hired. You're more likely to end up working in retail than as an actual

fashion designer. Most up and coming designers need a
lot of start-up capital to begin a career on their own.[6]

The future of work is shrouded in mystery, and it will be difficult for
young people to navigate a world that increasingly looks dramatically different from that of their parents and grandparents. The current strategy
of directing young people to college and university in the hope that four
years of advanced education will provide direction fails on many fronts.
Many young people do poorly at university and leave without a credential.
Many others know as little about their career plans when they graduate as
they did when they started. A large number circulate back to a community college to get a practical training. And the promises of degrees seemingly perfectly aligned with the modern economy often prove illusory.

8

CONFRONTING THE DREAM INDUSTRY

North America is in many ways still a land of promise, a promoter's dream. Travelling across the country is in places like driving through a massive industrial zone, filled with get-rich-quick opportunities of many sizes, shapes, and purposes. From Powerball lotteries promising instant millionaires to the tawdry excesses of Las Vegas and Atlantic City, from the once-impressive American stock market and finance sector to the Russian roulette of college football, the USA provides endless opportunities for the average person to fantasize about a future of wealth and freedom.

The belief in the inevitability of prosperity—for most defined as middle- or even upper-class wealth—is profoundly engrained in American life. We saw this operating during the dot.com boom, when everyone with programming skills believed they would be the next Steve Jobs or Bill Gates, and in the ridiculous chaos of the American subprime housing market. How else can you explain a world where people with $20,000-a-year incomes saw nothing wrong in signing up for a $600,000 home, only to be forced out in humiliation when interest-rate reality hit? Or the others, with bigger incomes, who saw nothing wrong in lending them the money? This is, after all, the country where bankruptcy is as much a rite of passage as a sign of fiscal incompetence.

In this context, rolling the dice on a university education makes sense. People are willing to gamble on real estate, in the marketplace, and with their private businesses, to say nothing of lottery tickets and the gaming tables. Why wouldn't they gamble with a few years of their kids' lives? Even if college does not work out for everyone, it works for many. Why not invest four years and a couple of hundred thousand dollars on your children in the hope that they will find their feet academically and get a golden ticket to medical school, make friends with the next new age billionaire, marry brilliantly and into money, make the basketball team and the NBA, or any of the other unlikely miracles that are available to those few who play the game successfully. The dream of prosperity in the next river valley, across the mountain, in the next industry, or through a trip to the patent office is as American as apple pie, baseball, and the agony of the electoral system.

AMERICANS GAMBLE, CANADIANS HEDGE THEIR BETS

Canada, a country more cautious and risk-averse than its southern neigh-bour, is in many respects quite different. Most Canadian students go to a university close to home. The American pattern of applying across the coun-try and travelling on lengthy campus visits is not common in Canada. The country's publicly funded universities (there are almost no private ones) are mostly of good quality, with several of them in the top two hundred world-wide. While the country has lotteries (run by the government) and low-end gambling, it is not a risk-taking nation; it brags more about the security of its financial institutions than the success of its entrepreneurs. Where America celebrates quirky individualists, Canadians are more fond of mod-eration. Canada has its own minor-league Donald Trump—Rob Ford, the ex-mayor of Toronto—but his type doesn't last long in this country.

Canadians, as a consequence, do not dream the same college dream as Americans do. They do not head to leading institutions like McGill or the University of Toronto on the off-chance that they might rub shoulders with new generation superstars (although the writer Malcolm Gladwell and the Blackberry co-founder Jim Balsillie were in residence together at University of Toronto). They go for the Canadian promise: a solid educa-tion and a chance at a middle-class job, preferably with the federal gov-ernment, one of the country's large banks, or a major company. "Middle managers are us" is the Canadian mantra. Canadians love to plan, not dream, have moderate expectations of life, and focus, from an early age, on a unionized job, a decent wage, secure health care and a nice pension. The Canadian mantra does not get the heart pumping in the way that the American fantasy life does, but it matches a country of cold winters, sober lives, and a preoccupation with consensus.

These contrasting approaches have, however, led to roughly similar outcomes—American and Canadian high school graduates in the hundreds of thousands heading to college or university—with somewhat different thought processes backing up their decisions. For Canadians, a university education is a safe choice, providing the promise of entry into one of the nation's historical middle-class career streams. Americans, it seems, view college differently, like some grand lottery where the odds are best at the elite schools and less favourable as you travel down the institutional hierarchy. The reality of university outcomes—with substantial dropout rates, high unemployment rates, and serious problems with underemployment—suggests that the lottery odds are getting longer in the USA and the middle-class career paths are tightening up in Canada.

There is growing understanding—among analysts in the field rather than politicians and parents—that the college and university dream is eroding quickly. And Philip Lauder and his colleagues argued:

> [T]he American Dream needs to be reclaimed as people struggle to live the promise of education, jobs, and rising incomes. Occupational change over the last century has been remarkable. However, the idea that a global job market would accelerate the demand for highly paid knowledge workers and that Americans would monopolize the best jobs and leave emerging economies to become the new workshops of the world has proved false. We now confront the prospect of a high-skill, low wage work force that poses a challenge to all affluent economies.
>
> The vast chasm between middle class aspirations and the realities of the global auction reflects an explosion in education and know-how and the growing capacity for hi-tech work in low-cost locations. The rise of digital Taylorism involves the translation of various

forms of knowledge work into working knowledge that can digitally distributed worldwide. The war for talent, which focused on the outstanding performance of a global elite of employees, leads to steeper income differentials between the best and the rest. For many, including well-qualified Americans, these trends have conspired to undermine the value of their human capital that promised individual prosperity and social justice.[1]

One of the most important books on the intersection of education, technological change and employment is Claudia Goldin and Lawrence Katz's *The Race Between Education and Technology*. We quote them at length here because their study speaks directly to the most fundamental challenges in the twenty-first century effort to connect education and work:

> [W]e have emphasized the existence of an ongoing and relentless race between technology and education. Economic growth and inequality are the outcomes of the contest. As technological change races forward, demands for skills—some new and some old—are altered. If the workforce can rapidly make the adjustment, then economic growth is enhanced without greatly exacerbating inequality of economic outcomes. If, on the other hand, the skills that are currently demanded are produced slowly and if the workforce is less flexible in its skill set, then growth is slowed *and* inequality widens. Those who can make the adjustments as well as those who gain the new skills are rewarded. Others are left behind ...
>
> Today skills, no matter how complex, that can be exported through outsourcing or offshoring are vulnerable ... having desired skills for which there are only imperfect (domestic or international) substitutes provides the greatest security.
>
> ... College is no longer the automatic ticket to success. Rather, degrees in particular fields and advanced

training in certain areas are now exceedingly important. Interpersonal skills, possibly garnered from being
in diverse college peer groups and interacting with educated people, also matter a lot. The general point today is
somewhat different from the past. No longer does having
a high school or a college degree make you indispensable,
especially if your skills can be imported or emulated by a
computer program.[2]

While we agree with much of what Goldin and Katz have written,
we would add a caveat. The range and diversity of jobs threatened by
technological change is much greater than they assumed less than a decade ago. Major innovations in health care, from "tricorder"-like devices
(do you remember Bones from *Star Trek*?) to medical supervision provided through cellphones or nanomedicine have raised questions about
the potential dislocations of traditional medical practices, including
those of doctors and nurses. To use one simple example, the widespread
introduction of autonomous vehicles—in use as buses in a Greek village,
widely tested on North American roads, and coming soon to the highway
near you—will have the fortunate side effect of reducing car accidents
dramatically, meaning that fewer trauma surgeons and emergency room
nurses will be required. This is not something a late-career medical professional needs to worry about, but fifteen-year-olds planning on becoming doctors might well find a much-diminished demand for their services
as oversupply—the kind of thing now holding back the life ambitions of
history and biology graduates—spills over into health care and medicine.

As Goldin and Katz make clear, a major challenge lies ahead. The
promises, to say nothing of the reality, of college and university graduation are sounding more hollow every year. Opportunities are still present.
Dream Factories do produce substantial numbers of winners, even if many
of them came into college with many life advantages. But the workforce
is changing, job prospects are drying up, and the disconnect between the
education system and the workplace appears to be growing larger. Young
people and families must face the challenges directly and calibrate their
strategies for twenty-first-century realities. But what are they to do, when
the *Learning = Earning* formula is such an unreliable guide?

The error of valuing credentials over specific skills persisted because it was so politically pleasing. Parents pushed for university access for their children and the young adults went along. Governments got credit for providing opportunities, not for enforcing high standards—an element of North American education that has been driving down the quality of learning and basic skills for several generations. University faculty, particularly those in the basic sciences, Humanities, and Social Sciences, lauded the benefits of a general liberal-arts education. Rampant individualism—allowing young people to make their own decisions—took priority over government objectives and workforce needs. And how can you enforce national standards in a country based on freedom of action and enterprise? As a result, colleges and universities based their program management on student preferences—which helps explain why business schools have expanded dramatically from the 1970s to the present—rather than on the demonstrated needs of the economy or the abilities of the young adult population in the country. The USA and Canada had over nine hundred thousand undergraduate business students in 2013, representing 70 percent of the world's total business school enrolment; a strong testament to the power of consumer-driven education. But why is there not a cap on the number of marketing, human resource, and other business professionals? And do the USA and Canada really need to produce such a massive (over)supply of graduates? One wonders, to be frank, if the business schools have examined their own textbooks and prepared their students for the stark reality that many will face.

In *The Education Apocalypse*, Glenn Reynolds offers a caustic view of the reality of college education:

> Right now, a college degree is an expensive signifier that its holder has a basic ability to show up on time (mostly), to follow instructions (reasonably well), and to deal with others in close quarters without committing serious felonies. In some fields, it may also indicate important background knowledge and skills, but most students will require further on-the-job training. An institution that could provide similar certification without requiring four (or more) years and a six-figure investment would have a

huge advantage, especially if employers found that certification to be a more reliable indicator of competence than a college degree. Couple that with apprenticeship programs or internships, and you might not need college for many careers. The major problem with this plan is that college now serves largely as a status marker, a sign of membership in the educated "caste," and as a place for people to meet future spouses of commensurate status ... At any rate, American culture at its best values people more for what they do than for their membership in a caste—and now seems like a good time to reassert that preference.[3]

So, blunt talk is required. The surge of college and university degree completion has not been matched by a maintenance of academic standards and, even less, by high-value career opportunities. This observation is anecdotal rather than systematic, because national education systems have not kept records of the academic standards of graduating students. We do not, for example, know the percentage of degree holders in the USA and Canada who are literate in English. (If you think the answer is all of them, prepare yourself for bitter disappointment.) Having a degree does not mean the person who holds it has mathematical literacy, advanced research skills, public speaking ability, or another "core competency."

Here lies a national dilemma. To be competitive in the twenty-first century, a nation needs, among such things as venture capital, an entrepreneurial culture, and technological infrastructure, more engineers, computer scientists, environmental scientists, and the like. It does not necessarily need huge numbers of undergraduate degree holders in psychology, chemistry, literature, or cultural studies, regardless of how fine an education these fields provide. The economy needs highly skilled workers, and the demand for specialists and technical expertise is about to grow dramatically. Mass education may be excellent for citizenship—though we might ask how well this is serving the United States these days, with its plummeting level of political engagement—but it does not meet the needs of the economy.

To shift to a twenty-first-century economy and a supportive college and university system, governments must transform the transition from education to employment. North American society is shifting from a preoccupation with advanced education and its increasingly uncertain promises of careers and incomes, to a sharpened focus on employment with its implicit assumptions about specialized training, a strong work ethic, and personal motivation. The shift is subtle in definition but vital in impact. In the first instance, the *Learning = Earning* formulation helped convince people that going to college would set them up for life. In the second instance, the needs of the workforce take precedence, and young adults face the difficult challenge of determining which programs, degrees, or institutions will impress potential employers. In the first situation, the focus is on the institution, broad access, and credentialling. In the second scenario, the emphasis is on competence and real ability.

As the workforce experiences continued and potentially dramatic shifts due to technological change and continued globalization, national governments will be tasked with aligning their education and training systems with the needs of the new economy. This will be particularly challenging in North America, where governments have surrendered educational decisions to the collective choices of high school graduates and their parents. Given that private institutions are extremely attuned to student interest, you can bet that they would offer degrees in Penguin Studies if there were sufficient demand. Public institutions, which operate under more pressure to align with employers' needs and workforce realities, still fight back with a vengeance against any government interference with academic decisions. Governor Scott Walker of Wisconsin faced vigorous resistance to what were, in the end, comparatively small changes in the post-secondary system.

Governments can deal with these changes in a number of ways. Rather than taking resources away from existing programs and institutions, something that is fraught with political danger, they can dribble funding into new programs. They can create new institutions, such at the University of Ontario Institute of Technology (near Toronto). Or they can let the market dictate which institution thrives and which shrinks, a policy that doesn't threaten Harvard, but speaks doom for some small liberal-arts colleges.

NEW UNIVERSITIES AND COLLEGES IN TRANSITION

A *Times Higher Education Supplement* list of the best new universities in the world ("new" meaning less than fifty years old), included the following: Pohang University of Science and Technology (South Korea), École polytechnique fédérale de Lausanne (Switzerland), Hong Kong University of Science and Technology, University of California–Irving, Korea Advanced Institute of Science and Technology, Université de Pierre et Marie Curie (France), University of California–Santa Cruz, University of York (UK), Lancaster University (UK), the University of Calgary, and University of East Anglia (UK).[4]

Interestingly, the new entrants from the USA, Canada, and the UK tend to be multiversities, offering the full range of academic programs. Those in other countries are almost all polytechnics, focusing on science and technology. The North American preference for traditional institutions creating new opportunities for poorly covered areas or poorly served populations is clearly in evidence—just as the pattern of creation of new institutions in the rest of the world has a decided science, technology, business, and employment orientation. So, faced with the pressure to create more spaces, American and Canadian governments tend to create additional seats at existing universities or to add universities that look pretty much like the ones already in operation. This approach is driven much more by student interest and parental priorities—accounting over nanotechnology, psychology over robotics—which in turn reflects that naïve North American belief that following one's dream and personal interests is an appropriate preparation for joining a turbulent and fast-changing workforce.

The transition in the North American workforce will likely unfold in two stages. The first—over the next decade or so—will involve a difficult and slow change from the twentieth-century economy and jobs market to the twenty-first-century model. For this time period, and following a pattern that is already well established, young people may continue to cherish the fact that the time they spent on their degree in the Arts and Sciences was interesting and enriching—if indeed it was. But increasingly they will have to take employment in other fields in order to pay the rent and buy groceries. Everyone knows smart and capable twenty- and thirty-somethings with BAs and BScs making their living as bartenders and assistant retail managers. This is the contemporary reality. As technological change continues to erode middle-class work and undercut opportunities for the average person, the pace and nature of employment will shift dramatically. In this next stage—the 2030s and beyond—the decline of familiar work will accelerate and the challenge of creating personal opportunities will become more acute. Adjusting the expectations of young adults and their parents to these new realities will be difficult, and creating real opportunities, training programs, and sustainable careers will be even harder.

There must be greater public understanding of workplace realities. Colleges and universities will need to become much more responsive to the job market, something that likely means a sharp reduction in general education, and an equally sharp increase in the skills, motivational and preparatory requirements for incoming students. Governments will need to focus on retraining for workers, including those displaced by continuing technological change. Companies will be challenged to rethink fundamental business models, including corporate commitments to the maintenance and retraining of their labour force. Governments will be forced to radically rethink their approaches to education, social welfare, and technological transitions. Everyone will have to reexamine the most fundamental assumptions they have about work, leisure, and the functioning of advanced technology.

The twenty-first century requires a reimagining of the prospects and pathways for young adults. Today's college and university graduates are, in large measure, ill-prepared for the economy of 2015. It hardly needs to be said that the young will, if they continue along the current trajectory, find themselves even further disengaged from the workforce in 2025 and 2035, never mind 2060, when today's undergraduates will begin to reach the traditional retirement age. There is nothing easy about what lies ahead. The anticipated technological revolution will likely cause disruptions far greater than the ones experienced to date. There is every possibility that substantial political and social unrest will follow continued labour force transitions. Providing for the future of the young is one of the most fundamental challenges and responsibilities of parents and society at large. The global preoccupation with colleges and universities has dampened rather than enhanced planning for the future of work.

There is no need to panic, but complacency and clinging to the status quo are also not the answers. The technologies that disrupt current work can create new areas of economic activity. The global economy that has destroyed many jobs, companies, and entire sectors has created additional opportunities and allowed for greater entrepreneurial creativity. Done properly—with the right kind of elementary and secondary education, adaptive college and university systems, new approaches to entrepreneurship, inventive business models, a heightened sense of individual responsibility and motivation, and the acceptance of individual responsibility for economic success—the young adults of today and tomorrow can be prepared for a fast-changing, technology-rich global economy. Sticking with the current approach to higher education will perpetuate and accelerate the high costs, employment challenges, and societal frustrations of the present. It will not do to dismantle the Dream Factories without creating something in their place. Young people need futures—they need dreams—but ones with some chance of becoming real.

Not surprisingly, the early signs of the transitions and the dislocations are already evident. Parents are worried, teenagers are anxious, and university graduates have adopted either the Alfred E. Neuman (*Mad* magazine) approach—"What? Me Worry?"—or share their parents' growing concerns. The ones who do not worry should. But on the other hand, not all of those who are getting educational ulcers should be concerned. Colleges and universities produce wonderful outcomes for the "right degree, right time" graduates: the finance grads before the 2008 stock market collapse, the electrical engineers working on emerging digital technologies, the geological engineers who graduated in the ten years before the 2014 oil and gas crash, the high-end design and animation graduates who seemed assured of opportunities a decade ago, and the medical doctors confidently believing that their future will always be prosperous.

But, of course, the finance grads endured a shocking downturn from 2008 to 2010; many newbies lost their jobs and their financial dreams. And the engineers who found great job prospects—many were offered jobs before graduation—in the Bakken field of North Dakota and the many shale gas and oil projects under development globally saw the doors slam shut in their faces when the energy layoffs started in earnest in 2015. The electrical engineers are still doing well, because the digital media sector grows, bends, twists, and reforms as high-end electronic solutions emerge in countless sectors. Will they be the next doctors in terms of high incomes and job security? Will doctors enjoy high salaries, impressive status, and continuing benefits if, as many predict, digital medicine takes hold? Who would have thought that the quirky FitBit, now a decent heart, sleep, and exercise monitor but soon to be your 24/7 doctor and nurse, would threaten the careers of the seemingly most secure and stable profession around?

Colleges and universities have become like many service industries. While there are many elements an older generation would have considered intellectually pure—scholars in pursuit of grand ideas, scientists looking for profound medical advances, devoted teachers caring for the intellectual and social development of their students, counsellors eager to assist with the transition from the academy to the world of work—the primary reality is that these are important, often very large institutions that are concerned, first and foremost, with their own survival and growth. They, like all organizations, have bills to pay and responsibilities to meet. They have to pay faculty and staff, maintain expensive buildings, support research, and contribute to the world of ideas. And students are their primary source of income.

Most of us have the idea that colleges are separate from the grubbiness of twenty-first-century commerce—the "ivory tower" meme—but that is far from the truth. Colleges collectively spend hundreds of millions of dollars to attract applications. In the case of the elite schools, the exercise is probably a waste of money. The best colleges are well known, and they could get all the first-rate students they need without spending a dime. Indeed, the top schools are more interested in increasing their rejection rate to boost their ratings. Isn't that a perverse reason for sending hundreds of recruiters into the field and spending large sums on branding exercises and advertising? At most institutions, where there are not enough high-quality students to fill available spaces, recruiting has become an act of urgent necessity, leading to institutional exaggeration. Every institution issues colourful brochures and fancy recruiting videos and websites, promises dedicated teachers, diverse classes, fabulous learning opportunities, great career outcomes, and lots and lots of on-campus fun.

North American colleges and universities have a new recruiting field—international applicants—that they have attacked like wolves after a wounded moose. Foreign students pay fees that are significantly greater than those charged to domestic students, and if they struggle with English and with academic expectations, their failure is their tough luck, just some collateral damage in the student-numbers war. Many schools have agents and recruiters carpet-bombing East Asian high schools with recruiting material. The average and below-average schools, particularly those in demographically depressed areas, approach the international markets with the zealotry of the truly desperate. In the eyes of the international students, North American colleges remain Dream Factories and are promoted heavily to this end, in this case embellishing their sales pitch with promises of access to the United States, the potential for immigration, and the mystique of a world-leading university education, which they hope that they can convert into employment magic in the home country. They help pay the bills, they help keep the doors open, and they have not yet learned to blame the colleges for admitting them if they are below academic standard or if they struggle to pass their courses. All but the elite American and Canadian universities, however, delude themselves into thinking that there is an inexhaustible supply of foreign students, which, unfortunately for them is not the case.

> CONSUMERS RULE
>
> Students and prospective students will have an effect—and, indeed, already are doing so—simply by becoming better informed and less willing to pay top dollar for an inferior product. Ultimately, you can't run a college if you can't fill the seats with paying students, and that will be harder to do for schools that don't produce visible value. The schools that get ahead of the curve will prospect, while those that lag behind will not. The higher education bubble isn't bursting because of a shortage of money. It is bursting because of a shortage of value.[5]

AMERICA'S MEDIEVAL UNIVERSITIES

The liberal-arts curricula are fossils of the 1960s, the era of their professors' race, class, and gender activism. Such therapeutic courses short the very skills—written and oral proficiency, historical knowledge, and math and science mastery—that alone prepare graduates for a chance at a successful career trajectory.

Most disturbing is the inability of the modern university to adjust to the twenty-first-century workplace. Students are not graduating in four years. They are piling up crippling debt. They cannot figure out the byzantine nature of their high-interest student-loan packages. And they are hardly assured of jobs commensurate with their unsustainable investment in education.[6]

This all said—enough kind words about traditional universities and colleges, enough room for personal choice and eclecticism, and enough appreciation for the difficulties inherent in changing a large, multi-faceted, and deeply entrenched post-secondary system—steps have to be taken by national and subnational governments if they want the institutions of tomorrow to become real and sustainable Dream Factories. So, to quote Lenin, a political philosopher popular with radical professors in the 1960s, "What is to be done?"

LET THE MARKETPLACE DECIDE

The preferred approach—preferred because it is the easiest—is to let the market—in this case seventeen- to nineteen-year-old young people who have recently graduated from high school—decide. Politically palatable, this approach is a recipe for an ongoing disconnect between the workforce and the workers of the future. It avoids difficult decisions and has the benefit of preventing the government from attempting to pick educational winners and losers, a process that is often fraught with difficulties and bad choices. Over time—and there is evidence that this is happening now across North America, particularly in the shift away from market-insensitive programs toward business, technology, and professional courses—the college and university system will have to adjust to the new realities. This process will be time-consuming and will likely lag well behind the economy; unless, of course, there is a severe economic downturn that forces major and radical changes. The marketplace will decide. The only question is whether governments are comfortable allowing the conservative (in the sense of change-resistant) universities to take their time in adapting to new realities.

INVEST IN THE NEW ECONOMY

Innovation is expensive, and governments need to decide if they really want to invest properly in twenty-first-century education. Outfitting teaching and research facilities appropriately for the new economy is a lot more expensive than the old model, which relied heavily on massive first-year classes in the basic sciences, Social Sciences, and Humanities. To educate young people for the twenty-first-century world of work requires high-end equipment, routinely updated, intensive instruction (classes of twenty-five or fewer, not five hundred), specialized work placements and internships, and regular program revision. Governments that are not prepared to play at this level should probably stay out of the game, as partial investments will produce uneven results. These, of course, are the most fundamental challenges of the high-tech age: how much does a government spend, in what areas, and when? Making a substantial, nation-wide commitment to innovation through education (and research) would cost a great deal of money and would carry no assurance of economic success. Internships, incidentally, have emerged as a potential bridge between education and employment, providing earnest college graduates with the "first step" toward a career. They have also become a national and international scandal, as companies capitalize on the graduates' desperation and offer unpaid positions in return for what is supposed to be professional experience. Some employers are gracious and supportive; others exploitative. But the large and growing number of college graduates securing unpaid internships is actually an excellent sign of an education-to-employment system that is failing badly.[7]

KEEP TOP TALENT AT HOME OR AT LEAST NEARBY

Governments face a real dilemma in educating young people for the contemporary economy. In a globalized economy, truly talented individuals can sell their services almost anywhere. Governments wrestle with a basic question: is it their job to provide young people with life opportunities or is it their role to educate workers for the local economy? In general, the answer is both, but the North American balance is shifted far to the life opportunities side of the spectrum. Put more bluntly, do governments want to pay only to have their talented, highly skilled people move away? Some people are place-bound by language or culture (Japan, South Korea, and Finland), others by commitment to country (Israel), and others still by government funding policies (Singapore has elements of this). The problem is much more pronounced in Canada than the United States. Many more Canadians head south to California and Texas than Americans head north to southern Ontario and the lower mainland of British Columbia (although Americans would be surprised and pleased by the experience if they managed to cross the border). But much the same holds on a subnational level. Should North Dakota invest hundreds of millions to produce a work-ready graduating class, if most of the members of that class plan to relocate to San Diego or Boston? A shift of a skilled worker to a high-need area is a gain for the country, but might be seen differently by the state or provincial government that is covering much of the cost of the education. Major and ongoing government investment, ultimately, is justified by the return to the nation from enhanced competitiveness and productivity. But that is an outcome that is difficult to quantify.

Not all countries work on the same premise. Turkey expanded its university system dramatically, focusing largely on scientific and technological education, particularly in engineering. Producing many more engineers than the country's economy could absorb was, interestingly, part of the plan. The graduates left Turkey, with many heading to Germany and elsewhere in the European Union, producing sizable incomes that returned, in part, to support families in Turkey. Over time, the government hoped, the highly trained and now experienced engineers would return to Turkey to establish their own businesses and to improve the national economy. But the strategy of a developing nation does not work for a leading industrial economy. Educating young people so that they can leave the country is no solution. Training them for jobs within the nation is precisely the best way to proceed.

There is a sad codicil to this commentary. America, built by immigrants and famed the world over as a land of opportunity, has made it increasing difficult for immigrants to come to the country (leaving aside illegal immigrants) and, interestingly, for US-educated professionals to stay after graduation. Historically—and Silicon Valley is one of the best illustrations of this—foreign-born entrepreneurs have played a crucial role in the development of the country's high-tech economy. In recent years, highly trained international students have been unable to get the precious Green Card that would allow them to stay, meaning that their technical skills and entrepreneurial acumen go back to their country of birth or another, more welcoming nation. Given that first-generation immigrants played a crucial "founder" role in more than 40 percent of the Fortune 500 companies, the loss to America is considerable in terms of wealth, job creation, and opportunity. And isn't it odd that the USA's elite universities are, particularly in the scientific and technical fields, educating the leaders of tomorrow—for other countries. What is described as an "American brain drain" is at odds with the perceived role of colleges and universities in producing the wealth-generators for the United States.[8]

BUILD A CULTURE OF SCIENCE AND TECHNOLOGY

Popular culture to the contrary, today's young people are not technologically or scientifically savvy. Describing them as "digital natives" suggests a level of technological sophistication that is relatively uncommon among North American youth. Other countries—Finland, Japan, South Korea, and Germany—have strong S&T cultures built into their elementary and secondary schools and societies at large. Asian youth in the USA and Canada generally copy the experiences and approaches of East Asia and China, doing well in mathematics at high school and maintaining an interest in science and technology fields into university. The issue here is absolutely crucial. The twenty-first-century economy requires workers with advanced technological skills and, more generally, requires a scientifically literate workforce. Many of the workers of tomorrow will require advanced abilities in engineering, computer science, programming, health sciences, environmental science, mathematics, data mining, and on and on. Even those who do not have specific technical expertise in scientific areas should have more than a modicum of mathematical and scientific knowledge. Living in a technology-rich world requires the capacity to engage across the society. Stranding large numbers of people in a ghetto that is free of mathematics and science is likely to doom many of them to long-term marginalization. One of the realities of the modern era is what has been described as "people without jobs, jobs without people." It seems likely that technological ability, more than formal education, is one of the key factors in getting across the divide.

RAISE THE PROFILE OF COMMUNITY COLLEGES

Young people from wealthy and stable communities have excellent life advantages, including much greater opportunities to attend university. For students from disadvantaged homes—typically in areas with less parental involvement, poor schools, and fewer job opportunities—the jump from high school to university is often too big. While the talented and motivated can make the transitions, many founder along the way. Governments, high schools, and parents should put a much greater emphasis on community colleges, which offer better connections to the local job market, more practical education, and a closer focus on the abilities of individual students. As one study of the role of community colleges in the United States concludes, "The community colleges' potential is greater than that of any other institution because their concern is with the people most in need of assistance ... If the community colleges succeed in moving even a slightly greater proportion of their clients towards what the dominant society regards as achievement, it is as though they changed the world."[9] The continued overemphasis on universities as the avenue for advancement for all, as opposed to for those well-suited and well-prepared for the opportunity, is ironically harming many of the very young people they purport to be helping.

ACCEPT THE PERSONAL GROWTH ARGUMENT FOR COLLEGE

Governments do not have to take on total responsibility for colleges and universities. They could accept as a matter of policy that the primary purpose of a formal education is to learn and to develop the skills and attitudes of contemporary citizenship. Colleges would love a release of the pressure to prepare graduates for the workforce and would celebrate an official return to the age-old purpose of academic engagement. In this formulation, the *Learning = Earning* mantra would be replaced—as faculty the world over would prefer—by a *Learning = Personal Development* preoccupation. A large portion of the student population is already here. Enrolment in many academic programs (classical studies and theoretical mathematics) is focused more on individual ability and interests than on employment sensitivity. Thousands of graduate students, particularly those of more mature years, continue their studies out of personal interest more than a deliberate strategy of career development. This is certainly the case in the mid- and lower-tier MBA programs, which attract decent enrolments even if they provide a small return on investment (ROI). Of course, the largest graduate programs in North American are in Education, where union contracts guarantee teachers an immediate bump in salary if they complete a graduate program, thus providing a substantial ROI while having minimal impact on their actual jobs. But all this is probably idealistic, since refocusing college and university to emphasize personal growth—and not better jobs and higher incomes, and even less to meet the needs of the workforce—would likely result in a substantial decline in enrolments, major institutional reorganizations, and a flight of young adults to more career-focused options.

EMPHASIZE ENTREPRENEURSHIP

For several decades, colleges and universities focused on producing middle managers to run expanding government agencies, a rapidly growing retail sector, and a large and expanding industrial and resource economy. That shifted in a rush of enthusiasm for information technology and technology-based products and services, leading to the heavy promotion of scientific and technological education—what most called the "innovation economy." It turns out that ideas—brilliant, surprising, commercializable ideas—are in short supply. In an era of minimal communication costs, global reach, and the removal of distance, the old models of business and industry will become less significant. As James Clifton argued, "Entrepreneurship is more important than innovation. The supply and demand is backward here: Almost all countries, states and cities have bet everything on innovation. Innovation is critical, but it plays a supporting role to almighty entrepreneurship. The investments should follow rare entrepreneurs versus the worldwide oversupply of innovation. Put another way, it's far better to invest in entrepreneurial people than in great ideas."[10] And although some universities do extremely well in creating S&T based entrepreneurs—MIT, Stanford, Waterloo, CalTech—and although business schools have proliferated like the now-ubiquitous health studios across the land, the reality is that colleges and universities do much less well at fostering entrepreneurship than at fostering scientific research.

SHIFT TO A WORK AND LEARN APPROACH

National governments could, at least in part, lead the shift from the learn-work approach to the work-learn approach. By engaging with employers as partners in skills and career development, governments could encourage young adults to move from high school into the work-force, while continuing their studies on a part-time basis while employed. This model—which operates now among hundreds of thousands of young people who mix low-wage, non-career work at coffee shops, retail stores, and restaurants with "full-time" commitments to their college studies—would better meet the needs of employers and young adults alike. It would prioritize employment-related skills but would leave ample room for academic, intellectual, and professional development. This approach would require a dramatic shift in institutional structures and processes, for education would take a back seat to the pursuit of a degree. Instruction would change from semester- and year-long courses and four-year programs to online, just-in-time course delivery, modular instruction, workplace-focused and short-course formats. Employers, who have been freeloaders on personal and government investments in post-secondary education for generations, would have to move front and centre, using advanced evaluation processes to identify suitable candidates in high school and covering a substantial portion of the educational and employment costs for workers in training.

Engaging in this new approach would privilege the needs of employers over the choices of individuals and would represent a departure from the standard approach to post-secondary education. Furthermore, and in sharp contrast to the high level of business-government-education collaboration that exists in such nations as Japan, Germany, and Singapore, this system would rely on American companies adopting a country-first strategy that is anathema to the current generation of business leaders (including the financial institutions whose pursuit of self-interest nearly crippled the global economy and those, like Apple, that keep hundreds of billions of dollars in overseas tax havens). In sum, it's a nice idea that is unlikely to work well in Canada or the United States.

TACKLING SCIENCE AND TECHNOLOGY DEFICIENCIES

The growing inequalities in North American society have attracted a great deal of attention lately, and the structural and other barriers that block the pursuit of equality of opportunity in the United States, including access to career-ready education, have been thoroughly analyzed. But if mass access to education, and particularly university training, were the key to economic success and equality of opportunity, then the surge in enrolment and graduates should have contributed to a reduction in inequality, not an increase. Putnam's analysis applies to significant populations in Canada as well, particularly in the Aboriginal communities, although the extent of Canadian social programs has limited the growth in inequality significantly. But the problem is on the verge of getting much, much worse. The S&T economy requires strong foundations in mathematics and science, and access to computers and other digital tools.

Of course, the central characteristics of the lives of the poorest citizens include growing up in impoverished circumstances, enduring mediocre elementary and high schools (among the weakest among the world's wealthiest nations), being unable to afford top-flight post-secondary institutions, having weak job prospects, and difficulty finding their feet financially in a volatile economy. Any nation that wishes to be truly competitive cannot have a sizable percentage of the population disconnected from the emerging high-technology mainstream. This is a serious problem, one that defies easy solutions and that requires long-term, systematic change in social and educational policy. Such change would require,

among other initiatives, early childhood education for the poorest citizens, enhanced math and science programs in schools, S&T boot camps
for teenagers from underrepresented groups, and mentorship programs
for college and university students interested in the field.

ESTABLISH A NATIONAL COMPETENCY TEST

It is well understood that there are many ways to develop and demonstrate
competency in a wide range of technical and professional areas. For the
last few generations, we collectively shifted responsibility for these assessments to colleges and universities. Why should a company test potential
employees when their college grades and credentials would provide the
required information? Now, in a world of MOOCs (Massive Open Online
Courses) and inexhaustible amounts of rich content online, it is obvious
that people can gain real competency in a field without spending four
years and tens of thousands of dollars at university. As an aside, repositories of democratically accessible, widely dispersed, and regularly updated
professional and academic information has been readily available for generations. We call them libraries, and they used to be a valuable source
of self-education for working-class people, not just a place to borrow
romance novels. The convergence of two crucial elements—the uncertain quality of a college degree in terms of core competencies and the
proliferation of educational and training delivery systems—has rendered
the degree an uncertain (at best) indication of actual abilities. Employers
routinely complain about engineers who lack social and writing skills,
arts graduates who are scientifically illiterate, and business graduates who
have limited understanding of domestic or global affairs.

A growing number of companies brag of the hidden gems in their
ranks who lack specific credentials but have world-class skills and a tremendous work ethic. Governments can support and increase the numbers
of such people in a simple way, by establishing a national competency testing system, tied to specific skills from the basics (writing, reading, arithmetic, problem solving) to advanced and specialized skills (programming
languages, design abilities, artistic skills, specific engineering or health
science qualifications). People would have the opportunity to challenge
for a specific skill at any point in their lives. The test would be nationally

recognized and be accredited by employers who would quickly identify any weaknesses or shortcomings in the accreditation system. Some companies in the USA have developed their own testing systems that help them—without recourse to official transcripts or college credentials—identify potential employees who have the precise skills and aptitudes that they need.

The prospects of this happening at the national level and through a government program are very small, if for no other reason than the strong likelihood that the results would reveal serious differences among applicants of different cultural, ethnic, social, and economic groups. And schoolteachers and faculty unions are strongly opposed to such testing. But if there ever was an educational opening awaiting a healthy dose of American capitalist magic, this is it. Imagine if the top five hundred companies in the United States agreed to use a private or public evaluation system. Imagine if young adults discovered that many people could do well on the assessment based on current abilities or could study for specific skills tests in nonaccredited study programs (such as reading some books on their own). Imagine if these students skipped the expensive and time-consuming college programs and used the assessment tools as a means of accelerating their entrance to the paid and specialized workforce. Imagine how quickly young adults and their parents would—save for the truly gifted and the status-obsessed—gravitate toward personal assessment and self-taught skills development.

CREATING TWENTY-FIRST-CENTURY JOBS

The first debate of the Democratic nomination process in 2015 devoted a great deal of attention to the twin malignancies of North American life: growing inequality and the absence of good jobs for middle-class people. If the debate is any indication of the quality of American thought on this issue, the country is in for some stormy weather. Led by Senator Bernie Sanders, the discussion focused on major investments in infrastructure (brought to you by candidates who also favour radical action on climate change), lowering the cost of college and university tuition, raising the minimum wage, and otherwise rediscovering the policy innovations of the 1960s and 1970s. Hillary Clinton even referred to the need for a new "New

Deal" for America, as though a strategy that did not work all that well in the 1930s would save the country some eighty years later. Twenty-first-century thinking should look forward, not backward, toward a world of work transformed by technology and globalization. It considers how to create sustainable and highly paid jobs based on the new technologies, not on old-economy thinking. National governments need to bring together government agencies, major employers, new-economy thinkers, colleges, technical institutes, futurologists, and researchers to give serious thought to the future of work and to develop strategies for wealth creation (companies and individuals), skills acquisition and societal change in the face of the greatest explosion in high technology in world history. Few are doing this.

THE TRIPLE MATCH: FOCUS ON INDIVIDUAL OUTCOMES

Colleges and universities, at their best, produce excellent outcomes, preparing fortunate men and women for careers and for life. And, it should be added, far more women now than men, for women are considerably more likely to attend college and even more likely to graduate. Many of the fastest-growing careers—health sciences, for example—are dominated by women. The prospects for young men, who historically had the option of physical or outdoors work at good rates of pay, are diminishing quickly.[11] At their worst, the institutions exaggerate the work potential of their graduates, fail to graduate many students, and do a mediocre job of preparing many of their students for employment. Colleges and universities will have a major, even prominent, place in the post–high school experiences of young people. This will not change, but it should. Governments have to change the language of post–high school possibilities.

From a preoccupation with colleges, governments have to refocus the conversation on the education-to-employment transition. Young adults and their families who uncritically accept the *Learning = Earning* mantra, need to emphasize the need to coordinate education and workplace preparation. From the simplistic and inaccurate emphasis on colleges and universities, governments must focus instead on the full range of opportunities available to high school graduates, from entrepreneurship to international experiences, technical institutions and private career centres, apprenticeships and, of course, universities. The goal must be the Triple Match of individual abilities, workforce needs, and training/educational opportunities. This must be the priority of educational institutions, government agencies, individuals, and employers: to get young adults the right training for the right job. Put simply, national strategies have to change from the shotgun, one-solution-for-almost-everyone, approach to the more surgical and thoughtful Triple Match that creates opportunities for individuals by matching talent with jobs, for employers looking for young people with the right schools, and for educational and training institutes that seek people who need and will benefit from their programs.

REALITY CHECK ON YOUTH FUTURES

Permit us one more swift kick at our favourite *bête noire*: the mantra of self-actualization. Be anything you want to be! You are amazing and you can do anything you want in life! The world will respond to your needs and not the other way around, and will give you what you desire. This is nonsense now and always has been, unless you believe that the sharecropper loved heading out to pick cotton, that the prairie sodbuster leapt out of bed each morning filled with joy at the chance to break another acre of farmland, or that the night manager at Burger King takes professional pleasure in managing unruly and unreliable teenage cooks and servers. There are people who love their jobs—the generously paid university professor, the high-tech start-up employee who works with one eye on his stock price, or the columnist whose ideas are read by millions—but they are much fewer in number.

People work to pay the bills, to save for the future, to provide for their family, and to live as good a life as they can. Not very many have the pleasure of working for the love of the job. And not many people get to do the job that they thought that they would truly love. The pursuit of medical degrees is a case in point. Huge numbers of high school graduates head to college hoping to become a doctor. Many quickly fall by the wayside, done in by a handful of B grades rather than a propensity to faint at the sight of blood. But many thousand persist through their degrees and then battle, ferociously, for one of the few spaces in a good medical school. Some of those succeed, but the vast majority do not. They are now in their early twenties, dreams dashed, the career of choice closed off, and limited prospects for a comparable job with the same status, salary, and interest level. Many of these students are fine people, who fell just short of a very high bar. One suspects that most found their feet somewhere. But they did not get the career of their choice or their dreams.

Much as we would like it if every person found exactly the career he or she desired, at a substantial and stable income, with great prospects for advancement, that aspiration is unrealistic. Fewer than a third of people report that they like their jobs—in 2013 Gallup reported that "70% of Americans Hate Their Stupid Jobs."[12] Work, for most, is a means to an end and not an end in itself, and there is usually not much glamour in the life of the industrial worker, stockbroker, barista, postal carrier, farmer, logger, government official, or car salesperson. Most people head off to work with a significant level of resignation and do everything they can to leave their work behind at the end of the day. Gurus say "pursue your passion," but for a great many people this is neither possible nor practical. For almost everyone, work is about money, which in turn is about lifestyle and the pursuit of material and physical well-being. To the degree that this is the case—and research shows overwhelmingly that even the decision to go to college is driven primarily by the pursuit of income and a decent career—it is imperative that the education-to-employment transition become front and centre for national and subnational governments. Advanced education and training is not about self-actualization (nice when it happens), not about institutional stability and financial well-being, not about buffing up a politician's credentials as a person of the people. Advanced education should be very simple—and we return here to the Triple Match:

1. Realistically identify an individual's potential, motivation, aspirations, and core abilities;

2. Identify the prospects for work in the constantly evolving economy;

3. Align institutional programs and services to maximize the connection between ability and workforce need.

In an age of testing, digital personality evaluations, and the like, the first step is relatively easy—but hard for individuals and particularly for their parents to accept.

The second is extremely difficult and is the hardest part of the Triple Match, if only because of economic shifts and the unwillingness of most corporations to make future commitments.

The third should be the easiest, but only if the institutions place the good of the economy and the needs of individual students ahead of institutional priorities (including faculty preferences and disciplinary barriers).

Unless we undertake a true reality check, the current system will blunder on with its periodic successes and growing list of failures. Sadly, it is unlikely that any non-command economy will respond to the opportunities of the Triple Match, although Asian countries are likely to make moves in this direction soon. For, as we have seen, aspirations, individual and parental, are the major stumbling block. If you assume that every young women can be a world-class lawyer, if only she wants to be; every young man a top-notch surgeon, if he works hard enough; a brilliant writer, if only given sufficient chance to discover himself; or a world-changing entrepreneur, then you will want to keep the current system, particularly if you think the world of work will not change and, Bernie Sanders-like, that there are jobs galore to be found through massive government make-work programs. But if the patterns of the past few decades continue to manifest themselves—if not accelerate—the gap between aspiration and reality is going to become a huge chasm, destroying the dreams of yet another generation. Change is possible. Will it happen? Experience would suggest that it is unlikely to happen; but, on the other hand, reality tells us that it's going to have to, one way or another.

Consider the sober conclusion reached by Martin Ford on the intersection of a college degree and the technology-drive economy:

> Nearly everyone agrees that a college degree is generally a ticket to a brighter future … The unfortunate reality, however, is that the college dream is likely at some point to collide with the trends in offshoring and automation … The fact is that college graduates very often end up taking "software" jobs; they become knowledge workers

... At some point in the future, the high cost of a college education, together with diminishing prospects for college graduates, is likely to begin having a negative impact on college enrolment.[13]

We share Ford's concern about technological trends and jobs, but argue that some of the negative employment effects have already started to alter the reality of the college to work transition.

At the end we go back to the question that we asked earlier: "What shall we tell our children?" This is not an academic game, not a public-policy debating point, not a simple lunchroom disagreement about options. This speaks directly to the most fundamental of all parental and societal instincts: How to make our children's future as good as our own, if not better? We know of the turmoil and uncertainty on many fronts: environmental change, inequality, international terror, economic convulsions, ageing populations, stupendous government debt. But we thought we knew one thing at least, that *Learning = Earning*.

But it isn't true, not for the majority of young people who head off to college or university, and yet we continue to send them in large numbers. Meanwhile, a technological transformation of work greater than anything we have seen before is staring us in the face. Every parent wants to answer this question, and every young adult wants to know that there is a clear and unequivocal response. Would that there were. In the end, we do not know how things will unfold. And so we finish with some simple advice. Prepare your children for uncertainty. Arm them with the real skills that they will need: scientific understanding, mathematical competence, deep curiosity, writing ability, analytical skills, global awareness, creativity, integrity, determination, and energy. Convince them that there is no substitute for excellence in all that they do. Give them an entrepreneurial outlook and ensure that they know that the greatest opportunities emerge for those who create their own future and not for those who wait for the future to select them. Prepare them to be future makers, not future takers.

And do not fall prey to the idea that there is only one route, a certain though costly one, through college and university into middle-class security. In our complicated and rapidly changing world, nimbleness, drive, and an understanding of technological change will matter more than an expensive credential of undetermined value. Many of those who prosper in the future will have degrees from college or university. But they will have those degrees because they have a thirst for learning and understanding, not because they wanted a prepunched ticket to the middle class. These future adults will have learned that the value of a university degree lies not in the credential it bestows, but in the knowledge, insight, and excitement about old learning and new discoveries that should be at the centre of the university experience.

ACKNOWLEDGEMENTS

We have been writing about colleges and universities for a number of years now, a reflection of our deep interest in our chosen profession and our growing concern about the gap between the promises and the outcomes of post-secondary education. We have always believed that universities and colleges are special places, deserving of public and government support, but we also believe that they should never be above constructive criticism, nor should they pretend to be the answer to all of society's needs.

We are by no means newcomers to the field: our combined experience at universities as students, teachers, and administrators totals almost exactly 100 years, beginning when Bill became a freshman at McMaster University in 1959. He has taught at Brandon University, Lakehead University, and the University of Northern British Columbia, and has given courses at the University of Victoria and at Duke University as a Distinguished Visiting Professor. Ken started his career at Langara College and the University of British Columbia before joining Bill at Brandon University. He then moved to the University of Victoria before we connected again at the University of Northern British Columbia. Ken then taught at the University of Waikato (New Zealand), the University of New Brunswick at Saint John, the University of Saskatchewan, Quest University, and the University of Waterloo, before returning to the University of Saskatchewan in 2012. He has travelled extensively and has visited universities around the world, from Svalbard and Fairbanks,

Alaska in the north to Adelaide, South Australia, and South Africa in the south, from Nanjing, China, to Doha, Qatar.

Our travels have enriched our thinking greatly, for they have allowed us to meet a great many college and university students, faculty members, and academic administrators. We have learned much from these interactions, which alerted us to the achievements, the aspirations, the prospects and the shortcomings of one of the most profound global experiments of the past fifty years—the contemporary expansion of the modern college and university system. We are profoundly grateful to those whose ideas and insights have shaped our thinking, oftentimes more by disagreeing with our ideas than by sharing them. Colleges and universities are sustained by zeal and passion for learning that greatly exceeds what institutions, parents, and governments pay by way of tuition fees and grants. We are honoured to live in a global world of ideas, intellectual debate, and shared commitment for a better world.

This said, we must express particular thanks to several colleagues whose ideas and activities shaped our thinking: Nobina Robinson, Michael Atkinson, Peter McKinnon, Elizabeth Parr-Johnston, Geoff Weller, Rick Miner, Toby Day-Hamilton, Nancy Mattes, Aron Senkpiel, John Milloy, Bonita Beatty, John Wilkinson, Rob Norris, John McLaughlin, Bill Chesney, Frank, Alicia and Jean Colson, Hans Michelman, Keith Taylor, Judith Henderson, Stephen McLeod, Barb Gillis, Lawrence Marrz, Tom Steele, Jim Bassinger, Emanuel Carvalho, Bob Park, Terry Mitchell, Bruce Muirhead, Bud Walker, Sandra Burt, James Skidmore, Deep Sani, Don Morrison, Amit Chakma, Else-Grete Broderstad, David Johnson, Dave Hannah, Guy Lonechild, Karen Barnes, Greg Poelzer, and Ernie Barber.

This book is our third collaboration with Diane Young, editor-extraordinaire with TAP Books, and we are grateful for her guidance and encouragement. She does a remarkable job of leaving our ideas intact and improving our prose. We appreciate the support of the staff at TAP and Dundurn, whose interest in our work convinced us to expand on our earlier writings and to reflect more fully on what we believe to be the future of college and university training.

We have been aided in the preparation of this work by a great team of researchers, superbly coordinated by Paola Chistie. Joelena Leader is as talented at research as she is unfailingly happy. Cale Passmore provided detailed and timely assistance with the statistical research. Megan McDowell jumped in at the end of the project and helped with permissions and fact checking. Sherilee Diebold-Cooze, Ken's long-time assistant and friend, coordinated his hectic life and made sure that his part of the work was done.

Our wives, Linda Morrison and Carin Holroyd, remain tolerant beyond measure, and we remain eternally grateful for their love and support. Our families continue to grow, bringing enormous joy (and perhaps future post-secondary students) into our midst. We celebrate, in particular, our wonderful grandchildren, whose spirit provides us with hope for the future, and whose potential drives us to work toward a better and more thoughtful world. So, Ken sends big hugs to William, Spencer, Victoria, Hazel, Oliver, Christopher and Katie while Bill does the same to Graeme, Ella, James, Henry, Quinn, John, and George.

We would like to dedicate this book to the parents and taxpayers who subsidize universities and colleges in North America. While we think that their passion is sometimes misplaced and their expectations often unrealistic, we know that everyone wants the next generation to build on the quality of life of the present and to have an even more prosperous and happy future. May these institutions of higher learning and career preparation respond to your expectations and dreams, to those of the young adults of today and tomorrow, and to those of the countries whose prosperity hinges on the abilities and innovation of each successive generation.

—Ken S. Coates and Bill Morrison

SOURCES

BOOKS

Arum, Richard and Josipa Roksa. *Academically Adrift: Limited Learning on College Campuses.* Chicago: University of Chicago Press, 2011.

———. *Aspiring Adults Adrift: Tentative Transitions of College Graduates.* Chicago: University of Chicago Press, 2014.

Bessen, James. *Learning by Doing: The Real Connection between Innovation, Wages and Wealth.* New Haven: Yale University Press, 2015.

Boles, Blake. *Better than College: How to Build a Successful Life without a Four-Year Degree.* Tells Peak, 2012.

Brown, Philip, et al. *The Global Auction: The Broken Promises of Education, Jobs, and Incomes.* Oxford: Oxford University Press, 2011.

Brynjolfsson, Rik and Andrew McAfee. *The Second Machine Age: Work, Progress, and Prosperity in a Time of Brilliant Technologies.* New York: Norton, 2014.

Cappelli, Peter. *Will College Pay Off?: A Guide to the Most Important Financial Decision You'll Ever Make.* New York: Public Affairs, 2015.

Carey, Kevin. *The End of College: Creating the Future of Learning and the University of Everywhere.* New York: Penguin, 2015.

Clifton, Jim. *The Coming Jobs War.* New York: Gallup, 2011.

Cohen, Arthur and Florence Brawer. *The American Community College.* 5th ed. San Francisco: Jossey-Bass, 2008.

Cowen, Tyler. *Average Is Over: Powering America beyond the Age of the Great Stagnation.* New York, Dutton, 2013.

Delbanco, Andrew. *College: What It Was, Is, and Should Be.* Princeton: Princeton University Press, 2012.

Dolan, Simon. *How to Make Millions Without a Degree: And How to Get By Even If You Have One.* Leicester: Matador, 2011.

Ford, Martin. *The Lights in the Tunnel: Automation, Accelerating Technology and the Economy of the Future.* Accultant, 2009.

Goldin, Claudia and Lawrence Katz. *The Race between Education and Technology.* Cambridge: Harvard University Press, 2008.

Huhman, Heather. *Lies, Damned Lies & Internships: The Truth about Getting from Classroom to Cubicle.* Cupertine: Happy About, 2011.

Leslie, Ian. *Curious: The Desire to Know and Why Your Future Depends on It.* Toronto: Anansi, 2014.

Marsh, Peter. *The New Industrial Revolution: Consumers, Globalization and the End of Mass Production.* New Haven: Yale, 2012.

Perlin, Ross. *Intern Nation: How to Earn Nothing and Learn Little in the Brave New Economy.* New York: Verso, 2012.

Pink, Daniel. *Drive: The Surprising Truth about What Motivates Us.* New York: Riverhead, 2009.

Putnam, Robert D. *Our Kids: The American Dream in Crisis.* New York: Simon & Schuster, 2015.

Reynolds, Glenn Harland. *The Education Apocalypse.* New York: Encounter, 2014.

Rosin, Hanna. *The End of Men and the Rise of Women.* New York: Penguin, 2012.

Stephens, Dale. *Hacking Your Education: Ditch the Lectures, Save Tens of Thousands, and Learn More than Your Peers Ever Will.* New York: Penguin, 2013.

Wadha, Vivek with Alex Salkever. *The Immigrant Exodus; Why America Is Losing the Global Race to Capture Entrepreneurial Talent.* Philadelphia: Wharton Digital Press, 2012.

Wolf, Alison. *Does Education Matter?: Myths About Education and Economic Growth.* New York: Penguin, 2002.

NEWSPAPERS AND JOURNALS

Forbes Magazine

Maclean's Magazine

The American Scholar

The Atlantic

The Boston Globe

The Economist

The Huffington Post

The London Times Higher Education Supplement

The National Post

The New York Times

Toronto Globe and Mail

U.S. News & World Report

ENDNOTES

PREFACE

1   Andrew Delbanco, *College: What It Was, Is, and Should Be* (Princeton: Princeton University Press, 2012).
2   http://www.huffingtonpost.com/2012/10/18/study-shows-correlation-b_n_1981264.html
3   http://www.japantimes.co.jp/news/2012/01/10/reference/student-count-knowledge-sliding/#.Vqj_vdQrJkU

INTRODUCTION

1   http://wenr.wes.org/2013/07/an-overview-of-education-in-nigeria/

1 THE DREAM FACTORIES

1   http://america.aljazeera.com/articles/2014/5/7/high-school-seniorslackcriticalmathandreadingskills.html
2   http://www.oecd.org/edu/Education-at-a-Glance-2014.pdf (August 2015), p. 45.
3   Andrew Hacker, "Everyone Should Go to College," *The Daily Beast*, August 28, 2011, http://www.thedailybeast.com/articles/2011/08/28/college-rankings-2011-everyone-should-go-to-college.html
4   Speech by Chancellor Angela Merkel on Being Awarded the King Charles II Medal, Royal Society, https://royalsociety.org/~/media/Royal_Society_

Content/awards/medals-awards-prizes/king-charles-medal/Angela-Merkel-speech.pdf

5   (Leicester: Matador, 2011).

6   "Why You Should Really Go To College, In 2 Charts" *The Huffington Post*, February 21, 2015, http://www.huffingtonpost.com/2015/02/20/college-income-premium_n_6720902.html

7   Stephanie Owen and Isabel V. Sawhill, "Should Everyone Go to College?," *Brookings*, May 8, 2013, http://www.brookings.edu/research/papers/2013/05/08-should-everyone-go-to-college-owen-sawhill

8   http://priceonomics.com/the-iit-entrance-exam

9   http://www.universityworldnews.com/article.php?story=20120216105739999

10   http://www.modernlibrary.com/2010/09/14/100-of-the-best-books-on-shakespeare/

11   It is worth noting that scholars who are busy writing all of these books and articles are devoting less time to reading the work of others. Estimates suggest that scholarly reading has dropped by 30 percent in the past two decades.

12   According to the World Bank, the Cuban GDP per capita in 2013 was US$5,300; the American figure was $53,000.

13   "What do you do with millions of extra graduates?" BBC News July 1, 2014, http://www.bbc.com/news/business-28062071

14   Doug Bandow, "Transforming China from Within: Chinese Students Head to American Universities." Forbes Magazine, September 22, 2014, http://www.forbes.com/sites/dougbandow/2014/09/22/transforming-china-from-within-chinese-students-head-to-american-universities/

15   http://www.universityworldnews.com/article.php?story=20140213153927383

16   According to a fact sheet distributed by the US Embassy in Lagos. http://photos.state.gov/libraries/nigeria/487468/pdfs/JanuaryEducationFactSheet.pdf

17   http://jobs.aol.com/articles/2013/01/28/college-educated-over-qualified-study/

18   http://theconversation.com/international-student-report-emphasises-their-value-but-not-the-means-39626

19   As of 2010. http://www.international.gc.ca/education/report-rapport/economic-impact-economique/index.aspx?lang=eng

20   As of 2011–12. https://international.uoregon.edu/nafsa_economic_report

21   As of 2015. http://www.bbc.com/news/education-32779507

22   September 17, 2015.

23   "Is College Worth It?" and "College (Un)bound," *New York Times*, June 23, 2013.

24   http://www.thestar.com/news/world/2012/01/10/stampede_over_university_admissions_in_south_africa_leaves_one_dead.html

25   http://chronicle.com/article/Little-Known-Colleges-Make/126822/

2 AWAKENING FROM THE DREAM

1   http://qz.com/145217/its-harder-to-get-a-job-in-italy-with-a-college-degree-than-without-one/

2   "Why is Youth Unemployment so High," *The Economist*, May 8, 2013, http://www.economist.com/blogs/economist-explains/2013/05/economist-explains-why-youth-unemployment-so-high

3   http://centerforcollegeaffordability.org/uploads/Underemployed%20Report%202.pdf

4   "'I bought my degree, now I want my job!' Entitled students on fast track to becoming disgruntled employees: study," *National Post*, May 25, 2014.

5   http://collegequarterly.ca/2010-vol13-num03-summer/daley.html

6   https://www.youtube.com/watch?v=yRZZpk_9k8E

7   http://www.cnn.com/2014/10/22/us/unc-report-academic-fraud/

8   http://educationbythenumbers.org/content/underemployment-college-grads_1589/

9   George Leef, "The College Bubble Is Popping, So Shameless Sales Pitches Pick Up," *Forbes*, November 26, 2013.

10   Matt Gurney, "The easy fix to student indebtedness—go to school later," *The National Post*, July 30, 2013.

11   "America's New Aristocracy," *The Economist*, January 24, 2015.

12   http://www.theatlantic.com/business/archive/2014/01/heres-exactly-how-much-the-government-would-have-to-spend-to-make-public-college-tuition-free/282803/

13   http://www.yalebulldogs.com/information/alumni/notable_alumni

14   http://academica.ca/top-ten/us-sees-drop-law-school-applicants

15   *The Economist*, June 20, 2015.

16   https://www.aacu.org/nchems-report

17   Robert Putnam, *Our Kids*, Chapter One: The American Dream: Myths and Realities.

3 OUT OF SYNC

1   James Clinton, *The Coming Jobs War*, Introduction.

2   http://www.ibtimes.com/google-inc-races-apple-1-trillion-valuation-1704135

3   Martin Ford, *The Lights in the Tunnel: Automation, Accelerating Technology and the Economy of the Future* (Accultant, 2009).

4   http://www.bls.gov/iag/tgs/iag52.htm#workforce

5   http://www.forbes.com/sites/susanadams/2015/02/17/the-highest-paying-in-demand-jobs-in-america/

6   https://lawschooltuitionbubble.wordpress.com/original-research-updated/law-graduate-overproduction/

7   Michigan Department of Technology, Management, and Budget.

8   Daniel Pink, *Drive: The Surprising Truth About What Motivates Us* (New York: Riverhead, 2009), p. 28.

9   The figures for Masters and PhDs are from 2010. http://www.huffingtonpost.com/2012/05/07/food-stamps-phd-recipients-2007-2010_n_1495353.html

10   http://www.theatlantic.com/magazine/archive/2015/07/world-without-work/395294/

11   Peter Cappelli, *Will College Pay Off? A Guide to the Most Important Financial Decision You'll Ever Make* (New York: Public Affairs, 2015).

12   http://www.nationalreview.com/bench-memos/296273/elite-law-schools-gaming-postgraduate-employment-rates-ed-whelan

13   *New York Times*, October 24, 2015.

14   http://oncampus.macleans.ca/education/2012/10/02/10-backup-careers-for-new-teachers/

4 THE DEATH OF AVERAGE

1   http://www.wsj.com/articles/hillary-clinton-proposes-debt-free-tuition-at-public-colleges-1439179200. http://www.usnews.com/education/best-colleges/slideshows/11-public-schools-with-the-lowest-in-state-tuition

2   http://www.bestvalueschools.com/most-affordable-universities-america-2015/#chapter6

3   James Bessen, *Learning by Doing: The Real Connection between Innovation, Wages and Wealth* (New Haven: Yale University Press, 2015), Introduction.

4   Rik Brynjolfsson and Andrew McAfee, *The Second Machine Age: Work, Progress, and Prosperity in a Time of Brilliant Technologies* (New York: W.W. Norton, 2014).

5   Peter Marsh, *The New Industrial Revolution: Consumers, Globalization and the End of Mass Production* (New Haven: Yale, 2012), Chapter 10.

6   http://www.psychologicalscience.org/journals/cd/12_1/Taylor.cfm

7   CPL recruiting, https://www.cpl.ie/

8   http://careers2030.cst.org/jobs/

9   https://medium.com/basic-income/should-we-be-afraid-very-afraid-4f7013a5137c

5 UNPREPARED FOR WORK

1   Margaret Wente, "Access or Quality," Toronto *Globe and Mail*, October 20, 2012.

2   http://www.businessinsider.com/mba-students-are-deluded-about-salary-2013-7. The figures are from 2013.

3   Alison Wolf, *Does Education Matter?: Myths About Education and Economic Growth* (New York: Penguin, 2002), Chapter 7.

4   "Academic entitlement leads to negative consequences, student researchers find," University of Windsor *Daily News*, May 30, 2013.

5   http://blogs.stthomas.edu/careers/2015/02/11/preferred-employers-and-jobs-what-are-college-graduates-looking-for/

6   Ian Leslie, *Curious: The Desire to Know and Why Your Future Depends on It* (Toronto: Anansi, 2014).

7   Dale Stephens, *Hacking Your Education: Ditch the Lectures, Save Tens of Thousands, and Learn More than Your Peers Ever Will* (New York: Penguin, 2013).

8   There are many such rankings. This one is from the London *Times*. https://www.timeshighereducation.co.uk/world-university-rankings/2015/world-university-rankings" \l "/sort/0/direction/asc

6 ADJUSTING TO REALITY

1   http://www.bloomberg.com/news/videos/b/d0ee3ffd-f1df-4991-ad7c-e9ecfd668b14

2   http://colleges.usnews.rankingsandreviews.com/best-colleges/rankings/highest-grad-rate/page+5

3   http://www.businessinsider.com/college-closings-chart-2015-3

4   https://www.insidehighered.com/news/2015/09/28/moodys-predicts-
     college-closures-triple-2017?utm_source=Inside+Higher+Ed&utm_
     campaign=e7ec3744ca-DNU20150928&utm_medium=email&utm_
     term=0_1fcbc04421-e7ec3744ca-198196985

5   Hayley Peterson, "Urban Outfitters' Co-Founder Is Building a College
     Campus," *Business Insider*, October 17, 2013.

6   John Goyder, "Liberal Arts Education and Income Attainment: At a
     Crossroad" (presented at the CSSHE Conference, Waterloo, May 2012).

7   http://qz.com/358929/law-school-enrollment-decline/. http://blogs.wsj.
     com/law/2014/01/02/law-2014-paring-back-at-u-s-law-schools-continues/

8   "Middle-Aged Drowning in Student Debt," *The American Interest*, July
     18, 2012.

9   http://www.businessinsider.com/law-school-bubble-2012-9

10   Tyler Cowen, *Average Is Over: Powering America Beyond the Age of the
     Great Stagnation* (New York: Dutton, 2013).

11   http://academica.ca/top-ten/us-institutions-marketing-second-
     bachelors-way-improve-graduate-employability, November 18, 2014.

12   Dale Stephens, *Hacking Your Education*.

13   Blake Boles, *Better Than College: How to Build a Successful Life Without a
     Four Year Degree* (Tells Peak, 2012).

7 STRATEGIES FOR YOUTH SUCCESS

1   The figures are here: http://www.oecd.org/pisa/keyfindings/PISA-2012-
     results-snapshot-Volume-I-ENG.pdf

2   http://www.oecd.org/pisa/keyfindings/PISA-2012-results-US.pdf

3   http://www.capenet.org/facts.html

4   Kevin Carey, *The End of College: Creating the Future of Learning and the
     University of Everywhere* (New York: Penguin, 2015).

5   https://www.insidehighered.com/news/2014/08/20/acts-annual-score-
     report-shows-languishing-racial-gaps-mediocre-scores, August 20,
     2014. ACT was formerly American College Testing; now it's just an
     acronym.

6   http://careerdare.com/5-most-overrated-degrees/?utm_
     source=taboola#axzz2ctz6iccj July 17, 2013.

8 CONFRONTING THE DREAM INDUSTRY

1   Philip Lauder et al., *The Global Auction* (Oxford: Oxford University Press, 2010), pp. 147–148.

2   Claudia Goldin and Lawrence Katz, *The Race Between Education and Technology* (Cambridge: Harvard University Press, 2008), pp. 352–353.

3   Glenn Harland Reynolds, *The Education Apocalypse* (New York: Encounter, 2014).

4   https://www.timeshighereducation.com/world-university-rankings/2015/one-hundred-under-fifty#!/page/0/length/25

5   Glenn Reynolds, *The Education Apocalypse*.

6   Victor Davis Hanson, "America's Medieval Universities," https://lockerdome.com/nro/6680394078767636

7   Heather Huhman, *Lies, Damned Lies & Internships: The Truth About Getting from Classroom to Cubicle* (Cupertine: Happy About, 2011) and Ross Perlin, *Intern Nation: How to Earn Nothing and Learn Little in the Brave New Economy* (New York: Verso, 2012).

8   Vivek Wadha with Alex Salkever, *The Immigrant Exodus: Why America Is Losing the Global Race to Capture Entrepreneurial Talent* (Philadelphia: Wharton Digital Press, 2012).

9   Arthur Cohen and Florence Brawer, *The American Community College*, 5th Edition (San Francisco: Jossey-Bass, 2008), p. 444.

10   Clifton, *The Coming Jobs War*, Conclusion.

11   Hanna Rosin, *The End of Men and the Rise of Women* (New York: Penguin, 2012).

12   http://www.ryot.org/gallup-poll-70-americans-disengaged-jobs/376177

13   Martin Ford, *The Lights in the Tunnel*. "'Software' Jobs and Artificial Intelligence."

PERMISSIONS

8 CONFRONTING THE DREAM INDUSTRY

TAP
BOOKS

Visit us at
Dundurn.com/TAPBooks